Consuming Images

Robert Abel's *Bubbles* (1974)

Consuming Images

Film Art and the American Television Commercial

Gary D. Rhodes and
Robert Singer

EDINBURGH
University Press

Dedicated to
Barry Salt
and
Gerald "Jerry" Schnitzer

Edinburgh University Press is one of the leading university presses in the UK. We publish academic books and journals in our selected subject areas across the humanities and social sciences, combining cutting-edge scholarship with high editorial and production values to produce academic works of lasting importance. For more information visit our website: edinburghuniversitypress.com

© Gary D. Rhodes and Robert Singer, 2020, 2021

Edinburgh University Press Ltd
The Tun—Holyrood Road
12 (2f) Jackson's Entry
Edinburgh EH8 8PJ

First published in hardback by Edinburgh University Press 2020

Typeset in 11/13 Monotype Ehrhardt by
IDSUK (DataConnection) Ltd

A CIP record for this book is available from the British Library

ISBN 978 1 4744 6068 2 (hardback)
ISBN 978 1 4744 6069 9 (paperback)
ISBN 978 1 4744 6070 5 (webready PDF)
ISBN 978 1 4744 6071 2 (epub)

The right of Gary D. Rhodes and Robert Singer to be identified as authors of this work has been asserted in accordance with the Copyright, Designs and Patents Act 1988 and the Copyright and Related Rights Regulations 2003 (SI No. 2498).

Contents

List of Figures	vi
Acknowledgments	ix
Introduction	1
1. Origins	16
2. Narrative	36
3. Mise-en-scène	62
4. Cinematography	92
5. Editing	129
6. Sound	154
Conclusion	178
Index	183

Figures

I.1	William Heise's *Admiral Cigarette* (1897)	2
I.2, I.3	Errol Morris's *Photobooth* (2001)	4
I.4	Michel Gondry's *Smarienberg* (1996)	12
1.1	Krinkles the Clown: "shock, entertain and sell": Post Cereal commercial (1953)	18
1.2–1.6	Gerald Schnitzer's *Going to the Dance* (1958)	19–21
1.7	Gerald "Jerry" Schnitzer	24
1.8, 1.9	Schnitzer's *Sunrise, Sunset* (1966)	30
2.1, 2.2	David Lynch's *Obsession for Men* (1990), featuring prose by Flaubert	38
2.3, 2.4	Michel Gondry's *Drugstore* (1994)	42
2.5, 2.6	Nicolas Winding Refn's 2014 commercial for Lincoln MKC	46
2.7	Lance Acord's *The Force* (2011)	49
2.8–2.10	Aldo Ray, Broderick Crawford, and Jack Palance in a 1977 commercial for Canada Dry Ginger Ale	56–7
2.11	*The G.I. Bill* (1987)	58
3.1	Dennis Quaid promotes Esurance in 2018	63
3.2	Ridley Scott's *1984* (1984)	64
3.3	Ozon Fluid Net Hairspray (1964)	66
3.4	Prestone commercial from 1974	67
3.5	*I'm You* (2010), featuring Christine O'Donnell	70
3.6	Scottie Tissues commercial from the 1960s	77
3.7	Micrin Oral Antiseptic from the early 1960s	77
3.8	Animation promotes Muriel cigars in 1951	79
3.9	Robert Abel's *Brand Name* (1977)	83
3.10	Robert Abel's *Brilliance* (1985)	84
3.11	Mike Dahlquist's 2017 commercial for Halo Top	87
4.1	Remco's *Hi, Heidi* commercial of 1964	93
4.2	Viz Eye Drops (1965)	97
4.3	*When There's No Man Around* (circa 1966)	99
4.4, 4.5	*Isn't It Cool in Pink* (1988), featuring Matt LeBlanc	103

4.6	Kodak's *Turn Around* (1963)	107
4.7, 4.8	*Daisy Girl* (1964)	111
4.9	Published in *Advertising Age* in March of 1977	117
4.10	Kentucky Fried Chicken and the Steadicam in 1979	118
4.11	Matthew Rolston's *Khakis Swing* (1998)	122
5.1	Steve Horn's 1985 commercial for Honda Scooters	130
5.2	Chemstrand Corporation's *A Lady Isn't Dressed Unless Her Legs Are Too* (1958)	134
5.3	Tarsem Singh's *Washroom* (1996)	137
5.4	Joe Pytka's *Two Kids* (1991)	141
5.5	Paxton cigarette commercial from 1963	143
5.6	Chills & Thrills commercial from 1970	145
5.7	Olan Soule promotes prune juice in the late 1960s/early 1970s	148
5.8	Maybelline's *Shine Free Mascara* (1986)	150
6.1	Roberto Malenotti's *Hilltop* (1971)	155
6.2	Hans Knaapen's *Thief* (2012)	160
6.3	Noxzema shaving cream commercial (1967)	163
6.4	Stan Freberg's 1968 commercial for Jeno's Pizza Rolls	166
6.5	Humira's *Not Always Where I Needed to Be* (2018)	169
6.6	*By the Pool* (2015)	173
C.1, C.2	The culmination of Ridley Scott's *1984* (1984)	180

Serenading sardines

Silly sardines come to life in a 30-second TV commercial for Season sardines, airing in the New York market. The Irvington, N.J.-based company's first TV campaign features five fishy characters—men dressed as sardines—who are "cast" as sombrero and serape-sporting Mexicans to promote Season's sardines in tomato sauce. Voiceover reminds sardine supporters that the brand is "loaded with protein, calcium and Omega 3." Furman Roth, New York, handles.

Surreal sardines from 1987

Acknowledgments

It takes a great deal of time and devotion to write a book. There are many people who actively contributed to the presentation and publication of our work, and we wish to acknowledge their generosity, and their reading and rereading of the material, and also to note the critical thinkers and lost narratives we discovered along the way. You are all no longer the secret heroes of our work.

We would like to offer sincere thanks to the various archives, libraries, museums, and universities that kindly offered assistance during the research phase of this project: the American Heritage Center at the University of Wyoming, the Ardmore Public Library of Oklahoma, the Bancroft Library at the University of California at Berkeley, the Billy Rose Theatre Division of the New York Public Library, the British Film Institute in London, the Charles E. Young Research Library at the University of California/Los Angeles, the Harry Ransom Center at the University of Texas at Austin, the Louis B. Mayer Film and Television Study Center in the Doheny Library at the University of Southern California, the Margaret Herrick Library of the Academy of Motion Picture Arts and Sciences in Beverly Hills, the Motion Picture, Broadcasting and Recorded Sound Division/Moving Image Section at the Library of Congress in Washington, D. C., the Museum of the Moving Image in New York, and the National Archives of the United States. The staff at the Kingsborough/CUNY library in particular were amazing in their resources and in their kindness.

In addition, we want to express gratitude to the following individuals whose encouragement has helped make this book possible: Kevin Brownlow, Wendy Chu, William Collins, Kristin Dewey, Steve Haberman, Michael Lee, Joseph H. Lewis, Bob Murawski, Charles Musser, Victor Pierce, Stephen Rivkin, Ellen Schnitzer, Haskell Wexler, Tony Williams, and Robert Wise.

Our deepest appreciation also goes to Gillian Leslie, our guiding spirit at Edinburgh University Press; Barry Salt, whose work acted as a model for our own and whose suggested revisions were crucial; and the late Gerald "Jerry" Schnitzer, who shared his personal archive and memories.

Introduction

"The best TV commercials create a
tremendously vivid sense of mood, of a
complex presentation of something."[1]

—Stanley Kubrick in 1987

In 1897, while employed at the Edison Studios, William Heise created one of the earliest filmed commercials, *Admiral Cigarette* (Fig. I.1). Heise, a director and (mostly) cinematographer of such Edison moving pictures as *The Kiss* (1896), *Serpentine Dance, Annabelle* (1897), and *McKinley Taking the Oath* (1897), shot the thirty-second moving picture, *Admiral Cigarette*, in one static, wide shot characteristic of the early cinema, but for the contemporary audience, this advertisement proved to be of historical significance: *Admiral Cigarette* helped inaugurate the ongoing and dynamic relationship between film culture and the advertisement–commercial, to be further exploited by the television medium.

Four men, dressed in costumes humorously suggesting various social and ethnic strata, posed in front of a billboard prominently featuring the name of the tobacco company; they sit and converse. Then, a large box to the left of the frame opens and exposes a woman, who promptly distributes cigarettes and casually tosses them all over the set. Near the end of this commercial, the men unfurl a large banner stating the inclusive ad copy "we all smoke," even Native Americans and women. All can watch, and all can purchase. The relationship between film and advertising, from an aesthetic and technical perspective, with consumerism and commerce as practiced in commercial advertisements, remains an intact industrial standard.

Appearing at an event held at Queen's University of Belfast in 2007, David Lynch fielded numerous questions from attendees. One of them asked why he had decided to direct television commercials, which he has occasionally done since first making a series of four commercials for Calvin Klein's Obsession in 1988. Smiling, Lynch quickly responded that he accepted the job offer for the large salary it provided, an answer that pleased the audience due to his honesty and good-natured demeanor.

Figure I.1 William Heise's *Admiral Cigarette* (1897)

Implicit in the question was a disdain for the TV commercial, not surprising given the fact that many critics view certain kinds of filmmaking as inferior to others, particularly those that are—in the larger sense of the word—"commercial." Likewise, Lynch's light-hearted answer operated on the level of money over issues of film style or art. The exchange was not surprising, as other discussions of the same topic emphasize the financial above all else. For example, a 2017 web-based article about Lynch's TV commercials was entitled "The Ringing of the Surreal Cash Till."[2] It was published 120 years after Heise filmed *Admiral Cigarette*.

To be sure, Lynch is only one of a large number of feature film directors who have made television commercials. Ridley Scott famously directed the dystopian *1984*, a commercial for Apple Macintosh that aired during the National Football League (NFL) Super Bowl in 1984. And such directors as Woody Allen, Robert Altman, Wes Anderson, Darren Aronofsky, John Badham, Carroll Ballard, Michael Bay, Ingmar Bergman, Michael Cimino, Sofia Coppola, Stan Dragoti, David Fincher, Terry Gilliam, Jean-Luc Godard, Michel Gondry, Hugh Hudson, Harmony Korine, Spike Jonze, Spike Lee, Baz Luhrmann, Adrian Lyne, Penny Marshall, Albert Maysles, Alan Parker, Alex Proyas, Martin Scorsese, Tony Scott,

Gore Verbinski, and Wim Wenders have also made TV commercials, either before or after their fame in feature films. These are all in addition to directors like Carlton Chase, Leslie Dektor, Stu Hagmann, Matthew Harris, Joe Pytka, and Joe Sedelmaier, who have made their names specifically in TV commercials.

And then there is the important case of documentary filmmaker Errol Morris, who has directed many TV commercials, including the Emmy Award-winning *Photobooth* promotion for PBS in 2001 (Figs I.2 and I.3). Morris has claimed that his documentaries have been dependent financially on his commercials, to the extent that money generated by them gives him a degree of artistic freedom.[3] But when speaking about whether or not he believes that his commercials have intrinsic value, Morris offered a compelling insight:

> It's very hard to make good commercials, and I work almost entirely with the same cameraman, Peter Donahue (who was the main cameraman on *Mr. Death* [Errol Morris, 1999]), and the same crew. And we've learned to work really, really fast together. We've made a pledge never to do bad work in commercials, and I've never looked at them as something that is just simply a job. It's always been an attempt to really do something interesting and to do something well.
> ... Part of going out and shooting anything is thinking about how it's going to be put together as a piece of filmmaking, and I feel pretty much the same way about commercials as I feel about everything else.[4]

Morris has also indicated that he uses the same approach to edit his documentaries and commercials, their narrative structures representing a "process of discovery" that occurs during post-production.[5] The ringing of the cash till need not impede cinematic creativity.

Nevertheless, the television commercial has received little scholarly attention from those working in Film Studies (as opposed to those working in the areas of marketing, advertising, and mass media). According to media critic Arthur Berger, this is an acute oversight:

> Commercials—in my opinion the most interesting and powerful form of advertising—should be seen as works of art that have their own conventions; they might best be thought of as mini-dramas that employ all the techniques of the theater and the cinema to achieve their aims . . . [T]hey are dramatic, they employ the most sophisticated techniques of lighting and editing [and] they often cost enormous amounts of money, relatively speaking, to produce . . . [which often] outstrip those of the programs during which they are shown.[6]

Though commercials are generally ignored by Film Studies and despised by some audience members, others have taken a more positive view, including popular-audience critics like Gene Siskel and Roger Ebert.[7]

Figures I.2 and I.3 Errol Morris's *Photobooth* (2001)

Consider also the attention paid annually to the commercials broadcast during the NFL Super Bowl. As Walter Cummins and George Gordon have observed, "For many TV viewers ... commercials are not bitter medicine. Many become mini-treats, lively and clever sources of pleasure in their inventiveness."[8] And then there is the dialogue spoken by Drake (Joe Swanberg) to a budding young filmmaker in Adam Wingard's *You're Next* (2015). "Do you do commercials, because those are my favorite? ... I just think that is just the height of the art form these days."

We believe that two key reasons explain the absence of literature devoted to the American television commercial as an art form sharing certain aesthetic formations and precepts with cinema culture. For one, Film Studies has long privileged the feature film, whether in terms of Hollywood or otherwise, and particularly with regard to scholars engaging in critical studies of mainstream filmmaking during the post-1915 era (as opposed to avant-garde and experimental cinema). Literature on the Hollywood short subject is, for example, woefully sparse.

The second reason that the cinematic importance of the television commercial has received limited attention is likely the more dominant of the two. The fact that television commercials exist to sell certain products—whether retail goods, political candidates and messages, or ideas (as in public service announcements)—might well lead some to view them not in terms of film or art, but only (or predominantly) in terms of advertising and marketing. As if to excuse the fact that he had directed a television commercial for Campari, Federico Fellini explained, "So now I've decided to do spots myself, so that [television stations] can interrupt *my* films with *my* spots. At least that way, there will be uniformity of style."[9] In Jean-Luc Godard's *Tout va bien* (1972), a TV commercial director (Yves Montand) makes excuses for his career, which was once aligned with more prestigious filmmaking. And the aforementioned exchange between David Lynch and the questioner further reveal the suspicion (and sometimes scorn) that film critics and scholars often have for television commercials, perceiving them as flawed or less worthy of attention because their primary goal is sales.

However, we should remind ourselves that most Hollywood feature films exist for commercial reasons. In their textbook *Film Art: An Introduction*, David Bordwell and Kristin Thompson interrogate the contempt some viewers have for "commercial" cinema:

> Take the distinction between *art* and *entertainment*. Some people would say that blockbusters playing at the multiplex are merely "entertainment," whereas films for a narrower public—perhaps independent films, of festival fare, or specialized experimental works—are true art. Usually, the art/entertainment split carries a

not-so-hidden valued judgment: art is high-brow, where entertainment is superficial. Yet things aren't that simple.

. . . The crucial point is that considerations of money don't necessarily make the artist any less creative or the project any less worthwhile.[10]

We would suggest that their explanation could easily be extended to encompass the American television commercial.

Another approach to this issue would be to consider the various ways in which American cinema has actively tried to sell products since the late nineteenth century, as previously noted with Heise's *Admiral Cigarette*. In some cases, these represent precursors to the television commercial, meaning short films intended to generate sales for retail products, such as those produced in 1895 and 1896 to promote Dewar's scotch, Maillard's chocolates, Columbia bicycles, and Piel's beer. By way of another example, in May 1898, the American trade publication *The Phonoscope* told readers:

> With the advent of warm weather comes the awakening of a new feature in metropolitan advertising, the use of moving pictures. This device has been hibernating somewhat through the cold season, when it is difficult to collect a crowd on the streets of New York, but now when the hazy evenings descend again over Broadway, large canvas screens are unfolded in every place where passers-by can obtain a good view, and with the turning of a bright light upon the canvas, the people begin to gather.
>
> Presently a picture appears on the screen, which we immediately recognize as having stared at us all winter long from the fences or streetcars. We have even wondered if that girl offering us some new brand of cigars didn't sometimes get tired of holding out her arm that way . . . we feel glad that she is at least going to move from her cramped position. She walks about the picture in a most lifelike way, and we go our way feeling as if we are quite well acquainted with the young lady.[11]

Such an example underscores not only the roots of the American television commercial, but also the fact that cinema engaged in commercial sales from an early point in its history, which continued as an industrial practice with the rise of television culture in postwar America.

With regard to Hollywood films, the coming attraction trailer represents a type of commercial used to promote forthcoming features, whether in their earliest incarnation as lantern slides or in the narrative film form they assumed in the 1920s and 1930s, one whose ultimate goal remains much the same in the twenty-first century. Here the message is clear, and it is one that (like advertising for so many other kinds of products) is often reinforced by radio and print advertisements, posters, and billboards: the consumer should buy an admission ticket to the advertised film.

INTRODUCTION 7

The regular convergence of Hollywood cinema and advertising also occurs through product placement, which historian Kerry Segrave defines as "the deliberate insertion into an entertainment film script of a product, its signage, a verbal mention of a product, and so on."[12] As Segrave has shown, the practice dates to the early talkie era, but gained particular momentum from the late 1970s to the present. Perhaps the most famous example remains the promotion of Reese's Pieces in *E. T. The Extra-Terrestrial* (Steven Spielberg, 1982), Hershey having paid $1 million for the product's insertion into the film. Within a month of *E. T.*'s release, sales of Reese's Pieces increased by 70 percent. Discussing these practices, Segrave writes:

> Hardly a film [in the modern era has been] released without the placement of items within it, often dozens of items. Hollywood studios were very open about the practice, even going so far as to sometimes issue price lists outlining how much it cost for a verbal mention or hands-on use by a star, and so forth. Critics of the practice were all outside the industry and carried no weight at all. Lining up manufacturers to have their products placed in a film took on almost as much importance as did the lining up of a big-name star and director.[13]

Whether inserted carefully or clumsily into a given film's plot, product placement represents little more than an embedded sales pitch for a retail product.

As a third and final example of the sales impetus of feature filmmaking, we believe it would be difficult to ignore the fact that—while the Hollywood blockbuster may be many things—each is certainly a commercial for *itself*, meaning its larger existence outside the confines of its running time, a galaxy in which everything from children's toys and videogames to T-shirts and McDonald's Happy Meals orbit the specific film. Indeed, the omnipresence of what have been called "ancillary" products before, during, and after a blockbuster's release could lead us to rethink which really constitutes the "ancillary," the film or the myriad products reflecting its existence.

Those working in the advertising industry and those studying the same have certainly exerted much effort in analyzing the marketing value of particular television commercials. Some scholars have also stressed the need to examine commercials, whether for their importance to cultural history, their use of certain genres of music, or even as indicators of the secularization of American life.[14] On rare occasions, scholars have also investigated the narrative form that the television commercial assumes, notably Martin Esslin, who posed the question, "is [the commercial] not too short, too trivial, too contemptible altogether to deserve serious consideration?" Esslin answered his own question by exploring the commercial's dramatic form, concluding that "not only must the television commercial be regarded as a species of drama, but that, indeed, it comes very close to the most basic forms of the theatre, near its very roots."[15] Approaching the subject from the standpoint of Film Studies, we would answer Esslin's question in a different manner, believing that the television commercial should receive serious consideration as an art form, in the manner that Bordwell and Thompson deploy the term. Put another way, we are guided by Stanley Kubrick, who told *Rolling Stone* in 1987, "Leave content out of it, and some of the most spectacular examples of film art are in the best TV commercials."[16]

It is important to note that there are various types of television commercial and, for that matter, print and radio advertisements. In 1978, for example, Donald Gunn of the Leo Burnett advertising agency famously outlined twelve types of advertisements, which ranged from "Testimonial" and "Demo" to the "Show the Need" commercial. Some directors have instead favored discussing TV commercials through the lens of only two categories, those that present a short narrative and those that are presentational (with, for example, on onscreen personality looking at the audience while extolling the virtures of a given product). While the present volume will investigate various genres that the TV commercial employs, we favor a more singular approach, especially given how amorphous all of these categories tend to be. Cross-genre efforts abound. After all, presentational commercials might sometimes include documentary-style segments about a product, or even fictional characters using the product that the presenter touts. While we will indeed discuss specific genres in this volume, we also believe that all commercials tell stories, just as they share other traits.

Lynn Spigel notes, "Sponsors' concerns with audience attention rose to new heights in the late 1950s and 1960s when they found themselves buying thirty- or sixty-second spots in programs."[17] In our view, the commercial is—or at least can be—a short film of substance, whether its running time is imprecise (as in live commercials of the 1940s and 1950s) or adheres to industry standards (which changed from 120 seconds and 60 seconds in the 1950s to the increasing dominance of 30 seconds in the 1960s and certainly thereafter). For us, the same holds true, whether the commercial was used to sponsor the entirety of a single program (as was usually the case in the 1940s and 1950s) or as one of a variety of sponsors juxtaposed against each other in the commercial breaks that became increasingly common in the 1960s, 1970s, and thereafter.

Vance Packard's *The Hidden Persuaders* (1957), published in the early days of American television and advertising history, remains a seminal study of the medium and its affective, socio-political agencies, consumer culture, and the omnipresent commercial. Packard documents multiple, prescient insights into the psychology of the mass sell—pervasive industrial merchandising strategies—engaging the postwar market audience, and he suggests that television's advertising tactics would have to address the audiences' "different levels of consciousness." He notes that there were "three main levels of interest" to initiate a dynamic, ongoing relationship between the new medium and its population of potential consumers. In a seemingly Freudian-inflected rhetoric and structural configuration, Packard observes how advertising may strategize its consumer messaging to succeed in producing desired psychological effects in terms that the surrealist André Breton would approve:

> The first level is the conscious, rational level, where people know what is going on and are able to tell why. The second and lower level is called, variously, preconscious and subconscious . . . [and] involves that area where a person may know in a vague way what is going on with his own feelings, sensations and attitudes . . . the third level is where we not only are not aware of our true attitudes and feelings but would not discuss them if we could.[18]

Packard then extends his analysis of this targeted method of communication between seller and buyer, and notes that "the sale of billions of dollars' worth of products [is] hinged to a large extent upon successfully manipulating or coping with our guilt feelings, fears, anxieties, hostilities, loneliness feelings, inner tensions."[19] Packard might have included in his list of potential, prompted audience reactions displays of humor, satire, absurdity, and occasionally, impressions of visual enchantment. We are moved, frequently transfixed internally by a psychological processing; what we experience, we potentially purchase, from detergents to automobiles.

Packard's thesis is informed historically by the well-documented rise of the popular-culture, postwar phenomenon that was network and local television, evidenced in American homes and audiences; for us, this thesis suggests that the psychology of media-based consumer manipulation may also serve as an entry point into examining the documents, records, and aesthetic praxis of TV commercials, to establish an ongoing relationship between film art and the television advertisement. TV commercials are dynamic, consumer-driven narratives reflecting and revealing aspects of modern-postmodern culture.

Understanding the television commercial's evolution from its inception to the late 1950s can allow us to understand how it was influenced by the classical Hollywood style, and how its very adoption of that style into a brief running time meant that it necessarily had to alter the style as well, particularly in terms of editing. The result meant that, even as the commercial borrowed conventions from Hollywood feature filmmaking, the two forms quickly became involved in a dialogue, with the television commercial influencing feature filmmaking, and vice versa. Chapter 1 initiates our exploration of these issues by focusing on early commercials and using the work of Gerald "Jerry" Schnitzer as an important case study. Schnitzer is the essential linking figure between the initial postwar broadcast commercial's direct appeal to the audience and its stylized evolution.

The dialogue between feature films and television commercials was not at all confined to the 1950s. Consider the following quotation from an article published in *Advertising Age* in 1988:

> In 1966, motion picture director John Frankenheimer prepared to make a film on Europe's prestigious Grand Prix auto racing series by watching car commercials. The feature film veteran wanted to analyze the way TV commercials photographed automobiles because, in his opinion, they were technically "miles ahead" of the work he had seen in feature films. The director of *The Manchurian Candidate* [1962], *Seven Days in May* [1964], and other cinematic milestones still holds that opinion . . . Mr. Frankenheimer believes the look of feature films has changed dramatically because of the presence of commercials.[20]

We argue that Frankenheimer's quotation is as true in the new millennium as it was in the twentieth century.

To explore these issues in depth, Chapter 2 covers narrative, specifically examining how television commercials operate in terms of scene, genre, cross-genre, and the remake. It is our contention that the narrative framework for producing the television commercial is arguably, shot by shot, second to second, as frequently creative as a full-length feature film. Some commercials utilize cinematic narrative forms of Hollywood; others diverge from the same. The product and its "message" might be realistic or wholly fantastic; nevertheless, the TV commercial is indeed a narrative, a critically substantial formation, whether it unfolds in the form of a slice-of-life story or a presentational style pitch.

Chapter 3 covers mise-en-scène, specifically examining sets and settings, blocking and direct address, special effects, and animation: all that the frame contains within its physical and visible parameters to create signifying, ideologically imbued images. While attempting to establish a sense of product differentiation in a highly competitive market, the commercial's mise-en-scène invokes the comfortability of the familiar, the shock of the unfamiliar, or even the convergence of the two.

Chapter 4 covers cinematography, specifically film stock, photofilms, the freeze-frame, moving camera, and bullet time/time slice. As *Sponsor* magazine declared in 1955, the "video portion" of the commercials needed to lead, with copywriters following.[21] Gerald Schnitzer often relied on some of the best camera operators of the classical and, later, post-classical Hollywood eras to shoot his TV commercials, beginning a practice in which cinematographers were able to explore and experiment within limitations dictated by advertising clients and television norms.

Chapter 5 covers editing, paying particular attention to average shot lengths (ASLs) and the influential role that the TV commercial has played in how they have decreased in Hollywood feature filmmaking. This chapter also explores the ways in which the TV commercial has approached cutting on camera movement, or in not using any editing, letting a single image remain on screen for the entire running time, a practice associated with nineteenth-century cinema and born anew for product sales. The chapter also examines the TV commercial's ability to eschew standard Hollywood editing practices, opting for decidely non-classical approaches, as in the exclusive use of closeups to tell a story.

Chapter 6 covers sound, offering discussions of how the television commercial has revived, fostered, and revitalized the musical and the silent film genres, integrating sound and image in particularized respects that are markedly different than most Hollywood feature films of the late twentieth and early twenty-first centuries. The chapter also addresses the TV commercial at its most experimental, meaning the use of intertextuality that dates to the 1960s, the disruption of aural teleology in the twenty-first century, and the unique (even if legally obligatory) forms of audio/visual dissonance in which beautiful images unfold while the voiceover explains the dire side effects of given pharmaceuticals.

While informed by rigorous historiographic research, these chapters are not meant to be exhaustive or purely chronological, but rather indexical, providing case studies of particular television commercials and aesthetic approaches that merit inquiry. For example, TV commercials have provided an important forum for the redeployment of aesthetics eschewed by Hollywood features films as being outmoded. Indeed, during the late twentieth and early twenty-first centuries, TV commercials have become the key mainstream proponents of black-and-white cinematography.

In other cases, from the famous (Michel Gondry's 1996 Smirnoff vodka commercial *Smarienberg* introducing the effect that became known as bullet time prior to its appearance in any feature film; Fig. I.4) to the overlooked (the influence of television commercials on the ASLs of Hollywood films), it is possible to view TV commercials as sometimes being at the vanguard of new and changing film aesthetics.

Whether advancing new technologies and aesthetic possiblities or reviving those of earlier eras, the television commercial's ubiquity is a crucial reason why it needs careful study as a form of film art. Prior to the rise of home video, viewers saw films at theatres or programs broadcast

Figure I.4 Michel Gondry's *Smarienberg* (1996)

on TV. Sometimes the films were revived, and sometimes programs were rebroadcast, but most viewers saw their content on a single occasion. By contrast, the television commercial was unique for the potentiality of far more repeat viewings than feature films or TV programs. To be sure, their sheer repetition was at times the source of viewer discontent.[22] The issue here, though, is that—far more than merely a litany of (albeit important) "firsts" or diffuse influences from TV commercials to Hollywood (and vice versa)—the TV commercial had the unique ability to do what it has in fact continued to do in a post-home video era: acclimate mass audiences to new, changing, and revived aesthetics. It has also done so in an isolated manner, meaning that such aesthetics can constitute the whole or bulk of given commercials, given their brief duration. In short, it is important historically that *Smarienberg* introduced bullet time before any feature film did so, but equally important given that such a commercial (and its successors, like *Khakis Swing* for Gap trousers in 1998) familiarized mainstream audiences (including those who do not attend movie theatres frequently) with a new aesthetic due to sheer broadcast repetition.

In tandem with the interactions and often-shared goals between feature films and television commercials is the need to analyze the television commercial as a valid art form on its own merits. While we do not mean to argue that all television commercials are equally artistic (any more than we would claim that all feature films are equally artistic), we do contend strongly that some of them represent examples of original, creative, and sometimes powerful filmmaking, including the aforementioned cases of David Lynch and Errol Morris. Director Howard Zieff once described television commercials as "little movies"; Adrian Lyne called them "minifilms."[23] We view TV commercials as films, short films to be sure, but films all the same, whether they were produced in 1897 or at the present time.

In terms of the urgent need for research in this area, it is fortunate that access to television commercials has never been greater. While some American TV commercials remain difficult to view, particularly many of those produced prior to the 1990s, an enormous number are readily available. More than one home video company has released compilations of them, ranging from collections of cigarette commercials to Taschen's DVD *Advertising Now*, which accompanies a book of the same name.[24] A number of filmmakers and advertising agencies post their commercials online, as do some of the clients that contract them. This is to say nothing of the internet, which is replete with television commercials of all kinds from the 1950s to the present.

Citing international archival print and media sources, with some previously "lost" or difficult-to-access material now available for critical analyses, we will establish that television commercials, whether hawking furniture sales, travel destinations, canned fruit, or cosmetic surgery, *are* short films. We believe these TV commercials—like newsreels, music videos, and trailers—are significant cultural artifacts to be considered as part of the modern visual media experience. According to William Boddy, we must address with increased zeal "the heretofore marginal critical and production practices excluded from traditional histories of cinema," and we now formally assert that commercials are integral parts of a common media history.[25] In "Historiography and Historiophoty," Hayden White also advocates a more inclusive processing of historical narrative:

> All too often, historians treat photographic, cinematic, and video data as if they could be read in the same way as a written document. We are inclined to treat the imagistic evidence as if it were at best a complement of verbal evidence, rather than as a supplement, which is to say, a discourse in its own right and one capable of telling us things about its referents that are both different from what can be told in verbal discourse and also of a kind that can only be told by means of visual images.[26]

In the present work, we note that many artists, filmmakers, and writers have pursued the same line of thought as Hayden White: television commercials—the "art of advertising"—do matter, and commercials have relevant technical and aesthetic historical criteria. More to his point, our monograph is accompanied by a compilation of key commercials we discuss, available online at more than one website.

The television commercial is a critically ignored short film narrative. *Consuming Images: Film Art and the American Television Commercial*, the first monograph devoted to the subject, examines and categorizes this aspect of postwar visual culture as an ideological, entertainment, and industrial staple of media production. Despite being critically and historically ignored in discussions of Film Studies, we wish to recover this enormous and enormously important corpus of films.

Notes

1. Quoted in Francis Clines, "Stanley Kubrick's Vietnam War," in *Stanley Kubrick Interviews*, ed. Gene D. Phillips (Jackson: University of Mississippi Press, 2001), p. 175.
2. David Seldon, "The Ringing of the Surreal Cash Till: David Lynch's Commercials," *Network Awesome*, August 25, 2017. Available at <http://networkawesome.com/mag/article/the-ringing-of-the-surreal-cash-till-david-lynchs-commercials/> (last accessed May 23, 2019).
3. Paul Cronin, "It Could All Be Wrong: An Unfinished Interview with Errol Morris," in *Errol Morris Interviews*, ed. Livia Bloom (Jackson: University of Mississippi Press, 2010), p. 149.
4. Tom Ryan, "Errol Morris Interview," *Senses of Cinema*, September 16, 2001. Available at <http://sensesofcinema.com/2001/feature-articles/morris/> (last accessed May 23, 2019).
5. Cronin, p. 187.
6. Arthur Asa Berger, *Ads, Fads, and Consumer Culture: Advertising's Impact on American Character and Society*, 5th edn (Lanham, MD: Rowman & Littlefield, 2015), p. 15.
7. See, for example: "At the Commercials," *Advertising Age*, October 3, 1983, pp. M4–M5, M46; "Siskel, Ebert Return to AA Workshop," *Advertising Age*, February 13, 1984, p. 52; "Critics Turn Guns on TV Ads," *Advertising Age*, August 25, 1986, p. 59.
8. Walter Cummins and George Gordon, *Programming Our Lives: Television and American Identity* (Westport, CT: Praeger, 2006), p. 58.
9. Quoted in Tony Shugaar, "Federico Fellini," *Advertising Age*, June 2, 1986, p. 59.
10. David Bordwell and Kristin Thompson, *Film Art: An Introduction*, 9th edn (New York: McGraw-Hill, 2010), pp. 2–3.
11. "Moving Picture Advertising," *The Phonoscope* (May 1898), p. 14.

12. Kerry Segrave, *Product Placement in Hollywood Films* (Jefferson, NC: McFarland, 2004), p. 1.
13. Segrave, p. 212.
14. See, for example: David Huron, "Music in Advertising: An Analytic Paradigm," *The Musical Quarterly*, vol. 73, no. 4 (1989), pp. 557–74; Brendan Maguire and Georgie Ann Weatherby, "Television Commercial Content: Religion Versus Science and Professional Expertise," *Sociology of Religion*, vol. 59, no. 2 (Summer 1998), pp. 171–8.
15. Martin Esslin, "Aristotle and the Advertisers: The Television Commercial Considered as a Form of Drama," *The Kenyon Review*, vol. 1, no. 4 (Autumn 1979), p. 107.
16. Quoted in Tim Cahill, "The *Rolling Stone* Interview: Stanley Kubrick," in *Stanley Kubrick Interviews*, ed. Gene D. Phillips (Jackson: University of Mississippi Press, 2001), p. 199.
17. Lynn Spigel, *TV By Design: Modern Art and the Rise of Network Television* (Chicago: University of Chicago Press, 2008), pp. 216–17.
18. Vance Packard, *The Hidden Persuaders* (New York: David McKay, 1957), pp. 24–5.
19. Packard, p. 57.
20. Jennifer Pendleton, "Hollywood Buys the Concept," *Advertising Age*, November 9, 1988, p. 158.
21. "Are Commercials Getting Picture Lazy?", *Sponsor*, February 7, 1955, pp. 42–3.
22. Lawrence R. Samuel, *Brought to You By: Postwar Television Advertising and the American Dream* (Austin: University of Texas Press, 2001), p. 111.
23. Quoted in Pendleton, p. 160; "Cover Story: Adrian Lyne," *Advertising Age*, August 1, 1985, p. 5.
24. Julius Wiedemann, *Advertising Now: TV Commercials* (Hong Kong: Taschen, 2008).
25. William Boddy, "Advertising Form: Technological Change and Screen Practices in the USA," in *Films That Sell*, ed. Bo Florin, Nico de Klerk, and Patrick Vonderau, (New York: Bloomsbury, 2016), p. 170.
26. Hayden White, "Historiography and Historiophoty," *The American Historical Review*, vol. 93, no. 5 (December 1988), p. 119x`x`3.

CHAPTER 1

Origins

American television commercials of the 1940s and early 1950s were often simple and presentational. Spokespersons sometimes held up or demonstrated a given product, instructing the audience to purchase the same. Surviving kinescopes reveal that many of these commercials gave limited consideration to mise-en-scène, cinematography, and editing. Many were performed live, an approach that *Sponsor* magazine endorsed in 1948, believing them to have a lower "fatigue" factor on viewers than repetitions of a filmed commercial.[1] Not unexpectedly, though, live commercials resulted at times in various snafus, as famously parodied on the television sitcom *I Love Lucy* in 1952, in which the inebriated title character (played by Lucille Ball) touts "Vitameatavegamin" to her broadcast audience.

William F. Baker and George Dessart have noted,

> For nearly a decade there would be no way to produce a broadcast-quality recording. Commercials had to be made live. Unable to summon up the grandeur of the Rockies, the allure of Paris, or the kinesthetic of water sports, advertisers were forced to rely on the product and its spokesperson, one of the most notable being Betty Furness.[2]

Many examples could be given, including the 1955 commercial for S.O.S. scouring pads. It consisted of one single shot lasting 148 seconds, during which 269 words were spoken and sung.[3] Looking back on such ads, the *Los Angeles Times* described them as "absurd product demonstrations."[4]

In fairness, these comments were hasty generalizations. From the late 1940s, a number of directors shot television commercials on 35mm film; as early as 1947, for example, Filmack of Chicago produced a film commercial for Dodge.[5] Such technology allowed directors to adopt the same possibilities as those employed by feature filmmakers, including the common usage of animation and/or various optical and special effects, ranging from wipe transitions to stop-motion. The trend towards film gained greater momentum as the 1950s progressed. Lincoln Diamant observed:

> Once TV commercials became more creatively complicated, the *filmed* commercial took center stage. *With a film camera, your studio was the world.* Commercial scenarios were *limited* only by the copywriter's or art director's imagination.
> . . . The 50s firmly established the era of the film commercial. Its keynote was not low cost, but simplicity, versatility, and control.[6]

Such control extended beyond the production process to distribution and exhibition, as film prints could be delivered to and used by American television stations with projection equipment ("telecines") that allowed them to broadcast the same with ease.

But shooting film did not necessarily result in cinematic commercials. In 1951, *Sponsor* reported that the bulk of the "people who are responsible for the original birth of the TV commercial are not film people."[7] In 1954, the same magazine wrote of the need for a greater emphasis on visuals, with "fewer commercials that could be described as 'radio with pictures.'"[8] And those voices were heard. Noticing the evolution under way, one journalist described the directors creating television commercials in 1956:

> His techniques are improving every day. Some of his singing commercials become popular hits. Actors of some repute and self respect are willing to accept his product-pushing scripts and perform them creditably. It is quite in order for the stars of the show to step out during breaks and tell us why they never use anything else except the sponsor's hair-oil, beer, dog food, foundation garments, or whatever it may be.[9]

The journalist concluded by declaring that "many of the commercials, particularly on the big name shows, are models of advertising, catchy, interesting, memorable."

Increasing budgets led to a greater emphasis on visual style, such that in 1956, *Sponsor* referred to the "Cecil B. DeMille touch" being "used increasingly" to "shock, entertain and sell"[10] (Fig. 1.1).

However, the transition to greater creativity in TV commercials did not occur quickly. In September 1958, screenwriter Ben Hecht complained virulently about them, believing that they induced a "sort of home-made catatonia" in audiences due to their uninteresting style and their broadcast frequency and repetition.[11] By that time, 40 percent of television commercials were being produced in Hollywood as opposed to New York, though the change in geography had not yet caused a drastic change in their narrative

Figure 1.1 Krinkles the Clown: "shock, entertain and sell": Post Cereal commercial (1953)

or aesthetic content.[12] Whether or not one enjoyed their jingles or onscreen talent, in other words, the TV commercial was not particularly cinematic, with many in the industry heralding the necessity of onscreen spokespersons undertaking product demonstrations.[13]

Enter Gerald "Jerry" Schnitzer, who transformed the television commercial during the very year of Hecht's complaint. Shooting on 35mm film, Schnitzer originated what became known as the "slice of life" commercial by creating short and relatable human-interest stories in which the product was featured, sometimes quite subtly.[14] The business side of his first commercial exemplified a standardized process that still exists in the twenty-first century: a client wishing to advertise (in this case General Motors) hired an advertising agency (in this case Campbell–Ewald), who contracted with a production company (in this case Robert Lawrence Productions, who hired Schnitzer) to create a commercial, one that had to adhere to broadcast standards and meet with the client's approval.

Schnitzer's cinematographer was Fred Gately, who was then best known for having shot episodes of such television programs as *Dragnet* (1951–9) and *The Adventures of Ozzie and Harriet* (1952–66). Immediately before working with Schnitzer, Gately had been cinematographer for the low-budget but extremely atmospheric horror movie *I Bury the Living* (Albert Band, 1958) with Richard Boone and Theodore Bikel.

In the space of two minutes, Schnitzer's commercial *Going to the Dance* (also known as *Boy Meets Impala*, 1958) touted Chevrolet by presenting a narrative about a modern family (Figs 1.2–1.6). It is prom night, and a male teenager heads out to his old car while mother, father, and little sister watch, all to the strains not of a jingle, but instead of non-diegetic jazz music composed specifically for the commercial and performed by electric guitar, vibraphone, and drums.

When he reaches his tired old clunker on the street, the teenager grimaces, and for the first time a voice is heard, in this case an offscreen announcer who says, "If it's happened once, it's happened a thousand times." Then the teenager glances in another direction and ogles a new 1958 convertible Impala. We quickly realize that it belongs to his father; both mother and little sister look up at him to see what he will do. After a number of glances back and forth, father finally smiles and takes the keys out of his pocket. The teenager runs back to grab them and to kiss his little sister before sprinting to the new car. Then he rushes back to his clunker to retrieve his prom date's nearly forgotten corsage. (Jump cut here to the next scene.) The boy and his date happily sit in the car before arriving at the prom. As the commercial ends, we hear the announcer speak again, for the first time since his initial voiceover: "What a gal! What a night! What a car! The New Chevrolet."

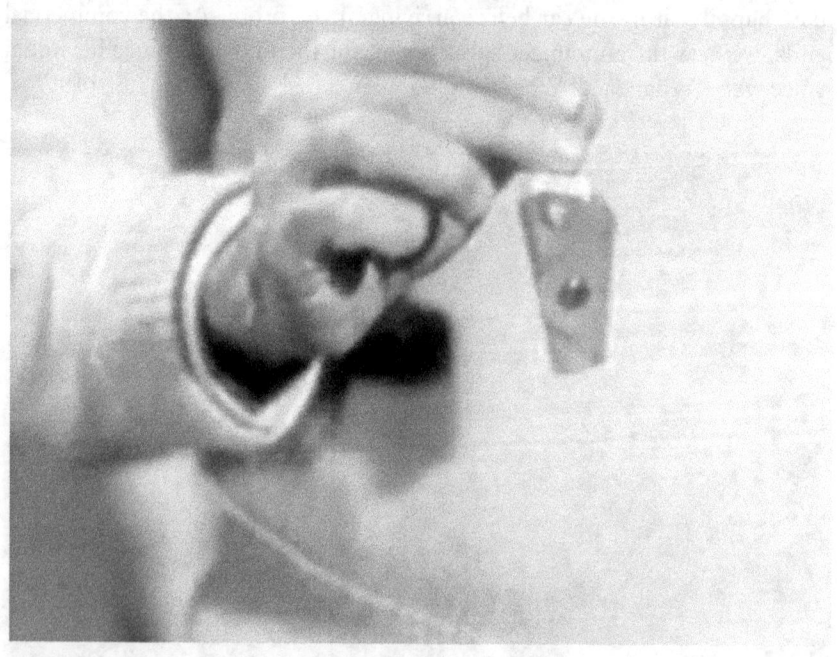

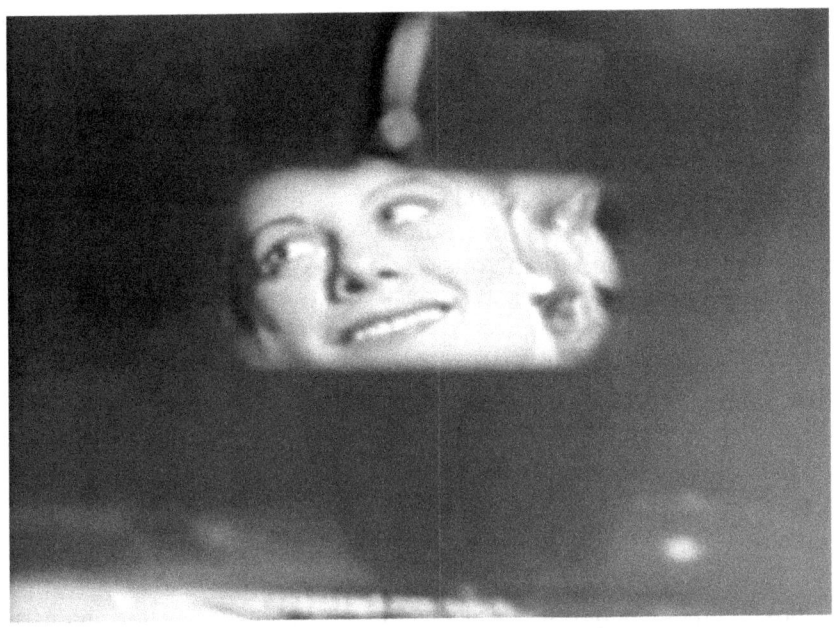

Figures 1.2, 1.3, 1.4, 1.5, and 1.6 Gerald Schnitzer's *Going to the Dance* (1958)

David Halberstam later wrote, "a new era was being announced and sold in a very new way."[15] First broadcast in June 1958, *Going to the Dance* was revolutionary for several reasons, ranging from its lack of dialogue and limited use of voiceover (only twenty-one words, in a period where some commercials used up to 120 per minute), to its amount of moving camera (four dolly shots) and its use of color film stock (which, granted, most viewers would not have seen in 1958 given the dominance of black-and-white television sets in American homes).[16] However, it was *Going to the Dance*'s narrative style that set it far apart from the past history of American television commercials. Here was a human-interest story in the form of a two-minute short subject, directed by a man who had no prior background in advertising or marketing.

Schnitzer was born in Brooklyn, New York, in 1917. His father worked in film sales, and Schnitzer would later suggest that his early viewing experiences of silent movies played an important role in his visual approach to TV commercials.[17] After working for documentary filmmaker John Grierson in 1939, Schnitzer was hired by the B-movie company Monogram Pictures in Hollywood, functioning as a dialogue director, assistant director, and part-time chauffeur before writing original stories and scripts, as he did for such films as *Bowery at Midnight* (Wallace Fox, 1942). In that case, the film begins with a prison break, immediately thrusting the audience into the middle of an action scene. Schnitzer later recalled, "That was almost a cardinal rule, although we writers tried to wean them off the stereotype. Action and motion were always the name of the game in low budget films."[18]

After serving in the Army Air Force from 1943 to 1946, Schnitzer returned to Monogram, writing a number of scripts for the Bowery Boys. Then he formed his own company, producing docudramas, as well as what he described as a "series of vignettes in the early fifties called *The Guitar and the Eye*, designed to encourage classroom discussion without a narrator's influence."[19] Heralding Schnitzer in his book *The Fifties*, David Halberstam describes *The Guitar and the Eye*:

> Schnitzer's stories were short and arresting, and in some way they reflected the essence of American life. They were the work of an original and very gifted man. One of them showed a mailman making his rounds, coming upon a hopscotch board and, when he thought no one was looking, playing a secret game of hopscotch. In another, Schnitzer had waited by a drawbridge and caught the idle moments of people in their cars as the bridge was up and their lives were momentarily interrupted.[20]

When Kensinger Jones of Campbell–Ewald saw *The Guitar and the Eye*, he quickly realized that Schnitzer could create a new type of television commercial. In 1961, O. W. Klose, Vice President of Campbell–Ewald, recounted the origins of *Going to the Dance*:

> Back in 1958, our TV department looked at a film produced and directed by Jerry Schnitzer. Not a commercial, simply a 'slice of life' vignette. It was wonderfully warm and revealing in the way it dealt with people. It was gently humorous. It was easy to identify yourself with the people on the screen. We got the client to look at the vignette. He saw the possibilities and agreed that it might be a way to go [for a new kind of television commercial].
>
> Trouble was, it was nearly impossible to write that kind of technique into a television script. All we could do was develop a situation, write a paragraph delineating it, and depend on Jerry's sensitivity, talent, and way with people to make it come alive.[21]

For Kensinger Jones, Schnitzer's work was reminiscent of the tone and approach seen in the paintings of Norman Rockwell.[22]

Critics agreed. In 1958, *Art Direction* judged *Going to the Dance* to be "indeed a step forward in the gradually growing art of the television communication . . ."[23] That same year, another journalist proclaimed Schnitzer had created an all-visual commercial: "the ice is broken and everything is set for the plunge," meaning that others should follow his lead.[24] *Going to the Dance* went on to become the "most awarded commercial of the year."[25] It won the Grand Prix at the Cannes International Advertising Film Festival in 1959, the first time an American ever received the award, and became an official selection at the first American TV Commercials Festival and Forum in 1960.

As one journalist realized, the "latest thing in TV commericals is something called 'non-verbal communications,'" and "one of non-V's strongest boosters is Jerry Schnitzer."[26] Schnitzer later recalled, "The result was phenomenal. General Motors led the way, followed by Kodak, Clairol, and Gallo Wine."[27] His large array of other clients would also include Alcoa, Bell Telephone, the Florida Citrus Commission, Kellogg, the American Tobacco Company, California Oil, and Security First National Bank & Trust Company.

Soon after becoming involved in TV commercials, Schnitzer stressed to the industry that his style arose from Hollywood feature filmmaking. In 1962, he explained:

> We're adopting a motion picture approach, making our commercials more like a little movie. We're giving them structure, a beginning, middle, and end. They're going to have characterization because we're learning how to use the tools of motion pictures in a very confined area.[28]

On a separate occasion, Schnitzer wrote, "Suffice it to say that all of the elements that go into a feature film must converge on the commercial if it is to fulfill its communicative mission."[29]

His success led him to become Vice President of Robert Lawrence Productions in 1959, the same company that had filmed *Going to the Dance* for Campbell–Ewald.[30] As of the summer of 1962, Schnitzer became head of his own company, which was located in Hollywood on Sunset Boulevard, very close to the location of his old employer, Monogram Pictures.[31] Though many others were producing commercials in Hollywood, most lacked what Schnitzer had: knowledge of Hollywood filmmaking *and* television advertising.[32] By late 1964, he had constructed a studio that featured a sound stage, an insert stage, viewing rooms, and built-in interiors.[33] He also became a key member of the West Coast Commercial Film Producers Association in 1967 (Fig. 1.7).[34]

Schnitzer railed against past practice in television commercials, arguing in 1962 that it would be "unpardonable to continue our coarse and artless ways."[35] He condemned "sloppy acting and cutting, heavy-handed music tracks and superfluous narration."[36] He believed the reliance on announcers was nothing more than the "voice of father, paternal and

Figure 1.7 Gerald "Jerry" Schnitzer (Courtesy of Ellen Schnitzer)

patronizing, in a fit of bombast."³⁷ In 1962, Schnitzer went so far as to write an article on the subject of narration:

> the commercial must be the confidant of the viewer rather than his counselor, his peer rather than his parent. It means that the commercial speaks *to* rather than *at* the viewer, in a tone more personable than paternal. It means that, instead of offending or deadening the viewer's sensibilities, the commercial befriends him. Instead of preaching to him, the commercial communicates with, socializes with, yes, even makes love to him.³⁸

In the cases that Schnitzer had to use voiceover, he experimented with new possibilities. For example, his 1962 series of commercials for Clairol Hair Color, *Do Blondes Really Have More Fun?* (also known as *The Clairol Story about the Adams Family*) relied on information spoken by an offscreen "stage manager," a device he adapted from Thornton Wilder's 1938 play, *Our Town*. The commercials unfolded in four acts over six minutes, featuring twelve cast members.³⁹ Schnitzer later described its narrative as "non-linear," one that showed "the activities of four generations of women who use the various Clairol Products. Original music heightened the shifting moods of each section."⁴⁰

Subtlety became a key hallmark of his narratives. For example, *Do Blondes Really Have More Fun?* placed its characters into everyday narrative situations in which their hair would be seen and admired, rather than concentrating on the packaged product. Similarly, while Schnitzer's 1963 commercials for Purina Dog Chow would show a dog eating the product, that was not its narrative focus. By contrast, the commercial depicted:

> several episodes in the day of a little girl and her pet dog, unfolding from the question and theme of the series, "What is a dog?" Scenes include a dog being brushed, fed, and sung to by a little girl . . . The commercial closes with the little girl in bed and her "best friend" sleeping beside her.⁴¹

These narratives exemplified Schnitzer's belief that there was "room for only one idea in a single commercial," an idea that would hook the viewer in much the same way as the opening scenes of his earlier B-movies had attempted to do, and to emphasize visuals to convey that single idea, in the style of silent cinema.⁴² Following general practice, these singular ideas normally unfolded in either thirty seconds, sixty seconds, or 120 seconds, though Schnitzer did create a six-minute commercial for Chevrolet that aired during *Bonanza* in 1964. *Back Stage* called it "breathtaking."⁴³

Schnitzer generally hired personnel with considerable experience in Hollywood filmmaking. His cinematic approach also included casting film actors to give performances similar to those seen in Hollywood movies. *Going to the Dance* starred two-time Academy Award nominee Shirley Knight in one of her earliest roles; Schnitzer subsequently directed various other film actors in his commercials, including Adam West, Lorne Greene, Sharon Tate, and Buster Keaton. In other cases, he discovered talent that would move from commercials to television and feature films, including Barbara Feldon, Donna Douglas, and Linda Evans. In 1965, Imogene Coca credited "artistic" directors like Schnitzer with helping to change the attitude of name actors towards agreeing to star in television commercials.[44]

Schnitzer also extolled the virtues of shooting on location. As one article in 1965 described, "Schnitzer runs off to Colorado to capture shots of cars zooming up mountain roads. He works outside of Denver, or Colorado Springs, and next year will probably have to find a new undiscovered country."[45] That same year, Schnitzer hired a professional location director.[46] "When you get outside with a camera," he explained, "things happen. Geography can add dimension to a scene." In 1962, Schnitzer directed a sixty-second commercial for Colgate–Palmolive's Halo shampoo that featured the following storyline:

> Last stop . . . New York. Among the passengers stepping down to the platform of Track 2 in Pennsylvania is a most attractive young lady, Miss Halo. But she is not seen by viewers of this new Halo commercial until she meets a friend at the gate. Up to that point the camera is busy picking up the admiring reactions of other travellers as she proceeds from the gate.[47]

Here again is an example of a Schnitzer commercial emphasizing narrative rather than a specific image of a retail product or even (for the bulk of its running time) the hair of the character who uses it. But in this case, Schnitzer filmed at Pennsylvania Station in New York rather than at a studio, a shoot that required two truckloads of equipment, a crew of twenty-five, four featured players, six supporting characters, and fifteen extras. He also praised the possibilities of natural lighting, so much so that he lobbied for faster color film stocks that would achieve better results outdoors, including in "adverse conditions."[48]

In other cases, Schnitzer constructed major sets, as in the case of a small Indiana town of the 1880s for one commercial, and a drugstore set featuring 1,100 different items of actual retail merchandise for another.[49] In early 1963, Gabriel Scognamillo joined his company as art director.[50] Scognamillo had begun his film career working for Jean Renoir and subsequently worked as a production designer and art director for MGM, Universal, Warner Bros., and Paramount. His resumé included films like

Love Happy (David Miller, 1949), *The Great Caruso* (Richard Thorpe, 1951), and *Tobor the Great* (Lee Sholem, 1954), as well as an Oscar nomination for Best Art Direction–Set Decoration for *The Story of Three Loves* (Vincente Minnelli and Gottfried Reinhardt, 1953). Scognamillo also served as art director for "Tomorrowland" during the construction of Disneyland in the 1950s.

As much as anything else, Schnitzer devoted his attentions to cinematography, ranging from his choice of 35mm film to achieve certain looks, but video for others, as well as his considered reasoning between black and white and color, becoming a leader in the adoption of the latter.[51] For example, Schnitzer's sixty-second commercial for Max Factor's Sheer Genius in 1965 placed its lead female character in a James Bond-style spy narrative. At a given moment, she takes out a tube of "005-style Sheer Genius" makeup and applies it before being captured by the enemy. In that shot, an out-of-focus candelabrum appears on screen left in the foreground while she is in sharp focus on screen right. Over her shoulder in the distance is the enemy, who appears in soft focus thanks to a shallow depth of field.[52]

Schnitzer regularly hired such cinematographers as Karl Struss, who filmed *Ben-Hur* (Fred Niblo, 1925), and *The Great Dictator* (Charlie Chaplin, 1940). Struss shared the Oscar for Best Cinematography in 1929 for *Sunrise: A Song of Two Humans* (F. W. Murnau, 1927), and was subsequently nominated for *Dr. Jekyll and Mr. Hyde* (Rouben Mamoulian, 1931), *The Sign of the Cross* (Cecil B. DeMille, 1934), and *Aloma of the South Seas* (Alfred Santell, 1941). Schnitzer also worked frequently with J. Peverell Marley, who had shot such films as *The Ten Commandments* (Cecil B. DeMille, 1923), *The Two Mrs. Carrolls* (Peter Godfrey, 1947), and *House of Wax* (André De Toth, 1953). He had been nominated for two Oscars for Best Cinematography for *Suez* (Allan Dwan, 1938) and *Life with Father* (Michael Curtiz, 1947). Their input allowed Schnitzer to achieve a cinematic look, with the ads Marley shot (*Do Blondes Really Have More Fun?* being one of them) featuring a greater use of depth than many television programs of the era.

In 1962, Schnitzer and Marley shot a commercial for the Gallo Wine Company on location in a vineyard, using a cast that combined professional actors with actual field workers.[53] Schnitzer recalled:

> You need a ballad, a ballsy story-telling ballad that'll synch with the movements of the workers, their faces, their hands, the reaching and bending, and gathering the grapes. You connect the sequence, panning with varied close angles of grapes, dissolving into a busy urban environment, and as the camera movement stops, the bottle of Gallo Wine fills the right portion of the screen.

> The second Act begins with highlights from the opening, adding a few new faces, followed with a med. shot, of a young boss-man type in work clothes, directing his men during the early selection and transferring the grapes into moving vehicles headed for the refinery.
>
> The Third act, the Closing, would reprise the harvesting from the previous two episodes with wider shots of the workers. The end sequence reveals a blend of the urban and upscale environment, in sharp focus along with a bottle of Gallo.
>
> With each following commercial, the ballad becomes more fully orchestrated as we reach the highlight, a handsome Padron on a white stallion, overseeing a wide expanse of his leafy lucrative vineyards. Naturally, you cover this sequence with juicy close ups of the rider, his horse and the grape pickers. And a lovely sunset shot as the name Gallo rises.[54]

Schnitzer hired folk singer Burl Ives to record a folk song to use as the background score.

Schnitzer also worked with Stanley Cortez, who had shot *The Magnificent Ambersons* (Orson Welles, 1942) and *The Night of the Hunter* (Charles Laughton, 1955). In his unpublished memoir, Schnitzer wrote:

> Reluctantly, I asked Mr. Cortez if he would consider such a menial assignment. His phone had not been ringing off the hook since *Night of The Hunter*. Stanley agreed to what would be a day's work, shooting mushrooms, the basic ingredient of the company's new campaign for its mushroom soup.
>
> The agency's producer and writer of the mushroom soup commercial warned us in advance that the mushrooms must look pure white as they tumble down a chute. (They may never look that white in the soup, but in the TV ad they must be whiter than white!)
>
> Before the miracle of today's space age imaging capability, not even Stanley Cortez, Pev Marley, Karl Struss nor any film processing company could make the mushrooms white enough to satisfy the agency producer.
>
> What began as a day's work for Stanly Cortez leisurely staring at mushrooms became a full week's nightmare. The mushrooms resisted vinegar rubs, varnish lights, full arc lamps.[55]

In other cases, Schnitzer achieved his aims by working with younger talent in the early stages of their careers, such as Ric Waite (who would go on to shoot *48 Hrs.* [Walter Hill] in 1982, *Footloose* [Herbert Ross] in 1984, and *Red Dawn* [John Milius] in 1984).[56]

Classical Hollywood editing also heavily influenced Schnitzer's commercials. His editors included David Saxon (who would go on to shoot *Willy Wonka & the Chocolate Factory* [Mel Stuart] in 1971) and Otho Lovering (whose career as a Hollywood editor began in 1928 and continued for four decades). Lovering edited such features as John Ford's *Stagecoach* in 1939, for which he shared an Oscar nomination with

Dorothy Spencer. Even more than cinematographers, editors played a key role at Schnitzer's company. In 1965, Schnitzer named Gary Freund, who had edited over fifty episodes of the TV show *Make Room for Daddy* (1953–65), as Vice President of his company.[57] The following year, Lin Ephraim, a former editor for Walt Disney, became Schnitzer's General Manager.[58]

Likewise, Schnitzer drew upon his knowledge of Hollywood soundtracks to hire a range of composers, among them André Previn, Mel Henke, and Laurindo Almeida, to create original background scores for his commercials that were carefully timed to the onscreen action.[59] The musicians hired to perform their music included the renowned flutist Arthur Gleghorn, saxophonist Benny Carter, and French hornist Vincent DeRosa, who was famed in the industry for the sheer number of feature film soundtracks on which he played.[60]

If *Going to the Dance* had been Schnitzer's breakthrough in the industry, the culmination of his efforts came as a result of his work for Kodak, which included commercials using the songs *Theme from A Summer Place* and *The Way You Look Tonight*.[61] He later remembered, "Based on the warmth and simple directness of a Kodak commercial I designed and directed, I was credited as the one who created 'The Kodak Moment.'"[62] Schnitzer's most praised work for the company came in 1966 with a two-minute commercial called *Sunrise, Sunset* (Figs 1.8 and 1.9). It begins with a medium shot of a beautiful, young bride. Her father is nearby. Schnitzer wrote:

> We zoom closer to father as the bride's face "lens dissolves" into his eyes, as the voice track, *Sunrise, Sunset* is narrated by the theatrical star, Howard Keel: "Is this the little girl I carried . . . ?"
> To me [a "lens dissolve," meaning racking the shot of eyes out of focus to lead to a transition] feels that when you move the lens by hand out of focus, it feels more like internal tears, instead of the usual optical house mechanically lacing adjacent scenes. We can use the normal dissolves as we follow the children through the growing phases. We'll see them at play, in intimate moments, and whatever the light and background suggest. To remind the viewer in the middle of the story, that the point of view of the father is always "present," physically, his shoulder and a part of his profile enter and rest against a tree, as he watches a young couple in the distant background racing across the lawn.[63]

Keel's dialogue was taken from Jerry Brock and Sheldon Harnick's song *Sunrise, Sunset*, as famously heard in the Broadway musical *Fiddler on the Roof* (1964), which at the time had not yet been adapted for the screen. He begins by speaking the words, with Laurindo Almeida's

Figures 1.8 and 1.9 Schnitzer's *Sunrise, Sunset* (1966)

guitar heard behind him. At approximately fifty seconds in, Keel—who is never seen—begins singing the lyrics rather than just speaking them, yet another Schnitzer innovation with regard to the problems he perceived with standard voiceovers. The word "Kodak" appears in the lower third of the screen during the first shot, but no Kodak snapshot camera is seen or mentioned until the final nine seconds of the commercial, at which time a different narrator says, "Keep the days you want to remember in pictures. All you need is a Kodak camera, Kodak film, and a little thoughtfulness." The camera is not shown on screen until the final three seconds, the visual emphasis being on Schnitzer's narrative.

Sunrise, Sunset first aired in May 1966, and proceeded to win the Grand Prix at the Venice International Advertising Film Festival.[64] It subsequently played during the Academy Awards broadcast in 1967, with Bosley Crowther remarking in the *New York Times* that it was "one of the most touching and agreeable interludes in the whole show."[65] Carl Reiner declared, "The commercial was better than the show!"[66] And a writer for the *New York Post* observed, "Seldom has a TV commercial found as much appreciation as the Kodak 'Sunrise–Sunset' sequence."[67]

Schnitzer's successes led him to consider the potential of television commercials. "He has the courage to say art and commercial in the same breath," a journalist said in 1963.[68] Speaking for himself, Schnitzer remarked:

> I submit that the filmed commercial can be, and, in notable instances, has been, art. And if it is ever going to mature as a vital means of communication, it will do so as an art form under the aegis of film men.
>
> Admittedly, it sounds like a preposterous notion: arty commercials! Yet few people will dispute the pretensions of other advertising forms to artistic consideration. If we are willing to acknowledge that the design of magazine and newspaper advertising can reach the heights, why not admit a similar potential for the filmed commercial?
>
> The source of one genuine doubt is in the inherent time limitations of the commercial. Can film, which has attained its most powerful expression as an art form in lengths of approximately 90 minutes—can it speak a meaningful and sensuous message in *60 seconds, or 150, or eight?*
>
> A print story may be 100,000 words, 25,000 words, 5,000 words, or 1,000 words. Whether it is called a novel, a novelette, a short story, or a short short, it is still a story and can be literature. The same holds true for the motion picture. None of its fundamental requisites depends for its fulfillment on any given duration of screen time.[69]

That Schnitzer's work received praise as artistic at the time is evident for many reasons, not least because some of his commercials were screened at the Museum of Modern Art as early as 1963.[70] By 1970, an article in

Entertainment World observed that he had transferred the "auteur theory into television commercials."[71]

One might consider Schnitzer's critical and creative work in the development of the postwar broadcast commercial as technologically pioneering both in its advancement of cinematic production values and overall industrial "professionalism," and, in Schnitzer's artfully stylized representation of "Americana," in his entertaining, milieu-specific, narrativized vignettes of life, which made the respective product—from automobiles to hair spray—desired by a consuming public. A reading of Schnitzer's TV commericals demonstrates that they were progressive–expansive in aesthetic design and sophisticated in the reading of its audiences' capacity, via a more "cinematic" narrative, to create a market for the product. It is not an exaggeration to conclude that Schnitzer, among other auteurs producing film in the 1950s and 1960s, altered how the American audience experienced visual culture and conceived of itself and everyday life. Schnitzer's commercial narratives largely initiated the industrial standard, the "human-interest story," and these stories and songs can be recalled decades later in the jingle-laced memory of the public, reliving favored shots of faces and places in personal Kodak moments, whether real or not, from postwar America: retrieved data, recalled director.

Certainly, there were many other persons in the industry who viewed television commercials as a form of film art. "Commercials are about to take a giant step on to a new plateau," *Sponsor* reported in 1959.[72] Others also value in them, as can be seen in the title of Norman Mailer's 1959 book *Advertisements for Myself* and in Marshall McLuhan's belief that advertisements constituted a type of folk art. These reactions were, in some measure, due to the commercial's adoption of the narrative and aesthetic devices of the Classical Hollywood Style.

In so doing, however, the television commercial's own attributes, including its sales remit and its brief running time, meant that it became a type of film short subject that necessarily altered that feature film style in terms of narrative, mise-en-scène, cinematography, editing, and sound. Rather than being a mere imitation, the television commercial was at times an experiment in form. Influenced by feature films, it came to influence them as well.

Notes

1. "Life Expectancy of a TV Commercial," *Sponsor*, November 1948, pp. 27–9.
2. William F. Baker and George Dessart, *Down the Tube: An Inside Account of the Failure of American Television* (New York: Basic Books, 1998), p. 86.

3. Lincoln Diamant, *Television's Classic Commercials: The Golden Years, 1948–1958* (New York: Hastings House, 1971), pp. 133–5.
4. Art Seidenbaum, "Visual 'Pitch' Replacing TV's Amateur Salesmen," *Los Angeles Times*, December 13, 1963, p. D21.
5. "Filmack Studios," *The Billboard*, April 14, 1956, p. 16.
6. Diamant, p. 8. Italics in original.
7. "Film Commercial Production Tip: Part Two," *Sponsor*, September 10, 1951, p. 39.
8. "1954 Splash in TV Film Commercials: $15 Million," *Sponsor*, February 8, 1954, p. 45.
9. Thomas Timmons, "The Television Commercial," *The Furrow*, vol. 7, no. 7 (July 1956), pp. 422, 423.
10. "Colossal Commercials," *Sponsor*, November 24, 1956, p. 30.
11. "Ben Hecht Blasts TV Commercials; Adds 3rd Sponsor," *Advertising Age*, September 22, 1958, p. 2.
12. "40% of TV Ads Now Are Made in Hollywood: Cole," *Advertising Age*, November 17, 1958.
13. See, for example: "Check Your TV Commercial Against These Five Schwerin Basics," *Sponsor*, November 17, 1952, p. 40.
14. "Monday Memo: Where Do You Get a 'Swinging' Idea?," *Broadcasting*, March 6, 1961, p. 22.
15. David Halberstam, *The Fifties* (New York: Fawcett Columbine, 1993), p. 634.
16. Charles W. Curran recommended in 1958 that "120 words per minute" should be the maximum in a TV commercial, adding that "even less is better." See Charles W. Curran, *Screen Writing and Production Techniques: The Non-Technical Handbook for TV, Film and Tape* (New York: Hastings House, 1958), p. 94.
17. Ralph Porter, "TV-Film Roundtable," *Art Direction* (October 1958), p. 16.
18. Gary D. Rhodes, "Gerald Schnitzer," *Filmfax Plus: The Magazine of Unusual Film, Television & Retro Pop Culture*, no. 129 (Winter 2012), p. 38.
19. Twice during the two minutes, the original background music features instrumental allusions to *See the USA in Your Chevrolet*, a Chevy jingle featured on many previous non-Schnitzer commercials.
20. Halberstam, pp. 631–2.
21. O. W. Kloser, "Monday Memo," *Broadcasting*, March 6, 1961, p. 22.
22. Halberstam, p. 632.
23. Porter, p. 16.
24. "Ears at Ease in Visual Sell," *Ohio State Journal* (Columbus, OH), June 3, 1958.
25. "Monday Memo: Where Do You Get a 'Swinging' Idea?," p. 22.
26. Clipping in Schnitzer's personal scrapbook, circa 1962.
27. Gerald Schnitzer, email to Gary D. Rhodes, October 5, 2011.
28. "Appraisal of Commercials: Vigor, Taste Blending in TV Ads," *Broadcasting*, January 22, 1962, p. 40.

29. Jerry Schnitzer, "The 90-Foot Dilemma," *Business Screen Magazine*. Clipping in Schnitzer's personal scrapbook.
30. "Programming," *Broadcasting*, March 9, 1959, p. 124.
31. "Programming," *Broadcasting*, August 6, 1962, p. 82; "East or West, Commercial Costs and Quality Are About the Same," *Broadcasting*, July 12, 1965, p. 35.
32. "40% of TV Ads Now Are Made in Hollywood: Cole," *Advertising Age*, November 17, 1958. See also: "Big Movie Studios Now Cater to TV," *Advertising Age*, January 12, 1959, p. 70.
33. "Schnitzer Completes New Studio," *Back Stage*, October 9, 1964.
34. "Commercial Makers Revive Association," *Broadcasting*, April 17, 1967, p. 37.
35. Jerry Schnitzer, "Too Much Father-Image in TV Sell?," *Madison Avenue* (May 1962), p. 24.
36. Quoted in "Jet-Age TV Commuter," *Weekly Television Digest*, September 3, 1962, p. 1.
37. "Trend to Tape," *Broadcasting*, November 9, 1959, p. 66.
38. Schnitzer, "Too Much Father-Image in TV Sell?," p. 24.
39. "Commercial Review: Story of a Family," *Broadcasting*, February 5, 1962, p. 32.
40. Gerald Schnitzer, unpublished memoir of directing television commercials.
41. "Commercial Preview: Purina Dog Chow," *Broadcasting*, March 11, 1963, p. 38.
42. "Schnitzer Favors Hollywood's 'Experience' for Commercials," p. 42.
43. "Schnitzer Shoots Six Minute Spot," *Back Stage*, April 24, 1964. At times, the press referred to the duration of this commercial as "5 and ½ minutes."
44. "TV Spots Qualify as Art, Says Coca," *Hollywood Reporter*, December 27, 1965.
45. "Commercials Booming," *Citizen Register* (Ossining, NY), June 23, 1965.
46. "Schnitzer Production Adds Murray." Clipping in Schnitzer's personal scrapbook dated December 20, 1965.
47. "Commercial Preview: A Slice of Life for Halo," *Broadcasting*, April 23, 1962, p. 36.
48. "Needed: Faster Color Film for Commercials," *Broadcasting*, August 16, 1965, p. 48.
49. Allen Rich, *Hollywood Citizen-News*, July 5, 1965, p. B12.
50. "Equipment and Engineering," *Broadcasting*, February 18, 1963, p. 34.
51. "B&W Commercials Will Soon be the Exception," *Broadcasting*, January 3, 1966, p. 80.
52. "A Common Bond Shared by Commercial Makers," *Broadcasting*, November 8, 1965, p. 36.
53. "Commercial Preview: Vineyard Backs Jingle," *Broadcasting*, August 27, 1962, p. 30.
54. Schnitzer, unpublished memoir.
55. Schnitzer, unpublished memoir.
56. "Saxon Joins Schnitzer," *Hollywood Reporter*, June 23, 1966; "But First: Word from the Sponsor," *Hollywood Reporter*, November 26, 1969, p. 12.
57. "Fates & Fortunes," *Broadcasting*, April 26, 1965, p. 68.
58. Clipping in Schnitzer's personal scrapbook, dated March 1966.

59. "Fates & Fortunes," *Broadcasting*, August 23, 1965, p. 78.
60. Bill Kennedy, "Mr. L.A.," *Los Angeles Herald Examiner*, August 2, 1965.
61. Schnitzer, unpublished memoir.
62. Gerald Schnitzer, email to Gary D. Rhodes, October 5, 2011.
63. Schnitzer, unpublished memoir.
64. "Big Budget Commercial," *The Hollywood Reporter*, April 28, 1966; "U.S. Commercial Voted No. 1 in TV at Venice Ad Fest," *Radio/Television Daily*, June 23, 1966.
65. Bosley Crowther, "The Shadow of the Box," *New York Times*, April 16, 1967.
66. Schnitzer, unpublished memoir.
67. Bob Williams, "On the Air," *New York Post*, April 13, 1967.
68. Clipping in Schnitzer's personal scrapbook, dated 1963.
69. Jerry Schnitzer, "The 90-Foot Dilemma," *Business Screen Magazine*. Clipping in Schnitzer's personal scrapbook.
70. Clippings in Schnitzer's personal scrapbook, dated 1963. Also, Richard Griffith, Film Library Curator, Museum of Modern Art, Letter to Gerald Schnitzer, March 1, 1963.
71. "Selling the Soft-Sell," *Entertainment World*, January 30, 1970, p. 15.
72. "The Commercial Is 'It' in 1959," *Sponsor*, January 17, 1959, p. 48.

CHAPTER 2

Narrative

Speaking to *Rolling Stone* magazine in 1987, the same year that *Full Metal Jacket* was released, director Stanley Kubrick enthused about the artistry of television commercials:

> [In a series of TV commercials for Michelob produced in 1986], the editing, the photography, was some of the most brilliant work I've ever seen. Forget what they're doing—selling beer—and it's visual poetry. Incredible eight-frame cuts. And you realize that in thirty seconds they've created an impression of something rather complex. If you could ever tell a story, something with some content, using that kind of visual poetry, you could handle vastly more complex and subtle material.[1]

Whether the storyline Kubrick alludes to is historical, fantastic, nonlinear, realistic, or documentary, narrative may be conceived and contextualized as, for example, a short story, novel, or feature-film release, and as an intertextually reified critical concept, as part of an unfolding whole of intergeneric potentialities.

In particular, television commercials may be categorized as short-film narratives as one examines comparative industrial practices and artistic accomplishments with feature-length film. Essentially, how do commerical narratives generate a reactive desire to consume, whether cereal flakes or sports cars, in the space and time afforded by the thirty-, sixty-, or 120-second format on the television screen? One notes the presence of familiar generic forms and recurring thematic and visual tropes, including stylizations and practices associated with horror, comedy, musical, documentary, and other forms of exposition, that are endemic to both full-length and short-film narratives. The TV commercial strategizes, informs, affects, and directs our overall range of perception in order to identify with objects, making them into subjects, and to stimulate a nascent desire to consume. We watch—we want.

In *Pleasure of the Text* and *S/Z*, Roland Barthes distinguished between two forms of narrative experience that we, as readers and viewers, encounter per text and among texts: the readerly and the writerly. Overall, a readerly text, such as Charles Dickens's nineteenth-century prose and filmmaker John Ford's *Fort Apache* (1948), does not challenge its audience's ideological preconceptions; the struggle for meaning and narrative clarity is passively resolved, in a familiar, settled world. The readerly text concludes, whereas, the writerly text, such as Kathy Acker's postmodern fiction, and Buñuel and Dalí's celebration of the comically irrational and symbolic in *Un Chien Andalou* (1929), remains unencoded, disruptive, and experiential, to be "rewritten" per reader or audience member. A readerly text is thus a meaningful, predetermined commodity; after one receives the product, messaging ends. Writerly texts are theoretically never-ending, unrestricted, unsettled, and fluid narratives; meaning produces more meanings.

Television commercials are overwhelmingly short-film, *readerly* texts, an ideologically articulated entry into industrial and generic narrative forms, in which space and time cohere, via plot, characterizations, dialogue, voiceover, and foundational technical precepts, as informative and strategized productions that begin and end per commercial segment. The readerly commercial is a singularly controlled narrative, and as a directed marketing strategy, the commercial incorporates codes and conventions indicating fixed meanings. However satirical, serious, artistic, or seemingly unconventional the commerical narrative, the product is the direct or inferred—but clear—subject. It is a controlled conversation between the observed and the observer, which ideally creates a purposeful, desiring consumer, even when involving unusual marketing strategies and products.

Relying on quotations from Gustave Flaubert's *Madame Bovary* (1856), one of David Lynch's four commercials, Calvin Klein's *Obsession for Men* (1990), never mentions the word "cologne" (Figs 2.1 and 2.2). This marketing strategy targets an active, "consuming for him," female audience, who frequently makes the purchase of such items for the heterosexual male in department stores, but who may also identify with the fantasies they share with a young woman wandering through her lover's room, alone with his possessions.[2] She is in his space, in momentary control of his things. Of course, the heightened erotics displayed in Lynch's commercial appropriation are not exclusively gendered images confined to heterosexual fantasies.

Lynch creates an intertextually multifaceted film production in this sophisticated production about female desire. This thirty-second commercial for a new male product, a chemically concocted "smell," is directed toward an audience of consuming females who do the smelling; of course, this does not exclude male consumers of all sexual orientations from the

Figures 2.1 and 2.2 David Lynch's *Obsession for Men* (1990), featuring prose by Flaubert

marketing and purchasing strategy, but commonly, *she* makes the purchase of such items for him, or at least is encouraged to do so in this commercial.

Lynch's *Obsession for Men* commercial is a fantasy-based short film about female desire, abetted by a collage of direct, translated quotations from *Madame Bovary*. According to Pat Sloan, directly citing Flaubert's realistic prose in this commercial involved the production goal of "preserv[ing] the intense sexuality of the brand's image," which it succeeds in translating visually via romantic, dissolving glimpses into her thoughts and feelings.[3] The commercial focuses on expressive images of female motion involving her heightened passion and its fulfillment, yet Lynch's short-film narrative—unlike full-length *Madame Bovary* feature films produced before and after Lynch's production—excludes the collateral issues of adultery and suicide from Flaubert's novel. Lynch's commercial, produced a year prior to Claude Chabrol's successful, relatively literal film adaptation of *Madame Bovary*, and three years prior to Ketan Mehta's *Maya Memsaab* (1993), an innovative, updated adaptation of Flaubert's novel set in contemporary, middle-class India, may be read as another intertextual reappropriation of Flaubert's literary source along with these cited adaptations.

Lynch's *Obsession for Men* is set in the boudoir of Emma's lover. After their consummation, he quickly exits, leaving Emma, portrayed by the actress Lara Flynn Boyle, to experience an unfixed and internalized space and time to freely associate her amatory feelings with objects in her lover's private space; his room reveals aspects of his identity. Flaubert's detailed, "objective" prose, in which a narrator's controlling male voice describes Emma's movement and activities, serves as the authorial voiceover:

> afterwards she would wander through the room exploring ... she would open drawers ... look at herself in his shaving mirror ... oftentimes she would raise his pipe between her teeth, the one he kept on his night table among the lemons, the lumps of sugar, and the jug of water ... it took them a good quarter of an hour to say goodbye ... Obsession for men ... Calvin Klein.

Lynch's nine-shot sequencing dissolves through her erotic, capricious daydreaming: the wistful, spoken, "breathy" tone links Flaubert's realistic eroticized language with Lynch's oneiric visualizations: (Shot 1) The two lovers embrace in a medium shot; Flaubert's name is superimposed over the image; (Shot 2) The non-reflecting mirror is centered on the night table; (Shot 3) The audience sees Emma as she sees herself in the mirror; she turns slightly away from its reflection; (Shot 4) Fruit on the table; (Shot 5) Her right hand takes his phallic pipe, while her left hand brushes against a piece of fruit; (Shot 6) She places the pipe in her mouth, as her shadow, another released "self" is revealed on the wall; (Shot 7) Her face appears in an extreme closeup; (Shot 8) The product bottle is in full view on the table—its name in print on the screen; (Shot 9) The camera gently zooms out to reveal related Calvin Klein commercial products. Thus, Lynch's dynamic appropriation of Flaubert's excerpted prose links the latter's realistic narrative technique to the former's stylized reinvigoration of erotic themes and images, an associative flow recalling Emma's interior life in the novel.

In his review of the Calvin Klein series of four "literary" commercials, media critic Bob Garfield seemingly misreads the aesthetic and technical processing involved with intertextual citation and renewal, in particular, between Flaubert's intimate prose and Lynch's visual interpretation, which both chronicle moments of unspoken female desire:

> As it turns out . . . Lynch's auteurship isn't much in evidence . . . They're 30 seconds long, so no time for prolonged close-ups of faces and inanimate objects . . . Lynch shoots grainy close-ups of handsome, mute people acting out the literary passages more or less word for word . . . The ardor and texture of Lynch's quite literal cine-interpretation nicely camouflages the fact not one of these excerpts really concerns obsession. They concern distraction, infatuation, fulfillment—none of them Calvin Klein scents, I don't believe.[4]

We do believe. Garfield's (mis)reading of Flaubert's *Madame Bovary* in relationship to the commercial's narrative schema misses the point; female obsession is one of several critical themes upon which the "Bovary experience" may reveal itself to an audience. In Flaubert's novel of observation and revelations, this boudoir-shot sequence brilliantly conjoins the sensual internal with the realistic setting; mundane objects resonate with sexual energy. This commercial is a romantic moment in a series of absorbing, introspective, and delusional moments in the life of a failed literary character. Garfield more correctly categorizes Lynch's series of adaptations for his Calvin Klein commercials as "notable," and that "what matters is catching the viewer's eye, creating an aura, defining a mood."[5] That mood is present within the commercial's compositional, dream-like strategy, for her private passion is revealed, via a controlling voiceover and by her movements within the frame. She touches, lifts, and observes objects that metonymically recall the lover-moment. This is especially evident in Shot 4, as we see her, seeing herself, in the mirror.

In "Of Other Spaces: Utopias and Heterotopias," Foucault presciently links the experience of the mirror as a transformative space for layers of complex relationships and exchanges for the self-image, which are applicable to Lynch's appropriated discourse from the novel:

NARRATIVE   41

> In the mirror, I see myself there where I am not, in an unreal, virtual space that opens up behind the surface . . . The heterotopia is capable of juxtaposing in a single real place several spaces, several sites that are in themselves incompatible . . . Heterotopias are most often linked to slices in time . . . their role is to create a space of illusion that exposes every real space, all the sites inside of which human life is partitioned, as still more illusory . . . or else, on the contrary, their role is to create a space that is other, another real space, as perfect, as meticulous, as well arranged as ours is messy, ill constructed, and jumbled.[6]

Slices in time, slices of life: in Lynch's narrative sequencing, the mirror, the privacy of the room, the departure of her lover, and, especially, Emma's aroused sentiments belie the outcome of this, and future, adulterous liaisons. What remains are the momentary impressions of the previously sensual: odor, objects, language, all associated with her interior life. We credit this as a notable directorial accomplishment for Lynch: the audience experiences her fleeting, dream-like impressions. Lynch's mirror shots reflect and reveal Emma's face, a stylized reverse affect shot, which invokes a time and space for her expression of these feelings to surface. Her lover's presence, then absence, renders the erotic moment real for Emma. In this commercial, Lynch emploits Flaubert's prose realism to suggest a brief glimpse into the space and time of Emma's fantasy landscape.

Here, in other words, is the kind of "visual poetry" that Kubrick described, a complex narrative, unfolding in the space of thirty seconds.

Tales for Sales

Grainy black-and-white footage is accompanied by music but no dialogue. In the 1920s, a car drives through a small town, arriving at the general store. The camera conveys the unseen driver's point of view. As various customers examine him, the driver purchases latex condoms from the storekeeper and inserts them in the watch pocket of his blue jeans. Day turns to night as he journeys to a rural, two-story home. A beautiful young woman appears on the outdoor balcony and smiles. The front door opens. It is the storekeeper who greets the driver, a handsome young man revealed to the viewer for the first time. The two men recognize one another, with the father trying to convince his daughter not to go on her date. She defiantly leaves with the young man. Along with the brand name Levi's, onscreen text announces: "Watch pocket created in 1873. Abused ever since."

So concludes the tale of *Drugstore* (1994), filmmaker Michel Gondry's ninety-second, tour-de-force commercial for Levi Strauss (Figs 2.3 and 2.4). It is emblematic of advice given in the pages of *Advertising Age* nearly three decades earlier, when a columnist counselled against copywriters being allowed to write commercials. "The truth is that words rarely

Figures 2.3 and 2.4 Michel Gondry's *Drugstore* (1994)

make a commercial memorable," he observed.[7] Stories told visually were the key, whether they were dramatic or comedic. Some members of the industry were convinced that such narratives constituted the most effective memory aids.[8] They certainly became the basis for a large array of artistic commercials.

Indeed, Gerald Schnitzer's "slice-of-life" narratives quickly influenced other television commercial directors, as well as those of subsequent generations. In 1992, documentary filmmaker Albert Maysles wrote:

> What if in their TV commercials, corporations, instead of seeming like strangers, threw bouquets to their potential customers? Not flowers, but elements of real-life experiences that serve to enhance a common interest, a human need, an act of recognition, a bond or symbol which currently results in a better image—and perhaps more sales.
>
> Henry Corra, Susan Froemke and I have been making "bouquet" commercials for some time. Like flowers, these "non-commercial commercials" come in many varieties and deliver different messages.[9]

Maysles was one of the many directors influenced, directly or indirectly, by Schnitzer. The same approach flourished in the years that followed. During the 1980s, Joe Pytka became known for commercials featuring "remarkably realistic dialogue" spoken by "remarkably ordinary-looking characters."[10]

"Narratives require action," Rick Altman declares.[11] There is cause and effect: three acts, with exposition, a problem, and a solution, often in the form of a happy ending. The structure of the feature film became, in many cases, the structure of the TV commercial. As Schnitzer freely admitted, he adopted the norms of Classical Hollywood narratives in his commercials. To make usage of the style overt, a number of commercials from the 1950s to the present have even gone so far as to feature cinematic, onscreen opening titles or the words "The End" as they conclude.

Running time is an unavoidable issue. Jib Fowles observed, "Speedily, in 28 ticks of the clock, the action shifts from confounding problem to heavenly solution courtesy of the advertiser's product."[12] But within that brief time frame narrative complexity can occur, to the extent that a few commercials have even parodied the same. *Lunch* (2017), a thirty-second spot promoting Progressive Insurance, features two unnamed male characters who work at a competing company. During their conversation, a female character speaks one line. Dialogue from one of the others refers to her as an "underdeveloped office character," a particularly ironic and humorous description given the sheer brevity of the narrative, as well as the fact that the two male characters are underdeveloped too, so much so that one of the two calls them "clichéd foil characters."

Whether simple or complex, though, the TV commercial has proven its ability to convey memorable narratives that evoke strong emotions. The "Crying Indian" (Iron Eyes Cody) in *Keep America Beautiful*, Marsteller's 1971 public service announcement, would be but one example of many. Considering these issues, Martin Esslin wrote in 1979:

> If the television commercial could be shown to be drama, it would be among the most ubiquitous and the most influential of its forms and hence deserve the attention of the serious critics and theoreticians of that art, most of whom paradoxically still seem to be spellbound by types of drama (such as tragedy) which are hallowed by age and tradition, though practically extint today.[13]

Most commercials represent an "excessively obvious cinema," to borrow the phrase used by David Bordwell, Janet Staiger, and Kristin Thompson to describe Classical Hollywood Cinema.[14] This is in addition to commercial narratives being intrinsically proleptic, to the extent that viewers know that the short film will try to sell them a product, service, or idea. After all, a large percentage of TV commercials end with a "pack shot" or title card that shows and/or names the product.

All that said, there can be a striking distance, even dissonance, between the product being advertised and the narrative used to promote it, particularly with regard to how much or little the product is displayed or mentioned. In 1982, Ridley Scott directed a Chanel No. 5 commercial in which the product was not named or even seen until the last four seconds of the thirty-second spot. However, as *Advertising Age* noted, its beautiful images of a woman and man poolside, along with "philosophical" voiceover by Catherine Deneuve, "made the viewer want to see it again," which was a "great accomplishment for any commercial."[15] A more extreme example would be director Larry Robins, who in 1989 tried to capture beautiful visual "moments" to promote Infiniti automobiles. His controversial thirty-second spots never showed the car.[16]

The Scene

Mean Joe Greene limps into a stadium dugout. A young boy (Tommy Okun) informs the football player that he is the "best ever." Mean Joe is unimpressed. The young boy offers him his Coca-Cola. After first turning it down, Mean Joe takes the bottle and drinks the beverage as a jingle plays in the background. "See ya around," the exasperated boy says before walking away. Calling after him, Mean Joe smiles and tosses the boy his jersey. "Wow! Thanks, Mean Joe," the kid exclaims happily. Text reading "Have a Coke and a Smile" appears onscreen as song lyrics complete the same phrase. Running for sixty seconds, *Hey Kid, Catch!* debuted in 1979.

Roger Mosconi and Penny Hawkey created the spot for McCann Erickson. N. Lee Lacy directed. Ken Bald drew the storyboards. It became one of the most popular TV commercials in history. For an audience very likely familiar with the myths of interracial cooperation and sportsmanship associated with American sports, as promulgated in films such as Buzz Kulik's *Brian's Song* (1971), Lacy's commercial reinforces these sentiments; feelings sell merchandise. And it does so relying on a single scene.

The brevity of TV commercials has for decades caused many to operate in much the same way. A commercial for the 1967 American Motors station wagon reworked the Biblical tale of Noah. An old, bearded man parks the vehicle in the great outdoors. A clap of thunder causes him to look upwards before opening the back of the vehicle. With the help of a ramp, pairs of leopards, rabbits, tigers, and other animals amble into the back of the car. That same year, a commercial for Kentucky Fried Chicken depicts a group of women walking into a darkened room. They have kidnapped Colonel Sanders, strapped him into a chair, and hooked a lie detector to his body. The women demand his famous recipe. He obliges, save for his secret combination of spices. The women have failed in their quest. While the two commercials are different, both narratives unfold as individual scenes.

Reliance on the single scene has continued into the twenty-first century. David Fincher's *Stairs* (2014), a thirty-second commercial shot in black and white and produced by Wieden+Kennedy for Gap, depicts a young man arriving in a building. He looks up and sees an admiring young woman. He begins running up the winding steps as she waits for him. His white shirt falls as onscreen text explains, "Simple clothes for you to complicate." No dialogue is heard, and yet the one-scene commercial is not only narratively legible, but also provocative. *The Huffington Post* called Fincher's Gap campaign (which totalled four commercials) "better than most of the feature films released this month."[17]

Tom Gunning and André Gaudreault have famously described the "cinema of attractions," meaning that, during their earliest years, films tended to focus on the presentational and the spectacular to incite "visual curiosity" and supply visual "pleasure."[18] Narrative storylines were minimal. Gunning also suggests, "Clearly in some sense recent spectacle cinema has reaffirmed its roots in stimulus and carnival rides, in what might be called the Spielberg–Lucas–Coppola cinema of effects."[19] Here is, as Wanda Strauven has noted, the "cinema of attractions reloaded."[20]

Given the similarities between the running times of late nineteenth-century films and TV commercials, as well as shared goals of exciting viewer interest, it is perhaps not unexpected that some commercials have provided a particular incarnation of the cinema of attractions. For example, film historians regularly cite *The Kiss* (Thomas Edison, 1896), in which May Irwin and

John Rice kiss on screen, as being an adaptation of the final scene of John J. McNally's 1895 play, *The Widow Jones*. In the space of approximately twenty seconds, the landmark film offers visual excitement through the single act of osculation. In 1960, Gerald Schnitzer directed a sixty-second commercial for Revlon that features a forty-seven-second kiss, interrupted—according to a review in *Printer's Ink*—"only by assorted murmurs, shifts in position, and a camera 'pan' to a blindfolded, blushing statutte of Cupid."[21]

Nicolas Winding Refn directed a sixty-second 2014 commercial for the Lincoln MKC, starring the American actor Matthew McConaughey, who has apparently driven right up to a large bull standing in the middle of an otherwise deserted highway (Figs 2.5 and 2.6). The opening shot of Refn's

Figures 2.5 and 2.6 Nicolas Winding Refn's 2014 commercial for Lincoln MKC

commercial frames a bull's massive head in closeup; then, as the camera dollies back, the commercial cuts to a reverse shot of McConaughey sitting behind the automobile's steering wheel, as he takes note of his predicament for himself and the audience. This is not a shot sequence excerpted from a bull-fighting, special effects-driven popular film. The camera cuts to a parodic western landscape painting: a shot of McConaughey in his car and the bull on the road, in a moment of self-reflexive posing.

The shot cuts to a side-angle, closeup profile of McConaughey. The action then cuts to a medium shot from inside the car, behind McConaughey's shoulder, in the passenger seat, so that the actor and the bull are in the frame within the frame (McConaughey's face is also seen in the rear-view mirror); this recalls the camera's framing within frames and positioning for visual referencing, as well as the uninterrupted action filming made famous in the heist sequence in *Gun Crazy* (Joseph H. Lewis, 1950), in which we gaze upon the gaze from the car to the street and back. Intertextual citations among narrative genre, movements, and forms suggest an ongoing aesthetic collaboration, in this case, involving art history and film noir.

In Refn's commercial, the camera cuts back to a frontal shot of McConaughey in the car, narrating, in a contemplative medium shot. A shifting movement affects the camera position to reveal a tight shot of the bull in front of the car, with a rack focus of McConaughey creating a sense of spatial perspective, and all the while, he continues narrating from his "safe" previous set-up. In a tight shot, the camera, set up behind the car, begins panning left (revealing the MKC insignia) located at the rear of car, but as the camera continues to pan left, the bull is seen again. Ultimately, discretion leads to its own driving rewards and the open road not taken. The shot cuts back to McConaughey's bemused, contemplative driving pose, then back to the conquering bull, then back to McConaughey, and finally cuts to a medium shot of the object of desire: the car, turning around and exiting the immediate frame, driving in a different, bull-free direction.

The images are playfully silly but entice the audience, as the narrative seeks to proscribe something "real" upon its pose. When McConaughey confidently speaks to himself, describing his respect for "1,800 pounds of do-whatever-I want." He, and now the audience, understand the bull's message: "Take the long way, huh?" The audience accepts that the actor–salesman turns his Lincoln automobile around and drives away into an American image of techno-pastoral happiness, leaving the bull where it stands. This humorously existential commercial narrative unfolds in a single scene, so memorable as to be parodied later on *The Ellen Show* by Ellen DeGeneres and by McConaughey himself on *Conan* with Conan

O'Brien. In 2013, Refn directed *Only God Forgives*, an excessively violent revenge crime narrative with complex Oedipal shadings, set in Bangkok's contemporary underworld; we believe that Refn's automobile commercial, with its impressive bull and western setting, self-conscious narration, and "star" performance, is another compelling film narrative he directed that same year.

In these cases, TV commercials distill narratives into memorable, single scenes, akin to the manner by which many viewers recall films, meaning not in their entirety, but in terms of particular scenes.

Remakes

Many commercials repeat narratives and the characters they feature, not only as part of the same campaign, but over a period of many years. Martin Esslin observes that the commercial

> resorts to the recurring personality . . . like the sweet little lady who embodies the spirit of relief from stomach acids and miraculously appears with her pills to bring comfort to a succession of truck drives, longshoremen, or crane operators suffering from upset tummies.[22]

These are not serials, meaning the same narrative continued episodically, though some commercials have relied on that approach. For example, *The Dog Strikes Back* (2012, also known as [aka] *The Bark Side*) became a sequel to director Lance Acord's *The Force* (2011, aka *Mini Darth Vader*; Fig. 2.7), a Donny Deutsch, Inc.-produced commercial for Volkswagen that *Advertising Age* called a "perfect piece of storytelling."[23]

In other cases, the TV commercial has remade prior narratives with minimal derivation. Anat Zanger's discussion of film remakes describes them as a form of both ritual and disguise:

> Cinema as a social institution knows what Scheherazade seems to have known all along: to narrate is to triumph over death. Hence, in an ongoing ceremony that occurs in the darkness of the movie theater (and lasts, ultimately, more than 1001 nights), society constantly delivers its encoded messages. The constant repetition of the same tale keeps it alive in social memory, continually transmitting its meaning and relevance.[24]

These repetitions allow for different film narratives, plotted and executed with much variance.

Harvey Roy Greenberg has importantly identified a typology of remakes.[25] One is the acknowledged, close remake, in which a new film

NARRATIVE   49

Figure 2.7 Lance Acord's *The Force* (2011)

reproduces an earlier film with few changes, particularly to the narrative. A second is the acknowledged, transformed remake, in which major changes to the earlier work are undertaken. Film history is rife with examples of both categories. That said, Rüdiger Heinze and Lucia Krämer remind us that "remaking is always more or less transformative."[26] Variations mark any examples of remakes one might give.

In some cases, the TV commercial has remade scenes of famous feature films. In 1974, the firm Dusenberry, Ruriani, & Kornhauser created a thirty-second parody of Marlene Dietrich in *The Blue Angel* (Josef von Sternberg, 1930) for Fruit of the Loom.[27] That same year, Weinstein Associates depicted the Getz termite exterminator as the "Getz-orcist," in a takeoff of *The Exorcist* (William Friedkin, 1974).[28] H. G. Willis & Associates created a takeoff of *The Phantom of the Opera* (Rupert Julian, 1925) for Hammond Organ dealers in 1976.[29] Warwick, Welsh & Miller created a takeoff of *King Kong* (Merian C. Cooper and Ernest B. Schoedsack, 1933) for So Soft, So Sheer pantyhose in 1980.[30] And, in 1985, Tracy Locke spliced the Tostitos' spokesperson into actual clips of such TV shows as *Dragnet* (1951–9, 1967–70), *Leave It to Beaver* (1957–63), and *Mr. Ed* (1961–7) for a Frito-Lay campaign.[31]

More commonly, though, commercials remake themselves. In 2009, for example, Crispin Porter Bogusky parodied the aforementioned *Hey Kid, Catch!* for Coke Zero.[32] Troy Polamalu played the role originally undertaken by Mean Joe Greene. A young boy exchanges the original dialogue with him for twenty-three seconds, at which time two "Coke Brand Managers" appear to grab the soda and announce, "Coke Zero stole our taste; they are not stealing our commercial!" Polamalu tackles one of them and finally gets to drink the soda. He then rips the shirt off of the Brand Manager and throws it to the young boy, saying, "Here Kid, Catch!"

Consider also the first two commercials in Joe Sedelmaier's popular *Where's the Beef* campaign for Wendy's in 1984. Both starred Clara Peller repeatedly spouting the tag line as she and two friends are at a fast-food counter. In the first ad, she asks the question to the counter, though no worker is present: "I don't think there is anybody back there," she says. In the second, the women are at the same counter, but this time talking to the owner on the phone. "I don't think there's anybody there," she says in a slight variation. Such commercials led everyone from Johnny Carson to Democratic presidential candidate Walter Mondale to parrot the question "Where's the beef?"[33]

Much more complex would be the case of Mr Whipple (Dick Wilson), a fictional grocery-store owner who promoted Charmin toilet paper in over 500 commercials, the bulk of them from 1964 to 1985.[34] Despite narrative variations both minor and major, a relatively consistent feature of the Benton & Bowles campaign was for Whipple to admonish his customers, "Don't Squeeze the Charmin" while regularly doing the same himself. The character became extremely popular, with *Advertising Age* dubbing him the "world's best-known toilet paper-squeezing fetishist."[35] The sheer repetition of the storyline even led to Wilson appearing in a commercial for A&W Cream Soda in which he squeezes the soft-drink can and apologizes for his "old habit."[36]

Some iterations of the Charmin spots from 1982 through 1984 found Whipple actively asking customers to squeeze the product. Other variations occurred when Whipple returned from "retirement" to tout the "new and improved" Charmin in commercials broadcast from 1999 to 2000.[37]

Genre

In the edited collection *TV Genres: A Handbook and Reference Guide* (1985), Deborah Franklin contributes a chapter entitled *The Television Commercial*.[38] The implication is that the TV commercial could be regarded as a genre, just as one might otherwise view, say, the novel as a literary genre, as Mikhail Bakhtin did. Or we could consider the simple division of, on the one hand, the presentational commercial with its ubiquitous spokesperson and, on the other hand, Gerald Schnitzer's "slice-of-life" narratives.

That said, it is also helpful to see the TV commercial as being comprised of many genres, some unique to the form, as in the case of the comparison genre. Voiceover or an onscreen presence compares the sponsored product to either a specific or a generic competitor. Cereal flakes, diapers, or paper towels are visually compared in demonstrations, sometimes relying on split-screen mise-en-scène. The sheer number of such commercials helped spawn related narratives in which two unlike objects or ideas are compared. In 1996, Chris Rock starred in a commercial for 1-800-Collect, in which the cost of most collect phone calls are compared to the US national debt. More famous is Joe Pytka's thirty-second public service announcement *This Is Your Brain on Drugs* (1987), in which an egg in a frying pan acts as a metaphor for the human brain on illegal narcotics.

In other cases, TV commercials have mimicked genres associated with television. Consider *Impromptu Interview, Dennis O'Keefe*, a 1950s commercial in which the title star describes his affinity for Camel cigarettes in the space of 120 seconds. The commercial unfolds as a Q&A not dissimilar to those conducted on such television programs as Edward R. Murrow's *See It Now* (1951–8) and *Person to Person* (1953–61). Though filmed and edited, the O'Keefe commercial strives to convey an unrehearsed, even "live" narrative, thanks to the star playing himself and attempting to speak off the cuff.

Before and certainly after Gerald Schnitzer, most television commercials have attempted to adopt and adapt genres associated with feature filmmaking, among them the documentary. In *Taxi Driver and Dog*, Dwight D. Eisenhower's 1956 re-election commercial, a cabbie extols the virtues of the President in an ad that runs for approximately four minutes and twenty seconds. While organ music plays in the background, the taxi driver walks his dog at night, stopping in front of the White House and contemplating what Eisenhower is thinking at that very moment. The commercial then cuts to a large array of nonfiction footage that depicts the various global problems and issues that are among Ike's responsibilities. The first-person documentary returns to onscreen footage of the taxi driver on two subsequent occasions; during the second, he turns to the camera to address the audience directly.

The appropriation of evolving documentary narratives and aesthetics became a common component of public service announcements and political advertisements. *Hope* (aka *Journey*), a 1992 campaign commercial for Bill Clinton, illustrates this point well. It begins with a black-and-white photograph of Hope, Arkansas, Clinton's home town. During the course of sixty seconds, Clinton speaks autobiographically about his life and his political aspiration to bring "hope back to the American dream." Piano music plays softly in the background. On four occasions, Clinton is seen on camera speaking what otherwise unfolds as voiceover; the first two are medium shots, while the second pair are closeups. His eyeline is to screen right of the camera, just as would have been the case on so many historical documentaries. The other images include seven still photographs, all of which feature movement akin to the type popularized by Ken Burns's *The Civil War* (1990). Ten other shots are live action, the first four in black and white, and the latter six in color, operating as a visual metaphor of the words Clinton speaks about his past and future accomplishments.

Most commercial narratives have appropriated fictional genres from Hollywood cinema. Martin Esslin writes:

> From the point of view of its *form* the range of the TV commercial drama can thus be seen as very large indeed: it extends from the chamber play to the grand spectacular musical; from the realistic to the utmost bounds of the allegorial, fantastic, and abstract.[39]

The aforementioned Mean Joe Greene commercial drew not only on Greene's personality, but also on the sports inspirational genre that became popular in 1970s Hollywood. Ridley Scott's *1984* is science fiction. Other commercials have relied on romance, action, horror, mystery, the western, the historical drama, and the musical. They have also invoked the melodrama, or, as *Advertising Age* called it in 1989, the "'sentimental' genre," a "peculiarly American tearjerker."[40]

Similar to American cinema, one of the most consistently popular commercial genres has been comedy. In 1959, Arthur Bellaire of Batten, Barton, Durstine & Osborn (BBDO) wrote, "For any advertiser determined to have his commercials noticed, talked about, and even praised, humor, well-handled, is a sure-fire formula."[41] Consider *Monkey Business* (2005), Cramer–Krasselt's thirty-second commercial for CareerBuilder. Chimpanzees dressed in business suits party and dance to music in an office that features a chart suggesting positive sales growth. A human stops the music and turns the chart over, clarifying that sales are actually down. One chimp turns the sign back to suggest growth is strong, causing another to restart the music. The partying begins again. Comedy films depicting monkeys dressed in human clothing date to the nineteenth century, as in the case of American Mutoscope's *Joe, the Educated Orangoutang* [sic] (1898) and *Joe, the Educated Orangoutang* [sic], *Undressing* (1898).

TV commercial comedies have cited early cinema by presenting visual attractions that are immediately humorous, needing little to no explanation from onscreen characters or voiceover narration. *Thanks, Easter Bunny* (1984) for M&M's features a series of eight vignettes of children thanking the holiday for giving them candy. The eighth shows two kids costumed as an Easter egg and a chick. "Thanks, Easter Bunny," the former says, with the latter adding "Bawk, bawk."

In other cases, commercials appropriate another approach used during the early cinema period, meaning simple jokes that culminate in a humorous payoff. The vast number of such films includes *How a Rat Interrupted Afternoon Tea* (American Mutoscope, 1897), *How a Bottle of Cocktails Was Smuggled into Camp* (American Mutoscope, 1898), *How the Dressmaker Got Even with a Dead Beat* (American Mutoscope, 1898), *How Farmer Jones Made a Hit at Pleasure Bay* (American Mutoscope, 1898), and *How Bridget Served the Salad Undressed* (American Mutoscope and Biograph, 1898). The film titles act as the first component of a form of cinematic joke in which the onscreen action provides the punch line. How did Bridget serve the salad undressed? With some of her clothes removed, of course.

Gerald Schnitzer's 1962 commercial for Del Monte catsup depicted children buying food at Joe's Diner. Voiceover touts how many hamburgers, hotdogs, and French fries a single bottle can dress. At the end of the commercial, after the children have all happily used a bottle, there is hardly enough left for Joe's own hamburger.

A 1996 commercial for Pepsi finds a policeman trying to find the missing soda pop. After fifty seconds of the one-minute ad, it becomes clear that the culprit is a cow. A 2006 commercial features a Godzilla-like creature rampaging through a city; a giant robot confronts him. The two fall in love and the creature becomes pregnant. Approximately forty-three seconds into sixty-second commerical, the viewer learns that the baby is a Hummer, which onscreen text identifies as a "little monster." And a 2011 commercial for Doritos set in the Garden of Eden finds Eve offering Adam an apple. Twenty-two seconds into the thirty-second ad, Adam turns her down, explaining, "Nah, I'm good," while revealing that he has a bag of Doritos to sate his appetite.

Cross-generic and Intertextual

In so many cases, the presentational commercial and the "slice-of-life" commercial are much more than what those terms suggest, as commercials so often feature elements of both. Reiterating the key concerns of genre-based cinema, Rick Altman explains:

> A cinema based on genre films depends not only on the regular production of recognizably similar films, and on the maintenance of a standardized distribution/exhibition system, but also on the constitution and maintenance of a stable, generically trained audience, sufficiently knowledgeable about genre systems to

recognize generic cues, sufficiently familiar with genre plots to exhibit generic expectations, and sufficiently commited to generic values to tolerate and even enjoy in genre films capricious, violent, or licentious behavior which they might disapprove of in "real life."[42]

Stability and standardization are crucial, even as genres evolve and even overlap.

Cross-generic efforts are common in mainstream feature films, even though the emphasis usually remains on excessive familiarity. David Bordwell observes, "In fictional filmmaking, one mode of narration has achieved predominance. Whether we call it mainstream, dominant, or classical cinema, we intuitively recognize an ordinary, easily comprehensible movie when we see it."[43] Peter Verstraten adds, "We can easily jump from A to C while omitting B because the visually literate viewer has already trodden that particular path many times."[44]

By contrast, Verstraten adds, "A narrative logic that is jarring or altogether lacking is primarily the domain of the avant-garde, underground, and independent film, as well as of European art cinema."[45] And yet, jarring logic and abrupt shifts in genre are at times present in American TV commercials. A Woolite commercial from the 1970s unfolds as two genres in four parts: a fictional scene in which one woman tells another about the virture of the product, a documentary scene displaying the product with male, voice-of-God narration, then back to the two fictional characters, and then a return to the voiceover.

A commercial for Jeno's Pizza Rolls from 1968 features Louise Clark hosting a party; she offers coffee to one male character, who turns it down. "I see your husband didn't like your coffee . . . you should try my coffee," Mrs Johnson says to Louise, a reference to Mrs Olson (portrayed by Virginia Christine), who said much the same in Folger's commercials during the 1960s and 1970s. Louise orders Mrs Johnson out of her home before inquiring if another male guest likes the pizza rolls. A voice-of-God narrator soon interrupts, asking Louise if she has bad breath; Mrs Clark responds by saying the narrator does. She speaks into the camera and slaps it in the "face." Then she resumes talking about pizza rolls until the still-unseen narrator hurls a white shirt at her and demands she start "wearing cleaner blouses." Louise karate-chops the camera, which falls backwards. "This is a wild party," the male guest says while eating another pizza roll.

Consider also a thirty-second commercial for Canada Dry ginger ale broadcast in 1977 (Figs 2.8–2.10). It begins with the tropes of a war movie: Aldo Ray, known for his "two-fisted" performances in war films such as *The Naked and the Dead* (Raoul Walsh, 1958) and *The Green Berets*

(Ray Kellogg and John Wayne, 1968), is appropriately costumed as a military officer, positioned in a tank in the desert. It cuts to a police procedural image, with Broderick Crawford, known for his performances in such television productions as *Highway Patrol* (1955–9) and filmmaker Larry Cohen's *The Private Files of J. Edgar Hoover* (1977). In the commercial, Crawford speaks into his police car's CB. Then it cuts to a Fu Manchu-style set, with Jack Palance, known for his performances in *The Mongols* (André De Toth, 1961) and *Sign of the Pagan* (Douglas Sirk, 1964), now wearing Asian makeup. All of them repeatedly sing the slogan, "It's not too sweet," which provides a degree of continuity to otherwise abrupt generic shifts that contradict the hypotextual, "tough male" images to humorously market the soft-drink product instead. Real men like fizz.

For the *Smell is Power* campaign produced by Wieden+Kennedy, Tim Heidecker and Eric Wareheim directed actor and football player Terry Crews in a genre-busting 2012 spot for Old Spice. The first nine seconds feature a woman extolling the virtues of a Bounce Dryer Bar. The serenity ends abruptly. Crews literally explodes through the wall, riding a jet ski and yelling about Old Spice. "It's so powerful it sells itself in other people's commercials," he roars. In terms of its marketing logic, the commercial does promote two products owned by Procter & Gamble. A followup commercial featuring Proctor & Gamble's Charmin Freshmates was also invaded by Crews, who announced, "Old Spice Body Spray is too powerful to stay in its own commercial." These became the first co-branded TV commercials in film history.[46]

Director Lance Acord's *The Longest Chase* (aka *Heck on Wheels*), a ninety-second Prius commercial, aired during the 2016 Super Bowl. It featured a group of bank robbers played by actors who had last appeared together on HBO's *The Wire* (2002–8). Exiting the bank, they discover their getaway car has been towed. From there, the thieves leave a thank-you note and bag of money at a car dealership in exchange for the Prius they take. A humorous car chase begins. Here is a heist comedy. But after some forty-five seconds, a new element is introduced. Two TV news anchors report on what now imitates a high-speed car chase of the type broadcast live on cable news, complete with helicopter images of the vehicles. Then, at sixty seconds, a news anchor reports that the chase has become a global phenomenon. A K-Pop band performs a song about the event, and a Mexican quiz show contestant answers a question about the car used during the getaway. A morning talk show covers proud Prius owners, and then a boy opens a birthday present that contains a Prius toy. The commercial concludes by returning to the bank robbers, who make their final escape from a police roadblock.

NARRATIVE   57

Figures 2.8, 2.9, and 2.10 Aldo Ray, Broderick Crawford, and Jack Palance in a 1977 commercial for Canada Dry Ginger Ale

Conclusion

The television commercial narrative traditionally provides resolution, a completion, to resolve ambiguities, but does not deactivate or stifle the audience's associations and citations. This chapter began with a reference to Stanley Kubrick's *Full Metal Jacket* (1987) and with Kubrick's statement of admiration for TV commercial aesthetics. In the second half of *Full Metal Jacket*, set during the violent historical period in Vietnam known as the Tet Offensive (1968), there are two shot sequences of critical and comparative relevance to the era in which some armed forces recruitment commercials were produced and extensively broadcast on television.

One of the shot sequences involves the simulated interview of several soldiers who were introduced in the first half of the film and are now in Vietnam, where they learn the art of obedience and slaughter. In these mock filmed interviews, presumably to be broadcast on American television's nightly news, several soldiers express rambling impressions and revealing insights into the Vietnam experience, ranging from the ironic to the oblivious. Each soldier makes direct eye contact with the camera, in medium framing, as the audience witnesses a full frontal expression of personal, strangely inconsequential thoughts. Kubrick's narrative simulates the first-person testimonial process associated with many commercials, like a consumer reviewing at that moment some merchandise, revealing positive or negative reactions, as if discussing a fruit drink or insurance company.

Another compelling shot sequence in *Full Metal Jacket* involves an extensive tracking shot in which these somewhat hardened soldiers react to the presence of a filmmaker's camera trolling them around the time of "real" live-action warfare; each soldier, lying down or sitting behind a defensive line, suggesting a future grave, recalls in a series of passing quips a derisive comment expressing his self-awareness of the unfiltered Vietnam "experience" in comical, ironic language. The underscore recycles The Trashmen's 1963 song *Surfin' Bird* as a form of caustic, mocking associative commentary. While Kubrick examined the absurdities of war in those two sequences, other narratives produced that year suggest alternative realities.

In 1987, the U.S. army produced *The G.I. Bill*, a thirty-second television commercial comprised of nine shots (Fig. 2.11). An integrated set

Figure 2.11 *The G.I. Bill* (1987)

of attractive young people, including a woman, sit in a diner somewhere in present-day America, lamenting their future: "I don't know. What are you going to do?" As if paraphrasing the dialogue from Delbert Mann's chronicle of lonely men with limited social and class prospects, *Marty* (1956), each person in this commercial queries the other in a variety of medium and closeup shots, with one young man in particular attesting to the promise, the lure, of the (GI) product. The messaging is directed not only at the youth sitting at the table, but also at those sitting at home. As the audience listens to the stilted dialogue, the young diner patrons discuss the new opportunities the army makes available for them. "It's a great place to start," the voiceover informs the audience near the conclusion of the commercial. Upon deconstructing the realistic middle-class diner table images and uncompelling discourse, the commercial may be read as a fictional, ironic "before" to Kubrick's "after" historical experience. A few years later, these imaginary diner patrons could also reflect upon their experiences during the Gulf War and beyond. The product remains the same; the sales pitch transforms per decade.

Whether they are slice-of-life or presentational, whether they are generic or cross-generic, television commericals are indeed short-film narratives, no less ideologically reflective than the culture that mediates and consumes them.

Notes

1. Quoted in Tim Cahill, "The *Rolling Stone* Interview: Stanley Kubrick," in *Stanley Kubrick Interviews*, ed. Gene D. Phillips (Jackson: University of Mississippi Press, 2001), p. 199.
2. Along with Flaubert's novel, prose excerpts of works by several modern authors were featured in a series of Calvin Klein commercials.
3. Pat Sloan, "Obsession's New Twist," *Advertising Age*, August 13, 1990, p. 49.
4. Bob Garfield, "Ad Review: Sticking to Text Becomes Obsession with Director Lynch," *Advertising Age*, August 27, 1990, p. 40.
5. Garfield, p. 40.
6. Michel Foucault, "Des espaces autres" [1967] ["Of Other Spaces: Utopias and Heterotopias"], *Architecture/Mouvement/Continuité*, trans. Jay Miskowiec, October, 1984.
7. Stephen Baker, "Should Copywriters Be Allowed to Write Television Commercials?," *Advertising Age*, August 22, 1966, p. 89.
8. Harry McMahan and Mark Kile, "'Slide' Sells With Drama," *Advertising Age*, September 14, 1981, p. 68.
9. Albert Maysles, "Persistence of Vision," *American Cinematographer*, September 1992, pp. 22, 24.

10. Bob Garfield, "Pytka's Style Moving Toward Cliché," *Advertising Age*, April 27, 1987, p. 52.
11. Rick Altman, *A Theory of Narrative* (New York: Columbia University Press, 2008), p. 11.
12. Jib Fowles, *Why Viewers Watch: A Reappraisal of Television's Effects*, revised edn (Newbury Park, CA: Sage, 1992), pp. 204–5.
13. Martin Esslin, "Aristotle and the Advertisers: The Television Commercial Considered as a Form of Drama," *The Kenyon Review*, vol. 1, no. 4 (Autumn 1979), p. 96.
14. David Bordwell, Janet Staiger, and Kristin Thompson, *The Classical Hollywood Cinema: Film Style & Mode of Production to 1960* (New York: Columbia University Press, 1985), p. 3.
15. Theodore Halaki, "Reflections on a New Wave," *Advertising Age*, March 8, 1982, p. 27.
16. "Silent Spring," *Advertising Age*, October 2, 1989, p. 6.
17. Jessica Goodman, "David Fincher's Gap Ads Are Better than Most of the Movies Released this Month," *The Huffington Post*, August 28, 2014. Available at <https://www.huffingtonpost.com/2014/08/28/david-fincher-gap-ads_n_5729240.html> (last accessed May 23, 2019).
18. Tom Gunning, "The Cinema of Attractions: Early Film, Its Spectator and the Avant-Garde," in *Early Cinema: Space, Frame, Narrative*, ed. Thomas Elsaesser with Adam Barker (London: British Film Institute, 1990), p. 56.
19. Gunning, p. 59.
20. Wanda Strauven, editor, *The Cinema of Attractions Reloaded* (Amsterdam: Amsterdam University Press, 2006).
21. "Revlon Enchants World with One Selling Technique," *Printer's Ink*, June 3, 1960, p. 40.
22. Esslin, p. 100.
23. "10 Ads Creativity Loved," *Advertising Age*, December 12, 2011, p. 12.
24. Anat Zanger, *Film Remakes as Ritual and Disguise: From Carmen to Ripley* (Amsterdam: Amsterdam University Press, 2006), p. 9.
25. Harvey Roy Greenberg, "Raiders of the Lost Text: Remaking as Contested Homage in *Always*," *Journal of Popular Film and Television*, vol. 18, no. 4 (1991), pp. 164–71.
26. Rüdiger Heinze and Lucia Krämer, "Introduction: Remakes and Remaking—Preliminary Reflections," in *Remakes and Remaking: Concepts—Media—Practices*, ed. Rüdiger Heinze and Lucia Krämer (Bielefeld: Transcript, 2015), p. 12.
27. Untitled, *Advertising Age*, July 23, 1974, p. 1.
28. "Termites," *Advertising Age*, February 25, 1974, p. 2.
29. "Newest TV Spot," *Advertising Age*, August 8, 1976, p. 3.
30. "Beauty and the Pantyhose," *Advertising Age*, October 20, 1980, p. 38.
31. "Old Slips, New Chips," *Advertising Age*, November 14, 1985, p. 2.
32. Bob Garfield, "Ed McMahon's Bad Ad Steals the Super Bowl," *Advertising Age*, February 2, 2009, p. 1.

33. "'Where's the Beef?' Star Dies," *Advertising Age*, August 17, 1987, p. 47.
34. "10 People We'll Miss," *Advertising Age*, December 17, 2007, p. 32.
35. Joe Madese, "Sorry, Jolly: The Media Loved Betty; Spindex Special; Elsie Lags the Pack as a Parade of Ad Icons Are Relaunched," *Advertising Age*, September 6, 1999, p. 9.
36. Patricia Winters, "Madge, Whipple Dip and Squeeze in New A&W Ads," *Advertising Age*, December 10, 1990, p. 1.
37. "Whipple Goes Back to Work," *Advertising Age*, June 28, 1999, p. 6.
38. Deborah Franklin, "The Television Commercial," in *TV Genres: A Handbook and Reference Guide*, ed. Brian G. Rose (Westport, CT: Greenwood Press, 1985), pp. 401–14.
39. Esslin, p. 104. Italics in original.
40. Stephen Meyer, "Get Your Handkerchiefs Out," *Advertising Age*, February 6, 1989, p. 8.
41. Arthur Bellaire, "When to Use Humor in TV Commercials," *Sponsor*, September 5, 1959, p. 34.
42. Quoted in Barry Langford, *Film Genre: Hollywood and Beyond* (Edinburgh: Edinburgh University Press, 2005), p. 11.
43. David Bordwell, *Narration in the Fiction Film* (Madison: University of Wisconsin Press, 1985), p. 156.
44. Peter Verstraten, *Film Narratology* (Toronto: University of Toronto Press, 2009), pp. 4–5.
45. Verstraten, p. 3.
46. Malysa Stratton Louk, "Old Spice Hijacks Bounce and Charmin in Co-Branded Commercials," *Digital Journal*, February 3, 2012. Available at <http://www.digitaljournal.com/article/318975> (last accessed June 3, 2018).

CHAPTER 3

Mise-en-scène

In David Shane's sixty-second Esurance commercial *It's Surprisingly Painless* (2018), American actor Dennis Quaid speaks directly into the camera and addresses the audience, explicitly telling them, "This is a commercial about insurance" (Fig. 3.1). Quaid's self-reflexive performance as narrator–actor shifts between two standpoints as he continues speaking with the audience and (with various in-character performers) operating within numerous set designs. The camera follows Quaid throughout the narrative, panning along with him or centering him in the shot: this is his film. Evident throughout the commercial is a marketing strategy that depends upon an audience familiarity with Quaid's "nice guy" screen persona. One character even tells us, "I like Dennis Quaid." The audience can trust the imagery and messaging.

The staging of this *Esurance* commercial is notably cinematic. There are ten shot sequences, each with an effectively rendered mise-en-scène: multiple characters passively and interactively move across the screen; the lighting per sequence is realistic and only backlit when appropriate; the blocking follows the physical space and time of the respective indoor–outdoor setting; and camera angles, movement, and placement establish an overall sense of familiarity and humor.

One especially noteworthy shot sequence involves a cut from one set (the sound stage of a city street) into a slovenly male viewer's living room. Here is a mise-en-abyme shot, in which Quaid on the city street appears on the man's TV. After another cut, we see the face of the incredulous man, who mouths the dialogue "I don't want to hear about insurance" while we hear Quaid speaking the same words. Thanks to a pan to the right, we see Quaid sitting on the man's couch. The commercial then cuts to the same city street staging prior to this sequence. Quaid never stops talking to the audience or to other potential customers he meets in the dynamic set of unfolding, obvious, make-believe situations.

Figure 3.1 Dennis Quaid promotes Esurance in 2018

The camera work in this commercial is visually compelling and includes medium closeup and wide shots, an over-the-shoulder shot, a handheld shot, high-angle placement, eyeline matching, camera pans, camera flare, and more. Perhaps most noteworthy about this commercial is its seamless, overall mise-en-scène: a humorous self-awareness. Quaid even tries to eat a "prop apple." There is an overall feeling that we, the audience, know this is a pleasant make-believe moment about buying insurance, but it still pleases the eye and mind.

Mise-en-scène specifically examines sets and settings, blocking and direct/indirect address, special effects, performance, lighting, and animation—all that the frame contains within its physical and visible parameters to create signifying, ideologically imbued images. How might these and other aesthetic devices effectively be used to market a product like computers in a visually arresting commercial? How can an impersonal object like an Apple computer—a complicated and expensive device back in 1984 for most middle-class people to afford or utilize—become the subject of consumer desire? How could a commercial's mise-en-scène invoke the shock of the unfamiliar and unsettling, while drawing on comprehensible intertextual associations?

In Apple's *1984* (1984; Fig. 3.2), one of America's most successful and creatively produced commercials, director Ridley Scott captured a uniquely inflected dystopian narrative for the most hyperinflated sports spectacle on television, the Super Bowl. In reality, it was a revelatory

Figure 3.2 Ridley Scott's *1984* (1984)

minute in the history of the commercial as short-film narrative because it invokes personal and collective memories, both real and imagined, of the Cold War and its popular culture narratives, psychological alienation, and the questionable promise of technology to lead into an advanced age. This Apple computer commercial stands in contradistinction to those commercials produced throughout the postwar era, in which American middle-class lives and homes are entitled domestic spaces of utopian potential; if only the consumer would buy the improved soap detergent or newest car model, what could life be like in America?

Dank, dark, and bleak: in Apple's *1984*, the future is here, televised, and it is an Orwellian nightmare, colorless and impersonal. Workers march and function in lockstep while government troops rally into action, in this highly manipulative shot sequence. An imperious leader projects the rhetoric of power via bellowing commands, while the camera cuts to reaction shots of intimidated subjects. The image of totalizing passivity recalls the "shift change" shot sequence in Fritz Lang's *Metropolis* (1927), in which workers silently pass each other, sheepishly marching into the gates of a prison-factory, heads bowed and silent.

In the Apple commercial, workers sit and watch their leader's flickering face dominate their lives as the troops chase an athletic, unidentified woman. Dressed in colorful clothing, she uses Olympian skill to hurl a sledgehammer at the screen. The leader's face explodes. Wind gales at the workers as onscreen text is spoken in voiceover: "On January 24th, Apple Computer will introduce Macintosh. And you'll see why 1984 won't be like *1984*." Directed by Scott for Chiat/Day, the sixty-second commercial, which cost between $400,000 and $600,000 to produce, aired during the Super Bowl of 1984. It won more than thirty awards, including the Grand Prix at the International Advertising Festival at Cannes.[1] A critic at *Advertising Age* called it the greatest commercial ever made.[2] In his article, "Nineteen Eighty-Four and '1984,'" media critic Thijs van den Berg comments on this phenomenal, complex narrative:

> The *1984* commercial was to a large extent prompted by the poetics of dystopian discourse. By engaging with Orwell's classic fiction Apple's advertisement was able to activate paradigms of spatial coherency and subversion that are associated with utopian and dystopian constructions, and so effectively managed the commercial space into which Macintosh could emerge . . . Apple's decision to quote what is perhaps the most canonical example of dystopian discourse appears to have been inspired by the company's sales strategy for its new Macintosh computer.[3]

Van den Berg suggestively references an intertextual framing of the Apple commercial's dystopian setting:

> the mise-en-scène is dominated by shades of grey. Almost no colour is present in the picture. The marchers are men who share the same outfit of loosely fitting overalls and have shaved heads, giving the impression of a prison colony.[4]

Technology provides an escape from this imprisonment, but it demands a price, or at least a price tag. Van den Berg concludes:

> Scott's work on *Alien* (1979) and *Bladerunner* [sic] (1982) put Apple's dystopian vision of the computer marketplace in the art style and visual language that audiences associated with the large-scale tech-noir Hollywood productions of the late 1970s and early 1980s. As a result, *1984* seems less like an advertisement with a target audience than it does a miniature film for popular, mainstream cinema: its production value, visual style and soundscape bespeak a heritage of Hollywood film production rather than that of an advertisement for a niche electronics device.[5]

Scott's messaging is clear: the audience must confront its individual and collective anxieties concerning innovative technology—rebel—and experience new freedom. It is an unforgettable mise-en-scène, framing desire for the home viewer.

Performance and Blocking

What is in a face? Does it have to be a human face, special effect, known celebrity, or some creative concoction to inspire the audience? Whether artfully recreating the myth of the saintly, suffering fifteenth-century peasant-hero Joan of Arc, in Carl Dreyer's *La Passion de Jeanne d'Arc/ The Passion of Joan of Arc* (1928) or in the humorous–horrifying IHOP commercial produced in 2018 to sell pumpkin spiced products, the face sells. Philip Drake's article, "Reconceptualizing Screen Performance," comprehensively examines the function of the cinematic single-shot closeup: "the deployment of bodily or facial expression is often coded in order to present particular emotional states (anger, sadness, surprise, and so on)."[6] This has been a production staple, an axiomatic insight, in both film and commercial marketing cultures.

Other commercials could eschew Hollywood filmmaking and the cinematic, compositional strategies associated with classic filmmaking: visualizing the abstracted face and body. For example, in 1964, a commercial for Ozon Fluid Net hairspray showed an attractive young mother with her child embracing just before leaving the home for a night out. Two heads merge as one emotional unit, framing home, family, and product. But her husband exists largely off screen, with only his arms entering the frame to give her a comb and then help her with her coat (Fig. 3.3).

Figure 3.3 Ozon Fluid Net Hairspray (1964)

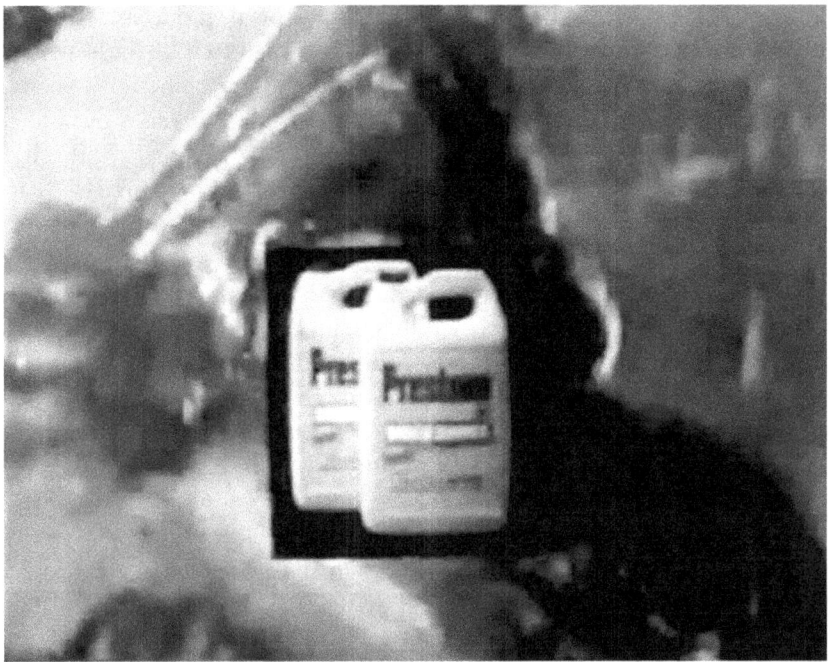

Figure 3.4 Prestone commercial from 1974

Not surprisingly, the human form at times surrenders its position as the center of the visual spectacle to the product being advertised. In a 1974 commercial for Prestone, a closeup of a worker's face becomes heavily obscured behind a rectangular graphic that depicts two bottles of the antifreeze/coolant (Fig. 3.4). It is strangely off-putting enough for the viewer to qualify as an eccentric and nontraditional composition; it is obvious enough for the viewer to convey its consumerist message, to sell a product. In 1966, Andy Warhol's *Screen Test* series of hipster near-still portraiture produced "Coke," in which the musician Lou Reed drank from a bottle of coke, in one continuous closeup, shot in black and white. There is no specific consumer message involved; Warhol's short film, unlike the Prestone short commercial film, is an open-ended narrative inviting interpretation. The Prestone commercial reflects one approach of many that television commercial blocking can assume: to be influenced by Hollywood filmmaking, to influence Hollywood filmmaking, or to diverge from it altogether, a creative strategy Warhol might have appreciated.

A large degree of attention has been paid to such concerns as lighting and blocking since the 1950s, usually in an effort to make products and the actors who promote them look as good as possible.[7] Casting choices, with particular consideration at times paid to actors' hands and face, if the same will hold or use the product, have also proven important.[8] As with Classical Hollywood Cinema, the human form is often at the center of the spectacle, frequently in the form of famous stars, sometimes playing themselves, sometimes in character. The cult of celebrity has proven to be a consistent feature of commercials since the 1950s.[9] From 1979 through the first half of the 1980s, Orson Welles's slogan on commercials, "Paul Masson will sell no wine before its time" was one of the best known in advertising.[10]

In 1973, Helena Rubinstein, Inc. announced plans to drop Katharine Ross as its spokesperson, intrigued by the idea of "going with something different."[11] What other possibilities were there? Unknown actors, of course, but for the TV commercials they directed in the 1970s and 1980s, the Maysles Brothers favored using "real people," believing "untrained, uncoaxed people will come up with great copy—in less time, and for less money—than you'd spend on a script." They had "credibility."[12] By contrast, many automobile commercials obscure the faces of actors by use of shadows and tinted windows in an effort to allow the viewer greater ease in imagining themselves in the role of driver. The face remains a constant image and industrial staple to attract and define a market.

Sets and Settings

Following the lead of Gerald Schnitzer and his colleagues, directors increasingly shot commercials on locations during the 1960s. In 1961, *Sponsor* noted that location shooting was a key reason for ever-increasing commercial budgets.[13] Four years later, *Advertising Age* reported an industry belief that the "trend today is to realism."[14] In 1969, for example, Ed Carr productions travelled to Jamaica to produce commercials for Nestlé's Milo, an instant chocolate drink.[15] Some three years later, Chevrolet airlifted a 1973 model Impala to the top of Castle Rock, Utah.[16] A 1977 article in *Advertising Age* extolled the virtues of shooting commercials overseas.[17] Usually, these expensive locations were chosen due to their natural beauty, but that was not always the case. In 1969, Cole Swimwear filmed model Pat McGuire "amid a slew of white wrecked cars," some of which had to be spray-painted for the shot.[18] Others used exteriors to create unexpected visual juxtapositions. In 1989, a thirty-second spot for Ovation Marketing featured the company's President sitting behind an office desk in the middle of a cornfield.[19]

But many directors continued to rely on studio spaces, whether outside of Southern California and New York, in an effort to keep production costs down, or—when it saved money—shooting at major studios like 20th Century Fox, as the studio-owned Wylde Films would do in the 1970s.[20] The possibilities were vast, whether in the absurd recreation of Grant Wood's 1930 painting *American Gothic* for a parodic commercial for Country Corn Flakes in 1963; or in a prison scene with George Raft for a 1969 Alka-Seltzer commercial, which invokes every George Raft prison-gangster film narrative known to the audience; or the fantastical, theme-park sets for McDonald's 1987 campaign *Mac Tonight*, which *Advertising Age* described as "Ronald McDonald meets Bertolt Brecht."[21] Set designers like Alan Roderick-Jones made major names for themselves in the industry for creating all manner of studio sets, ranging from jungles to lunar landscapes.[22]

As early as 1893, the Edison Manufacturing Company filmed indoors at its Black Maria studio. The roof could be opened to receive the sunlight necessary to obtain usable images. Under the studio was a revolving platform that allowed the building to rotate and thus take advantage of the sun as it moved across the sky. W. K. L. Dickson, who headed the company's motion picture team, once likened the Black Maria to a dungeon due to its "portentous black" background.[23] In February 1895, *Frank Leslie's Popular Monthly* described the background as being one of "Stygian gloom."[24] Here were not real-world locations or elaborate sets, but the deliberate absence of the same. According to Charles Musser, the black background "eliminated extraneous visual distractions" and "placed its subjects in bold relief."[25] This cinematic world was, at least to a degree, removed from the real world. Seldom used in the Classical Hollywood era, the mise-en-scène returned in the age of television.

From *The Mike Wallace Interview* (1958–9) to *Charlie Rose* (1991–2017), interview programs have at times used solid black backgrounds akin to the Black Maria's, which places particular focus on the interviewees, and—to a much lesser degree—the sparse number of props, which include the likes of chairs, tables, and coffee mugs. But the black background, as well as variations on the same, such as in the use of different and sometimes gradient colors, has found particular and repeated usage in television commercials, which, given their brief running times and efforts to emphasize the center of the spectacle in "bold relief," recall the Edison films.

Consider the case of Christine O'Donnell, a Republican candidate for a US Senate seat from Delaware in 2010. Years earlier, in 1998, when she appeared on Bill Maher's *Politically Incorrect* (1993–2002), O'Donnell revealed, "I dabbled into witchcraft. [But] I never joined a coven." When the clip resurfaced during the 2010 campaign, O'Donnell—who had positioned herself as an evangelical voice for right-wing conservatism—was subjected to a barrage of attacks.

Figure 3.5 *I'm You* (2010), featuring Christine O'Donnell

O'Donnell then appeared in a campaign ad response, speaking to the camera in a medium closeup. "I am not a witch," she began, in a phrase rarely heard in America since the seventeenth century (Fig. 3.5). O'Donnell proceeded to explain that she was "you," meaning the viewer, while piano music played softly in the background. *Time* magazine wrote, "Only in the ever-wackier 2010 election cycle would a campaign video start with such an assertion."[26] Within a few weeks of its first broadcast, O'Donnell told NBC that she regretted appearing in the commercial, admitting it had given renewed life to the story.[27]

Given that the purpose of *I'm You* (aka *I Am Not a Witch*) was to deny being a witch, it is surprising that its creator Fred Davis had O'Donnell wear black clothing in the advertisement and filmed her against a solid black background, save for a small amount of ethereal dark blue light behind her. The background takes O'Donnell out of the world, its Stygian darkness serving as a potential contradiction to her words.

Though usually reserved for spokespersons, the black background has served props as well, just as it did in the Edison films. A circa 1964 commercial for Chevrolet automobiles promoted a range of their vehicles, "from the '64 Stingray to the '59 Impala." It unfolds in twenty-seven shots, the first six being nighttime exteriors filmed on location in Hollywood. The commercial also includes one subsequent exterior, as well as a closing shot that asks the viewer to see their local Chevrolet dealer. But the bulk of the commercial is filmed inside a studio. These nineteen shots feature different camera moves, tilts, and fast zooms to display the cars.

The lighting scheme is near-psychedelic, intended to mimic the look of colorful neon signs in Hollywood. But the cars are very definitely inside a studio. The black background accentuates the nighttime setting, while simultaneously forcing full attention onto the automobiles.

By contrast, other commercials have employed a solid white background, one similar to the mise-en-scène of George Lucas's *THX 1138* (1971). Evoking a clean, sterile environment, the white background has been featured in many spots, notably in the Apple *Get a Mac* (aka *Mac vs. PC*) campaign that ran on TV stations from 2006 to 2009.[28] Directed by Phil Morrison, the extensive number of commercials featured Justin Long as the human embodiment of a Mac, a cool guy wearing casual dress, and John Hodgman as a PC, a boring person dressed in formal wear, somewhat resembling Bill Gates.[29] In some cases, other characters appear, including, in one commercial, a football referee. Rather than the tone of friendly denial that O'Donnell adopts, the *Get a Mac* commercials are humorous, comically drawing contrasts between the two types of computers.

Direct Address

In presentational television commercials, direct address to the camera, the returned gaze of the cinema, is so common as to be a cliché. Reverse-angle cutting and point-of-view shots are largely the purview of narrative commercials, while characters staring into the camera lens often dominate the presentational approach. "It looks at you," as Wheeler Winston Dixon's monograph suggests.[30] Marc Vernet writes:

> According to traditional approaches, the look at the camera has a double effect: it foregrounds the enunciative instance of the filmic text and attacks the spectator's voyeurism by putting the space of the film and the space of the movie theater briefly in contact.[31]

Here Vernet's explanation could be meaningfully augmented by consideration of the space that is the home, the traditional site of television viewing.

The "look back" can operate for various reasons, including for the sake of humor in mainstream cinema. With regard to such examples as Oliver Hardy or the Marx Brothers, Vernet writes that they turn the viewer "into a witness for an ironic commentary on the actions or attitudes of other characters. Here the address to the spectator is a forming of the spectator as witness."[32] The "look back" occurs in other genres as well, including pornography. In all of these cases, such a staging position and reciprocal acknowledgment assigns, according to Dagrada, "the spectator a place *in* the film."[33] The staging position yields a subject position. Here is not voyeurism, or for that matter reverse voyeurism, but an intended dialogue. More specifically, Nick Browne observes:

> The spectator's place, the locus around which the spatiotemporal structures of presentation are organized, is a construction of the text which is ultimately the product of the narrator's disposition toward the tale.[34]

The television commercial provides an important and recurrent example, one in which the disposition is sales, whether of products or services or ideas. It is a particularized version of what Dixon calls the "commodity of spectacle."[35]

Actors looking into the camera became commonplace on television, their appearance and returned gaze creating shared recognition. In 1983, for example, *Advertising Age* bemoaned the death of Arthur Godfrey, claiming that his "ad style was revolutionary."[36] Godfrey's renown resulted from many projects, but among them were certainly his direct address commercials for Lipton tea, Chase & Sanborn coffee, Chesterfield cigarettes, and many other products. "His manner of delivery of commercials ... captivated audiences and earned him, besides millions of dollars, honored status as a legendary communicator," the magazine remarked.[37] For some, the spokesperson commercial created boredom.[38]

Nevertheless, the sheer number of actors who have cultivated their own careers by appearing in TV commercials would be hard to list, but they begin with such luminaries as Godfrey and Betty Furness, and include a large number of persons known mainly by their commercial personas. Examples include the Maytag Repairman (played by Jesse White) and Joe Isuzu (played by David Leisure) for Isuzu Motors, Ltd. Each commercial positions the actor in a medium closeup shot, surrounded by a credibly realistic, character-centered setting; the audience engages with the image and a sense of familiarity settles. In other cases, the anonymity of actor and character is a potential strength, building trust and credibility due to the appearance of being an everyday person. The audience knows that these are actors but accepts their respective commercial identity and willingly participates in the comedic narrative: washing machines will break, and Joe's smarmy, self-conscious pitch to buy a car is obvious.

There is a long and established production tradition to consider. For example, *1-USA '57 Chevrolet* (1957) features a medium shot of an unknown actor directly addressing the viewer, expounding on the virtues of the new Chevy automobile. As he continues to talk, the commercial cuts to shots of admiring customers in a faux-showroom, as well as static images of the particular features he describes, ranging from the car's instrument panel to its fuel injection. Here the commercial unfolds akin to a lecture, with the knowledgeable teacher speaking to us while projecting slides.

Unknown actors can also try to build a different, more friendly relationship with the viewer. A 1950s commercial for Robt. Burns cigars begins with four shots of a boy at the beach with his uncle. Against sentimental music, the first-person voiceover remembers happy occasions from years gone by, those of an uncle who smoked Robt. Burns cigars. Following from a slow dissolve, the fifth shot in the spot depicts a man sitting in a chair and smoking a cigar. He looks to screen left and then turns his head to speak directly into the camera. His fond memories have led him to choose the same cigars, he explains, proceeding to outline the product's virtues. "Why don't you smoke a Robt. Burns cigar soon?", he suggests in a friendly voice.

More unique is a commercial for Budweiser from the late 1950s. In it, the actor looks directly into the camera, extolling the virtues of the beer's foam and the fact that it is beechwood-aged. "You can taste the difference," he explains, and then almost literally hands a glass of beer to the viewer. It obscures the screen for approximately three seconds. Soon the "viewer" hands an empty glass back to the talent. The use of props in tandem with the direct address draws upon such films as Robert Montgomery's *Lady in the Lake* (1947).

Commercials can intensify these friendly relations by making the direct address intentionally secretive or confidential, thus placing the viewer in a position of privilege. A 1978 commercial for Hidden Valley Ranch exemplifies this point. A wife in the kitchen addresses the viewer; her husband is visible in the background, sitting at a dining-room table. She explains, "If I told him how I make Hidden Valley Ranch salad dressing, he'd never try it." Thanks to an edit, the husband immediately responds to her, explaining that he did try it and enjoys it. His gaze is at her; an eyeline match clarifies that he is oblivious to the viewer. The wife proceeds to tell us that the packet of "fixings" combines with mayonnaise and buttermilk. Overhearing, he asks her "What did you say?" She responds that they are out of butter, as she does not want him to know that buttermilk is one of the ingredients. She then reassures us that the resulting salad dressing is "delicious," prompting the puzzled husband to ask, "Edith, who are you talking to?"

Direct address can even unfold in situations where the talent cannot see the viewer. Consider Democrat Jason Kander's political advertisement for a US Senate seat from Missouri when he ran against Republican incumbent Roy Blunt. First broadcast in 2016, the commercial depicts Kander wearing a blindfold—therefore, not looking into the camera—for the first twenty-three seconds of the half-minute commercial. While speaking about gun rights and his opponent, Kander's face looks towards the camera as he puts together a rifle. Once the firearm is complete, he lifts the blindfold, continuing to look in our direction, but for the first time with his eyes revealed, as he suggestively reveals himself, with renewed, clarified "vision," to the audience.

Direct address is a favored approach in many political ads, including a number of those featuring US Senator Bob Dole, whether for his congressional campaigns from the 1970s to the 1990s, or for his presidential bids, including most famously his tenure as the Republican Party's nominee in 1996. In one commercial, he speaks to the camera in a thirty-second commercial about his commitment to Medicare. The camera tracks slowly inward. No edits occur. The entire ad features his unbroken gaze, reassuring the viewer about a political position on which he had been attacked.

Such ads, as well as Dole's celebrity status, meant that he was quite the opposite of, say, actors in the aforementioned commercials for Chevrolet and Robt. Burns. How he might appear (meaning suits and ties, shaking hands with supporters amid American flags) and how he might be heard (meaning delivering impassioned speeches, speaking to the camera, at times with patriotic background music) formed a cliché, quite similar to most politicians and most political advertisements.

Having lost the 1996 election, Dole then appeared in a thirty-second 1997 commercial, giving a political retirement speech with all of the expected audiovisual pomp and circumstance. He returns to his hometown, where he is imminently recognizable. Half-way through the commercial, he asks if he can pay by check at a restaurant. "Of course, Bob," the friendly waitress replies, before changing to a stern tone. "Can I see some ID?" What seemed to be a political ad for fifteen seconds transforms unexpectedly into a promotion for Visa Check Cards.[39] Dole does not have one, which leads him to look directly into the camera and humorously explain, "I just can't win."

The use of direct address in subverting viewer expectations continued to be an important part of Bob Dole's advertising career. Beginning in 1998, Dole appeared in commercials for Pfizer's drug Viagra, produced by Cline, David & Mann.[40] In them, Dole speaks plainly and sincerely to the camera with first-hand experience about how it helped him after a prostatectomy, and how it could help others with erectile dysfunction. *Medical Marketing and Media* later observed:

> Dole's first Viagra spot looks an awful lot like a political ad. He wears the traditional uniform of dark suit and red power tie; the background music could well have been lifted from a military procession. But the message Dole delivers could

not have been any more straightforward: "It's a little embarrassing to talk about ED, but it's so important to millions of men and their partners that I decided to talk about it publicly."[41]

Rather than lampoon the political commercials for which he was known, he relied on the gravitas of their mise-en-scène to discuss another topic seriously.

Then, in 2001, Dole starred in a forty-five-second Super Bowl commercial produced by BBDO for Pepsi Cola. Soft music plays in the background. Dole wears a jacket and open-collared shirt. As he walks along the beach with his dog, his voiceover explains, "Hi, I'm Bob Dole, and I've always spoken to you frankly, no matter what the subject." The camera cuts to a closeup of Dole looking into the camera. He continues, "That's why I'm eager to tell you about a product that put real joy back in my life." The image dissolves to Dole on the beach. Slow-motion footage of his dog running and waves crashing is seen. Given Dole's words and his association with Viagra, the commercial creates a mise-en-scène akin to that of a pharmaceutical ad. Dole's voiceover strengthens the connection: "What is this amazing product? My faithful little blue friend." The reference seems more suggestive of Viagra than ever, given that it is a small blue pill. But then, after twenty-five seconds, the commercial offers its humorous, ironic punch line. Dole is actually describing an "ice-cold Pepsi Cola." Its conclusion features another actor in a laboratory coat speaking to the camera, advising viewers to "check with your local convenient store counter clerk" to determine if the "revitalizing effects of Pepsi-Cola are right for you."

Animation

In *The Technique of Film Animation* (1971), John Halas and Roger Manvell explained:

> Cartoons have particular advantages as commercials; among these advantages are their immediate entertainment value, their speed at making points against the severe limitations of time, and their ability to stand up to repetition when most live-action commercials tend to lose "face" by being repeated.[42]

Halas and Manvell also observed the economic advantages, meaning that, while animation could be more expensive to produce than live-action commercials, animated characters with unseen voice actors did not require such costly repeat fees to performers as live-action performers. They could also visualize what was otherwise impossible, like two personified pieces of popcorn talking in a 1954 commercial for E-Z Pop popcorn.[43]

Animated television commercials date to late 1946, if not earlier.[44] As *Television Age* once observed, animation became a "strong factor" in TV commercials during the 1950s, before being largely displaced by the Schnitzer-style live-action commercials during the following decade.[45] In its discussion of the "ten most outstanding" commercials of 1957, for example, *Sponsor* magazine chose four that were animated.[46] And few commercials of the decade were more popular than Young and Rubicam's campaign for Piel's beer, which featured the animated characters Bert (Bob Elliott) and Harry (Ray Goulding).[47]

Consider the case of famed animator and one-time Disney employee John Hubley, who was fired from United Productions of America in 1952 due to his unwillingness to assist the Communist witch-hunts.[48] The lack of screen credits featured on commercials allowed him to find a new outlet for his talents. He most famously created a series of animated commercials for the Ford Motor Company, but also did the same for E-Z Popcorn, Western Airlines, Speedway, and Maypo Oat Cereal.[49] Hubley was one of the many animators who worked in the industry from the 1950s to the twenty-first century. Indeed, animation returned to greater prominence in TV commercials from the late 1960s.

Writing in *Advertising Age* in 1981, Hooper White offered specific reasons why producers and directors should select animation over live-action commercials. He suggested, "If going *inside* a product or service to watch how it works is key to your selling idea, the animator's pencil will get you there immediately."[50] For example, a 1960s commercial for Scotties tissues depicted their "new magic oval box" in closeup (Fig. 3.6). Three live-action shots feature superimposed, animated dashes outlining the perimeter of the box. The image thus reveals the interior of the box, the manner by which the product is stacked inside to allow them to "float up gently, one at a time" or "come out in neat handfuls," depending on what the user desires, "because there's a magic oval inside every new Scotties box." Commercials that decided to "go inside" predated the effect as employed by filmmakers in the 1990s and beyond, as in such cases as the gunshot wound scene in *Three Kings* (David O. Russell, 1999).

An early 1960s commercial for Johnson & Johnson's Micrin Oral Antiseptic serves as another example of how animation could unveil an otherwise unseen world, in this case a live-action commercial that includes one animated shot, an iris image of various fonts depicting the letter "G" for "germ" (Fig. 3.7). They bounce into one another, appearing akin to a microscopic image of bacteria. Then the commercial compares Micrin

MISE-EN-SCÈNE 77

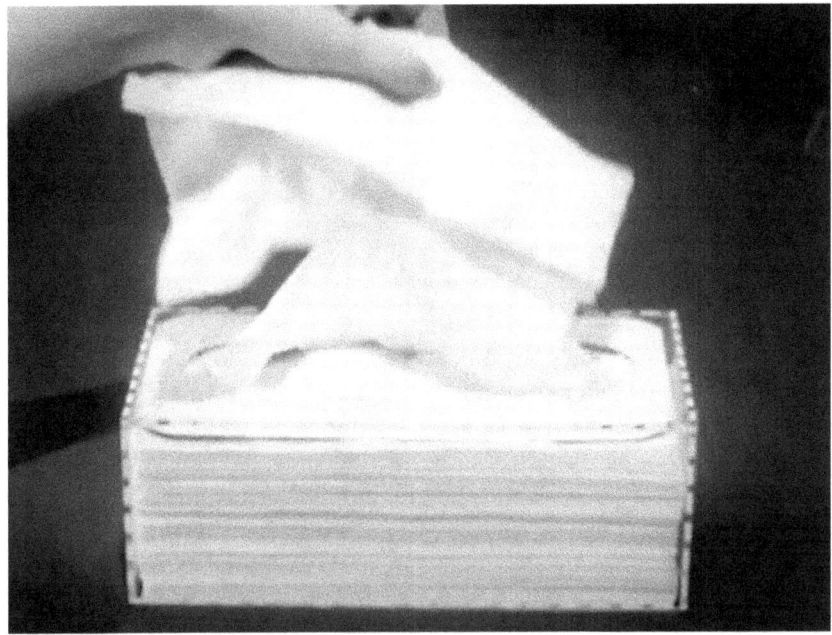

Figure 3.6 Scottie Tissues commercial from the 1960s

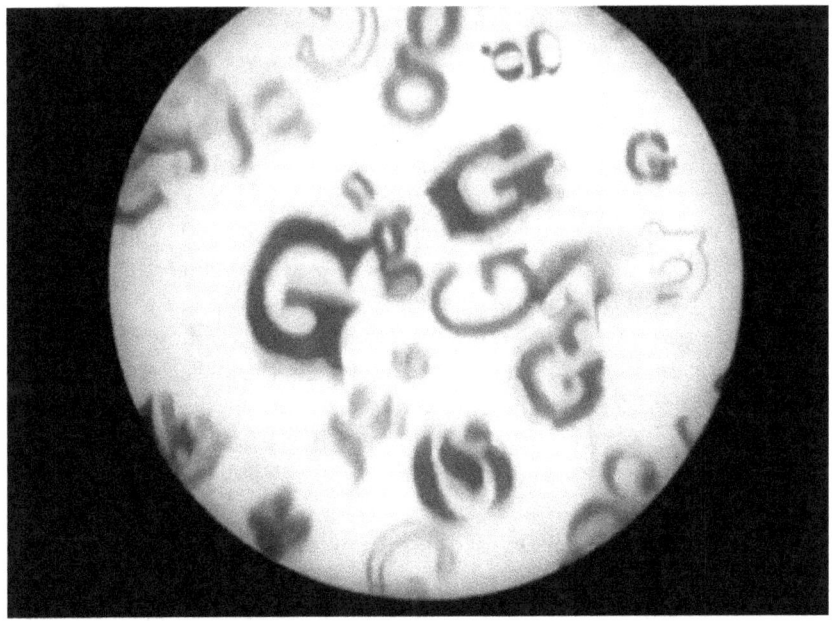

Figure 3.7 Micrin Oral Antiseptic from the early 1960s

with the "other mouthwash," the animation visualizing how quickly bad breath might return.

White also suggested animation's usefulness for other narrative and thematic purposes:

> If exaggeration would help you make a sales point, animation offers you visual opportunities denied you in live action.
>
> If humor aids the selling force of your commercial, animation offers you an unlimited source of very funny sight-and-sound combinations.[51]

These reasons are rather obvious, and extend to far too many commercials to chronicle. One salient example would be *Take Stock in America*, a 1977 commercial for US Savings Bonds. A cartoon ant works "day and night" while a grasshopper "fiddled away his free time." When Winter comes, the ant leaves on vacation and the grasshopper seems literally left out in the cold. But he is not. Voiceover by Paul Frees explains the grasshopper is "on the payroll savings plan, and by now all those US Savings Bonds added up to a big surprise." The grasshopper is able to join the surprised ant on Winter vacation. "Moral? Buy US Savings Bonds and you don't need a rich aunt."

Controversies over the use of cartoon characters to sell Camel cigarettes and other products might suggest that animation had solely been to appeal to children, whether in ads for toys and breakfast cereals or in those for adult products like tobacco that would inspire youthful interest in the same. As early as 1950, Pabst Blue Ribbon used animation to sell its beer. In 1951, Muriel cigars ran a commercial created by Lennen & Mitchell and Shamus Culhane, in which personified male and female cigars sing and dance together, the female being a parody of Mae West ("Why don't you pick me up and smoke me some time?") (Fig. 3.8).[52] Then, in the early 1960s, the animated Flintstones sold Winston cigarettes. Here are examples of what later provoked such concerns.

However, animation has often been the basis of commercials that were largely, or even solely, aimed at adults, including the aforementioned *Take Stock in America*. Indeed, there were animated commercials for such products as Crosley Corporation televisions in 1951, Ajax Cleanser in 1952, Raid House & Garden Bug Killer in 1955, and Hotpoint appliances in 1956, to name but a few.

In the 1960s, Alka-Seltzer used animation to depict a man unable to sleep because of the food he has eaten. In the middle of the night, a large number of angry personified foods attack him, all bearing various weapons. They

Figure 3.8 Animation promotes Muriel cigars in 1951

range from a clam with a rifle and an egg with a mace to a piece of bacon with snake-like fangs. Near the front of the pack is a Swiss cheese wielding a spear. "If there are little things still kicking around," the narrator explains, "your stomach is going to keep you awake . . . unless you take Alka-Seltzer." Its storyline recalls Edwin S. Porter's *Dream of a Rarebit Fiend* (1906), a trick film in which three little devils use a mallet, a trident, and a pickaxe to berate a sleeping man who has eaten too much cheese and liquor.

Perhaps the most influential animated commercial aimed at adults was broadcast in 1952. Rosser Reeves of the Ted Bates Agency created Dwight D. Eisenhower's famous 1952 campaign commercial *Ike for President*, which was produced by Walt Disney's brother Roy and Citizens for Eisenhower–Nixon. First broadcast three weeks before the election, the commercial featured a jingle composed by Irving Berlin: "You like Ike/I Like Ike/Everybody likes Ike—for President!" A cartoon version of Uncle Sam leads a parade of various citizens holding signs that read "Ike." They include a young couple pushing a stroller and a farmer riding a tractor. The tail of an animated elephant beats a drum. "Hang out the banner/Beat the drums/We'll take Ike to Washington!" Slogans were Reeves's key emphasis, with animation bringing "I Like Ike" to the masses. Some persons were aghast at merchandising the presidency, among them Eisenhower's opponent Adlai Stevenson, but the animated commercial helped determine the race's outcome.[53]

As Halas and Manvell note in 1971, "Any form of cartooning from stylized naturalism to the completely abstract can be readily adapted to positive salesmanship..."[54] The various possibilities have extended to the combination of animation with live-action footage. By 1959, the industry referred to these efforts as "hybrid" commercials, with studies suggesting that they could be more effective than either live action or animation used alone.[55] Here again, there are far too many examples to enumerate, many of which have been aimed at children, whether promotions for toys or for breakfast cereals. The result has made such cartoon characters as Tony the Tiger, Captain Crunch, Count Chocula, and many others famous.

But various others have targeted adults. A 1970s ad for Anacin's Arthritis Pain Formula featured a live-action woman putting dirty clothes into a washer. The image freezes. Animated lightning bolts illustrate how "occasional arthritis minor pain can strike any joint in your body." A subsequent shot depicts how Anacin is "circulated through your body in minutes" and "works all through your system." As those words are spoken, a shot of the laundry room features the woman's silhouetted body with a large pill shape in her stomach cavity. Inside the pill animated dots circulate. The outline of the pill disappears and the dots are visible everywhere inside her body, from head to foot.

Actress Gisele MacKenzie appeared on screen in a filmed commercial in 1956, conversing and playing music with Happy Joe, an animated mascot for Lucky Strike cigarettes. He even kisses her on the cheek. In 1983, Fox Photo launched a campaign that drew upon a scene in the feature film *Anchors Aweigh* (George Sidney, 1945), in which Gene Kelly's live-action character dances with Jerry, the cartoon mouse. Levenson & Levenson, who produced the commercial, tested approximately seventy dancers and careful choreography for what became a short story of a woman dancing with a fox.[56] A decade later, Michael Jordan played basketball with Bugs Bunny ("Hare Jordan") in Joe Pytka's sixty-second commercial for Nike. Debuting during the 1992 Super Bowl, the spot combined live action and animation for the sake of sports and even a nod to *Casablanca* (Michael Curtiz, 1942).

The combination of animation and live action has assumed other forms as well. In 1988, Avrett, Free & Ginsberg created a commercial for Chex cereal at Pan Productions in Brooklyn, New York. It painstakingly brought five Norman Rockwell paintings to life by carefully matching actors, wardrobes, and props, modifying the originals only to the extent of including boxes of the product.[57] Setups were matched against the original paintings using video assist with the 35mm camera. When the film was developed, every other frame was dropped in an effort "to create the feeling of a painting come to life." The remaining frames were blown up to VistaVision and then printed through a Canon laser printer. At that stage, twenty artists applied acrylics, pencils, pastels, and crayons to the live-action frames.[58] The final rotoscoped vignettes appeared in a thirty-second spot promoting the cereal's "classic crunch."

Special Effects

In 1982, magician David Copperfield appeared on screen in commercials promoting Kodak's instant Kodamatic camera. Along with touting the product and using it to take pictures, Copperfield performed magic tricks of the type that made him famous on stage. He returned in a 1984 commercial for Kodamatic Trimprint color film; however, this commercial incorporates digital special effects. Though featuring the same magician promoting the same company, the two commercials offer dramatically different approaches to achieve their cinematic tricks.

Special effects were a key component in the "cinema of attractions," as discussed in Chapter 2. It was spectacle over narrative. As Gunning notes, "this cinema differs from later narrative cinema through its fascination in the thrill of display rather than its construction of a story."[59] The most notable exponent of cinematic tricks in early cinema was Georges Méliès, famed for several hundred special effects-driven films produced between 1896 and 1913. Images from his *Le Voyage dans la Lune/A Trip to the Moon* (1902) rank among the most iconic in film history. The myth of Méliès was founded on such special effects as substitution splices, dissolves, and multiple exposures.

In the 1950s, Raleigh cigarette commercials employed special effects of the type earlier associated with Méliès, particularly in making props appear and disappear, all as part of an ongoing promotion for the inclusion of coupons in its packages that could be applied towards "free gifts." The same could be said of a 1960s commercial for Kleenex Man Size tissues, in which an offscreen character sneezes, causing all of the furniture and other props to literally blow across a living-room set. "Let's take back that sneeze," the voiceover tells us, causing the film to roll backwards and return the room to its former state. These special effects were not more advanced or "special" than those Méliès had employed five decades earlier, but they still resonated with some viewers.

Indeed, the commercials of the 1950s to the 1970s revived and repeated some of the most longstanding and arguably trite special effects in film history. At times, filmmakers found new and more economical approaches to old effects, but in most cases the outcomes were not dramatically different in appearance.[60] A 1953 commercial for the Pet Milk Company showed a chair pulling itself up to a table, a cup filling itself with coffee, a can pouring milk, and the cup emptying itself; the effects were strikingly similar to those used by J. Stuart Blackton in his 1907 Vitagraph film *The Haunted Hotel*.[61] And however sophisticated the Pillsbury Doughboy was when he debuted in 1966, his appearance comprised of "more than 100 separate bodies, head poses and expressions," he emerged from traditional stop-motion techniques that dated to Willis O'Brien and *The Lost World* (Harry O. Hoyt, 1925) and *King Kong* (Merian C. Cooper and Ernest B. Schoedsack, 1933).[62]

By contrast, in the late 1970s and 1980s, special effects in TV commercials became advanced enough to inspire regular articles in *Advertising Age* headlined "How Did They Shoot That?" At times, these constituted sophisticated variations of old tricks. In 1980, for example, Herb Loebel created an effect for Minolta in which a large number of pieces fly together at a fast speed to form a camera. He filmed it at 1,500 frames per second and reversed the footage.[63] But other tricks resulted from cutting-edge technologies. In 1979, for example, McCann–Erickson produced a commercial for Fanta in which "youngsters ride a merry-go-round amidst stars, planets, magical clouds, and floating bubbles." It relied on a new motion graphic technique created by Zeplin Productions.[64] Then, in 1984, Ian Leech directed a Jell-O commercial for Young & Rubicam that utilized an Ampex Digital Optics machine, a "Paint Box," and a VPR 3 switcher to manipulate the image of a surfer riding a wave and "wiping out the [product] box in its spray."[65]

Wanda Strauven has appropriately applied the term "cinema of attractions" to contemporary special effects, which include computer-generated imagery (CGI) and other digital effects.[66] Some commercial directors continued to rely on in-camera special effects, often achieving remarkable results, but many more turned to new possibilities present in post-production.[67]

As early as 1974, Robert Abel used a "computer production technique" to create *Bubbles*, a sixty-second commercial for 7-Up. Then, in 1977, he created the sixty-second spot *Brand Name* (1977) for Levi Strauss, a $250,000 visual tour-de-force in which the unseen lead character takes the company's logo for a walk as if it were a dog (Fig. 3.9). The result, relying

Figure 3.9 Robert Abel's *Brand Name* (1977)

in part on effects that Abel called "luminetics," was staggering for its time, and far ahead of any feature film. In 1980, Abel announced to colleagues:

> If there is one word for communications in the '80s, I'd say it was digital. It's a whole new concept for advertising as communication . . . We're going to have to find new, creative, dynamic ways to attract an audience . . . I went into digital because everything I saw looked alike. I knew I needed something unique.[68]

Abel proved his point well in *Brilliance*, a thirty-second spot he created for the Canned Food Information Council in 1985 (Fig. 3.10). Computer animation created a sexualized female robot. For accuracy, Randy Roberts invented what he called "brute force" animation, which filmed a live-action model with painted dots on her body. The computer used the spots to make a life-like vector graphic. After months of work, the commercial debuted during the Super Bowl on January 20, 1985. While full 3-D computer animation made its debut in feature films like *Star Trek II: The Wrath of Khan* (Nicholas Meyer, 1982) and appeared extensively in *The Last Starfighter* (Nick Castle, 1984), *Brilliance* brought to life the first 3-D computer animated human-like character on the screen. It remains a crucial, even if often overlooked, landmark in film history.

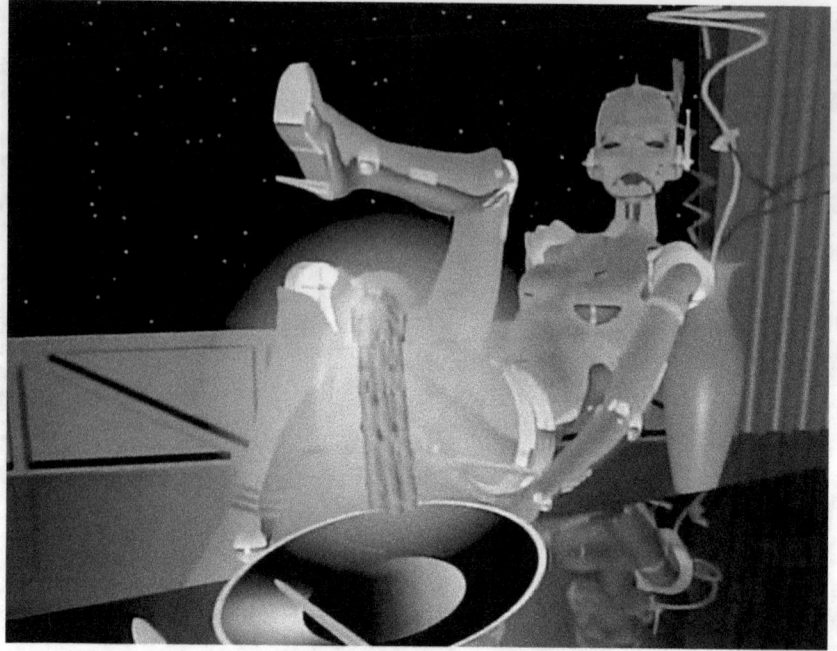

Figure 3.10 Robert Abel's *Brilliance* (1985)

During the 1990s and into the twenty-first century, commercials remained at the vanguard of CGI effects that do more than reconstitute the cinema of attractions. According to Andrew Darley in 2000:

> Most advertising now uses digital imaging techniques as a matter of course: these techniques involve both image manipulation (and image combination) and image synthesis . . . though not necessarily always together in the same advertisement . . . for some time, TV advertisements—among the shortest moving image texts in existence—have increasingly turned to using the new digital techniques to produce altogether new levels of arresting visual brilliance and allure.[69]

Darley adds that CGI allows for the "production of high-resolution photographic simulations of impossible or virtually impossible shots, actions and occurrences."[70]

Consider a trio of fifteen-second commercials for Dirt Devil's Broom Vac, Ultra Hand Vac, and Ultra MVP upright vacuum cleaner. They featured clips from two feature films starring Fred Astaire, *Easter Parade* (Charles Walters, 1948) and *Royal Wedding* (Stanley Donen, 1951), but with the sponsored product digitally inserted into his hands. The old became the new. The footage included the famous scene from *Royal*

Wedding in which Astaire appears to dance on the walls and ceiling, so memorable that it had earlier inspired director Mel Sokolsky to recreate the basic effect by building an elaborate revolving set for a Dr Pepper commercial in 1982.[71]

Atomic Films created the Dirt Devil commercials for Meldrum & Fewsmith at a production cost of over $1 million, to say nothing of the fees paid to Turner Entertainment and to Astaire's widow Robyn for the rights to the film clips and Astaire's likeness. Sight Effects designed the effects, which involved careful manipulation of approximately 1,000 frames of footage.[72] The result was, for its time, visually arresting, even startling.

By the summer of 1997, the Astaire commercials had resulted in a major controversy.[73] Astaire's daughter Ava complained to the Royal Appliance Manufacturing Company, who manufactured Dirt Devil vacuums, "Your paltry, unconscionable commercials are the antithesis of everything my lovely, gentle father represented."[74] She also bemoaned that her father had been "sold to the devil."[75] By contrast, Astaire's widow Robyn defended her actions, claiming, "I just feel Fred would have wanted me to do these commercials."[76] Astaire biographer Peter J. Levinson called them "tasteless."[77]

But concerns over digitally altering Astaire's art into a sales ad did little to dampen the overall excitement of the potential of CGI to transform pre-existing and iconic footage in such a convincing manner. Initial broadcasts of the commercials in 1997 resulted in approximately 1,100 newspaper and magazine stories, as well as positive reports on a large number of television programs.[78]

A related example would be a sixty-second commercial produced by Fallon McElligott and first broadcast during the Super Bowl in January 2000. The $4 million production promoted the Nuveen Investment Corporation, its closing voiceover explaining, "In the future, so many amazing things will happen in the world. What amazing things can you make happen?" Closing onscreen text clarified, "Invest well. Leave your mark."

The commercial's narrative features an onstage host speaking to a live audience, the depiction of a better future in the new millennium, one in which major advances have been made in the fight against AIDS and cancer. "And tonight," he explains, "tonight we celebrate a remarkable breakthrough in spinal cord injuries made possible by countless researchers and contributors." He then invites a special guest to present an award for this achievement.

Enter Christopher Reeve, the actor best known for playing the title role in *Superman* (Richard Donner, 1978). He had become a quadriplegic in 1995, the result of being thrown from a horse. Reeve never walked again, but he became an activist for research into paralysis and spinal cord injuries. And in the commercial, Reeve slowly strides to the podium, using what appear to be his real legs, all thanks to CGI effects. Computer imaging drew grid marks on an actor, lining it up to match Reeve's. To walk stiffly, the actor wore prosthetic weights on his legs. Put another way, Reeve's face was digitally inserted onto an actor's body to make possible the impossible.

Here was an effect that predated the digital usage of Nancy Marchand in *Proshai, Livushka*, a 2001 episode of HBO's *The Sopranos*. In it, Rhinoceros Visual Effects and Design "used tape editing and computer technology to craft a scene with Livia Soprano (Marchand) talking to her son, Tony (James Gandolfini), even though actress Nancy Marchand died last June before filming . . . began." To be sure, this example was more complex than the Reeve commercial, involving 8,000 frames and various pre-existing clips of Marchand talking. But not only did the Reeve commercial come first, it also spurred a greater response.

As Robert McRuer has written, the ad "garnered an unprecedented amount of media attention."[79] As a CBS news report asked immediately after the commercial aired, "Inspiring or Misleading?" The National Spinal Cord Injury Association was inundated with phone calls asking where Reeve had received his cure. Other advocates and researchers said they found the computerized image thrilling but worrisome, as it was so convincing that it raised false hopes about a quick cure."[80] *Advertising Age* noted, "If this futuristic look at a spinally rehabilitated Christopher Reeve . . . were a public service announcement, it would be inspiring, optimistic, and beautiful. But this spot is for an investment company, and, therefore, is crass and disgusting."[81] Nevertheless, its special effects were among the most talked about in the history of the American television commercial.

Conclusion

In 2017, Mike Dahlquist directed a Halo Top ice-cream commercial for the internet and movie theater audience (Fig. 3.11). The mise-en-scène is recognizably disturbing, humorous, and familiar: a dystopian narrative. "Eat the ice cream" is the message pleasingly and repeatedly intoned by the insistent robot that feeds an elderly, confined woman sitting in a spotless, isolated white kitchen of the foreseeable, undesired future; the entrapped older woman is an unwilling and intimidated participant in this parodic takeoff of dystopian narratives.

Dahlquist's commercial recalls not only Scott's *1984* commercial for Apple, but also the bedroom–dining table sequence near the end of Stanley

Figure 3.11 Mike Dahlquist's 2017 commercial for Halo Top

Kubrick's *2001: A Space Odyssey* (1968), in which an old man confronts himself and his mortality as he eats in a sterile, alienating space in an unknowable time. However, a more significant linkage is suggested with the factory lunch break, "feeding-machine" shot sequence in Chaplin's comedic workers' dystopia, *Modern Times* (1936). In all of these interrelated narratives, a filmic mise-en-scène establishes essential production considerations and recognizable intertextual–aesthetic parameters to create marketing strategies to sell tickets, computers, and even ice cream.

Notes

1. Alice Z. Cuneo, "Apple Concocts Homage to 1984; Famed Ad Turns 20 at Super Bowl," *Advertising Age*, December 8, 2003, p. 1.
2. "Technology Marketing; Landmark Campaigns; *1984*," *Advertising Age*, November 11, 1996, p. A22.
3. Thijs van den Berg, "Nineteen Eighty-Four and '1984,'" *Journal of Literature and Science*, vol. 5, no. 1 (2012), p. 98.
4. Van den Berg, p. 100.
5. Van den Berg, pp. 105–6.
6. Philip Drake, "Reconceptualizing Screen Performance," *Journal of Film and Video*, vol. 58, no. 1/2 (Spring/Summer 2006), p. 87.
7. "Make Your Commercial Look Its Best," *Sponsor*, January 12, 1957, pp. 29–31.
8. "The Art of Casting," *Sponsor*, January 19, 1957, pp. 29–31, 83.
9. See, for example: "How Valuable Is a Star's Name in a TV Commercial," *Sponsor*, April 19, 1958, p. 46.
10. Mitchell J. Shields, "Putting Wine to the Test-imonial," *Advertising Age*, January 6, 1984, p. M43.
11. "Rubinstein May Drop Katharine Ross from Ad Program," *Advertising Age*, October 15, 1973, p. 34.

12. "'Real People' Film Producers Catch Trend in Television Ads," *Advertising Age*, June 30, 1975, p. 50; James P. Forkan, "Maysles Finds 'Great' Copy from Mouths of Real People," *Advertising Age*, November 8, 1982, p. 80.
13. "What Price TV Commercials?", *Sponsor*, November 27, 1961, pp. 33–4.
14. "TV Ads Are Moving Towards Realism, FC&B's LaCava Says," *Advertising Age*, October 22, 1965, p. 96.
15. "Idyllic Jamaica Scenes Illumine Nestle Milo Ads," *Advertising Age*, April 14, 1969, p. 46.
16. "Chevy Short on Rocks," *Advertising Age*, September 25, 1972, p. 84.
17. Hooper White, "Shooting Overseas? You Don't Have to Take the Crew and Equipment with You," *Advertising Age*, June 6, 1977, pp. 53–4.
18. "Cole Swimwear TV Film Uses Wrecked Cars as Background," *Advertising Age*, December 1, 1969, p. 102.
19. Scott Hume, "Corny, but Earworthy," *Advertising Age*, September 18, 1989, p. 8.
20. Arthur Bellaire, "Take Time, See Studios Out of Town, Cut Cost," *Advertising Age*, July 10, 1972, p. 48; "Wylde Films Plans Greater Use of 20th Studios, Props," *Advertising Age*, May 14, 1973, p. 30.
21. Bob Garfield, "Could That *Hotel Hell* Someone Be Mac the Burger?", *Advertising Age*, August 31, 1987, p. 44.
22. "Conjuring the Here and Now," *Advertising Age*, July 3, 1989, pp. 18–19.
23. W. K. L. Dickson and Antonia Dickson, *History of the Kinetograph, Kinetoscope, and Kinetophonograph* (New York: Museum of Modern Art, 2000), p. 22. Originally published in 1895.
24. "Wonders of the Kinetoscope," *Frank Leslie's Popular Monthly* (February 1895), p. 245.
25. Charles Musser, *The Emergence of Cinema: The American Screen to 1907* (Berkeley: University of California Press, 1990), p. 78.
26. Katy Steinmetz, "Delaware Wiccan Speaks Out on Christine O'Donnell," *Time*, October 6, 2010. Available at <http://content.time.com/time/politics/article/0,8599,2023973,00.html> (last accessed May 23, 2019).
27. "Christine O'Donnell Regrets 'I'm Not a Witch' Ad," October 21, 2010. Available at <http://www.nbcnews.com/id/39775295/ns/politics-decision_2010/t/christine-odonnell-regrets-im-not-witch-ad/#.WdDeR0yZNQM> (last accessed July 26, 2017).
28. Beth Snyder Bulik, "Apple: With Design as Centerpiece, Apple Stands Out," *Advertising Age*, October 20, 2008, p. 29.
29. Beth Snyder Bulik, "Mac Owners Just Like, Well, the Mac Guy," *Advertising Age*, January 28, 2008, p. 6.
30. Wheeler Winston Dixon, *It Looks at You* (Albany: State University of New York Press, 1995).
31. Marc Vernet, "The Look at the Camera," *Cinema Journal*, vol. 28, no. 2 (Winter 1989), p. 48.
32. Vernet, p. 52.

33. Elena Dagrada, "Through the Keyhole: Spectators and Matte Shots in Early Cinema," *Iris*, vol. 11 (Summer 1990), p. 98.
34. Nick Browne, "The Spectator-in-the-Text: The Rhetoric of *Stagecoach*," in *Film Theory and Criticism*, 4th edn (New York: Oxford University Press, 1992), p. 221.
35. Dixon, p. 196.
36. James F. Forkan, "Godfrey's Ad Style Was Revolutionary," *Advertising Age*, March 21, 1983, p. 6.
37. Forkan, p. 6.
38. T. V. Byor, "Do Spokesmen Commercials Portend an Era of Boredom in TV Advertising?", *Advertising Age*, May 26, 1975, p. 35.
39. Rick Fizdale, "Stars Rise, Fall in a Turbulent Year," *Advertising Age*, December 22, 1997, p. 14.
40. Ira Teinowitz, "Bob Dole Talks 'Health Education' in Pfizer TV Spots," *Advertising Age*, December 21, 1998, p. 28.
41. Larry Dobrow, "7 Ways Viagra Changed How Drugs Are Marketed," *Medical Marketing & Media*, October 3, 2016. Available at <http://www.mmm-online.com/commercial/7-ways-viagra-changed-how-drugs-are-marketed/article/526011/> (last accessed May 23, 2019).
42. John Halas and Roger Manvell, *The Technique of Film Animation*, 3rd edn (New York: Focal Press, 1971), p. 109.
43. "I Like This TV Commercial Because . . . ," *Sponsor*, December 27, 1954, p. 38.
44. "Tele-Varieties," *Sponsor*, January 1947, pp. 40–1.
45. *Television Age*, January 13, 1969, pp. 34–5.
46. "The Year's Best TV Commercials," *Sponsor*, December 28, 1957, p. 32.
47. For more information, see: Larry Oakner, *And Now a Few Laughs from Our Sponsor* (New York: John Wiley & Sons, 2002), pp. 11–25.
48. Giannalberto Bendazzi, *Animation: A World History: Volume II, The Birth of a Style—The Three Markets* (Boca Raton, FL: CRC Press, 2016), p. 118.
49. Adam Abraham, *When Magoo Flew: The Rise and Fall of Animation Studio UPA* (Middletown, CT: Wesleyan University Press, 2012), pp. 130–1.
50. Hooper White, "How to Liven TV Spots: Animate," *Advertising Age*, March 9, 1981, p. 50. Italics ours.
51. White, "How to Liven TV Spots: Animate," p. 50.
52. "Muriel Cigars," *Sponsor*, April 23, 1951, p. 39.
53. Eric Burns, *Invasion of the Mind Snatchers: Television's Conquest of America in the Fifties* (Philadelphia: Temple University Press, 2010), pp. 196–8.
54. Halas and Manvell, p. 111.
55. "'Hybrid' Commercials Test the Best," *Sponsor*, January 10, 1959, p. 43.
56. Tom Bayer, "Shades of Gene Kelly—the Fox and the Lady," *Advertising Age*, July 12, 1983, p. 48.
57. "Chex Marks the Spot," *Advertising Age*, December 5, 1988, p. 6.
58. Hooper White, "Works Faithfully Reproduced," *Advertising Age*, November 28, 1988, p. 34.

59. Tom Gunning, "Primitive Cinema: A Frame-Up? Or the Trick's on Us," in *Early Cinema: Space, Frame, Narrative*, ed. by Thomas Elsaesser and Adam Barker (London: British Film Institute, 1990), p. 100.
60. See, for example: "New Technique Enables McCulloch to Put Giant in TV Ad at Low Cost," *Advertising Age*, December 18, 1967, p. 98.
61. "T.V. Storyboard," *Sponsor*, February 9, 1953, p. 65.
62. Jerry W. McMahan, "Pillsbury's 'Dough Boy' Stop-Motion Doll Is Perfect Symbol," *Advertising Age*, November 21, 1966, p. 116.
63. Hooper White, "Taking Apart the Minolta Spots," *Advertising Age*, October 20, 1980, p. 46.
64. "New Motion Graphic Technique," *Advertising Age*, May 28, 1979, p. 62.
65. Hooper White, "Postproduction Magic Making Waves," *Advertising Age*, August 16, 1984, p. 62.
66. Wanda Strauven, "Introduction to an Attractive Concept," in *The Cinema of Attractions Reloaded*, ed. Wanda Strauven (Amsterdam: Amsterdam University Press, 2006), p. 90.
67. Christine Demkowych, "Viewfinders' Keepers," *Advertising Age*, June 1, 1987, p. C16.
68. "One Word of Advice: Digital," *Advertising Age*, August 25, 1980, p. 68.
69. Andrew Darley, *Visual Digital Culture: Surface Play and Spectacle in New Media Genres* (London: Routledge, 2000), p. 90.
70. Darley, p. 90.
71. Hooper White, "'Round and 'Round It Goes . . . Where It Stops Dr. Pepper Knows," *Advertising Age*, February 8, 1982, p. 41.
72. Kris Goodfellow, "The Fleetest Feet in The Super Bowl Were Fred Astaire's," *New York Times*, January 27, 1997. Available at <http://www.nytimes.com/1997/01/27/business/the-fleetest-feet-in-the-super-bowl-were-fred-astaire-s.html?mcubz=1> (last accessed May 23, 2019).
73. See, for example: Iren Lacher, "Fred Is Her Co-Pilot," *Los Angeles Times*, August 17, 1997. Available at <http://articles.latimes.com/1997/aug/17/entertainment/ca-23118> (last accessed August 7, 2016).
74. "Astaire Won't Deal with the Devil," *Variety*, February 25, 1997. Available at <http://variety.com/1997/voices/columns/astaire-won-t-deal-with-the-devil-1117863031/> (last accessed May 23, 2019).
75. "Fred Astaire's Last Dance," *Entertainment Weekly*, June 18, 1999. Available at <http://ew.com/article/1999/06/18/fred-astaires-last-dance/> (last accessed August 7, 2016).
76. "Fred Astaire's Last Dance."
77. Peter J. Levinson, *Puttin' on the Ritz: Fred Astaire and the Fine Art of Panache, A Biography* (New York: St Martin's Press, 2009), p. 420.
78. "Dirt Devil & Fred Astaire Score Big in Super Bowl XXXI," *The Free Library* (1997). Available at <https://www.thefreelibrary.com/Dirt+Devil+%26+Fred+Astaire+Score+Big+in+Super+Bowl+XXXI-a019386920> (last accessed August 7, 2016).

79. Robert McRuer, "Critical Investments: AIDS, Christopher Reeve, and Queer/Disability Studies," in *Thinking the Limits of the Body*, ed. Jeffrey Jerome Cohen and Gail Weiss (Albany: State University of New York Press, 2003), p. 149.
80. "Reeve Ad—Inspiring or Misleading?", CBS News, January 28, 2000. Available at <https://www.cbsnews.com/news/reeve-ad-inspiring-or-misleading/> (last accessed August 7, 2016).
81. Bob Garfield, "Super Bowl Ad Standouts?", *Advertising Age*, February 14, 2000, p. 1.

CHAPTER 4

Cinematography

In 1964, film director and cinematographer Nicolas Roeg remarked that "you make the movie through the cinematography—it sounds like a simple idea, but it was like a huge revelation to me." That same year, Roeg worked as a cinematographer on *The Masque of the Red Death*, director Roger Corman's adaptation of Poe's 1842 short story. In his article, "The Phosphorescence of Edgar Allan Poe on Film: Roger Corman's *The Masque of the Red Death*," Mário Jorge Torres notes that Roeg's cinematography artistically achieves a "deep sense of richness and texture," especially as it facilitates the Poe narrative's "depths and ambiguities" of images and meaning:

> Poe's spirit and pervading beauty are omnipresent in the labyrinthine succession of the seven colored rooms, in the voluptuous way the camera follows this self-contained space with breathtaking tracking shots... One final effect adds up to Corman's phosphorescent vision: the Red Death unmasked has Vincent Price's face, in a terrifying construction of a *doppelgänger* reminiscent of German Expressionism.[1]

Dynamic cinematography may similarly be located in disparate horror narratives also produced in 1964, including *Hush . . . Hush, Sweet Charlotte* (directed by Robert Aldrich, shot by Joseph F. Biroc), *The Strangler* (directed by Burt Topper, shot by Jacques R. Marquette), and *Devil Doll* (directed by Lindsay Shonteff, shot by Gerald Gibb), as well as in other popular film genres: these include Robert Burks's use of the colored lens to instill mood into a sexually conflicted character in Alfred Hitchcock's psychological thriller of the same year, *Marnie*, but is especially true in the mid-1960s war narrative. For example, the low-angle, atmospheric framing in *Back Door to Hell* (directed by Monte Hellman, shot by Nonong Rasca) and the compelling two shot in *The Thin Red Line* (directed by Andrew Marton, shot by Manuel Berenguer) memorably illustrate filmmaker Robert Bresson's comment that: "Cinematography is a writing with images in movement and with sounds."[2]

These cinematographers, frequently working with proscriptive budgets and other creative restraints, focalize the perspective of the audience, to establish how one sees the film narrative.

Several television commercials produced in 1964 exhibit a stylized cinematography geared toward the respective gender and identity of the audience, especially its youngest consumers. From playing with dolls in the living room to playing with GI Joe soldiers on the imaginary battlefield, these commercials invite an aesthetic and formalist reading, linking them to the specifics of the horror and war genre, as well as to other cinematic industrial forms and movements. The Remco toy company produced *Hi, Heidi*, a sixty-second commercial that featured twenty-three camera shots, including a zoom, pan, dissolve, closeup, high–low angles, and medium shots, along with two voiceovers (male and female) and a song, but the doll is the focus of the gaze (Fig. 4.1). The narrative features gendered, targeted priorities, reassuring, familiar images such as a kitchen (play) stove and mirror, and live little girls at play to suggest a real world inside the fake world of the image.

But there is an uncanny feeling that one might experience when watching the toy commercial in retrospective analysis; it is somewhat creepy and, for the 1960s audience, the commercial involuntarily recalls, as an intertextual citation, references to *Living Doll*, a *Twilight Zone* episode broadcast in 1963, with the murderously inclined doll,

Figure 4.1 Remco's *Hi, Heidi* commercial of 1964

"Talking Tina," and also, with the violent and beleaguered performing dummy in Shontoff's *Devil Doll*, in reality a former living "essence" trapped within a dummy's (de)constructed body. A doll "speaks" to its owner–audience, regardless of whether the message is commercial or subversive. As Baudelaire notes in his essay, *The Philosophy of Toys*, "all children talk to their toys; the toys become actors in the great drama of life," even if the dialogue is curiously unsettling, and commercials produce dialogue and intertextual associations.[3] Cinematography reveals the depth and focus of the image and contextualizes the spoken exchange, the consumerist messaging; in fact, the final image to be viewed in the *Heidi* commercial is Heidi framed within a two shot of herself and the company trademark, a cinematic association made in marketing heaven.

To be sure, cinematography in TV commercials is part of a trialogue that included feature films and television programs. With regard to the latter, TV commercials have generally followed standard television practices that avoided low-key or overly contrasted cinematography. Part of this was expressed in terms of the lighting ratio, meaning the ratio of the brightness of the key light to that of the fill light. For much of television history, this was supposed to be no more than three to one, whereas feature films in the twenty-first century have become darker.[4] One reason for commercials following TV programs more than feature films in this respect is obvious: the advertisers want their products to be lit attractively and visibly.

All that said, television commercials have engaged in a meaningful dialogue with feature film cinematography, at times inaugurating effects that Hollywood would claim. Like short films, TV commercials communicate ideological and marketing strategies via form and content, drawing upon the nearly limitless aggregation of images and sounds absorbed and catalogued over one's lifetime in these brief acts of media messaging, to be reconfigured, "replayed," by the observer like favored shot sequences from any film narrative. Cinematography makes this possible, whether contextualized in a two-hour, studio-released film or in a thirty-second commercial.

Framing Motion

The art of cinematography is the indispensable creative factor in the production of film and commercial narrative; for the audience, wherever it is located, cinematography stimulates revelation, shock, anger, and delight, sometimes simultaneously. Consider once again the following quotation published in an article in *Advertising Age* in 1988:

In 1966, motion picture director John Frankenheimer prepared to make a film on Europe's prestigious Grand Prix auto racing series by watching car commercials. The feature film veteran wanted to analyze the way TV commercials photographed automobiles because, in his opinion, they were technically "miles ahead" of the work he had seen in feature films. The director of *The Manchurian Candidate* [1962], *Seven Days in May* [1964], and other cinematic milestones still holds that opinion . . . Mr. Frankenheimer believes the look of feature films has changed dramatically because of the presence of commercials.[5]

Frankenheimer's thesis is as applicable in the contemporary era as it was in the twentieth century. In fact, Frankenheimer's action film, *Grand Prix* (1966), a racing-car, James Bond-era male melodrama, is most notable for Lionel Lindon's stylized cinematography, which featured extensive medium and closeup shots of men, cars, the women who loved them, and the conflict-motion this all creates on the track. These shot sequences feature multiple camera placements and accelerated editing rates to simulate motion and speed. Lindon achieves a sensuous, realistic feel in his shot composition as the camera documents both the active track race and the drivers' points of view. This is not unique to advertising and its visual culture, but is certainly rooted in it.

A Ford Mustang commercial, also produced in 1966, engaged images of masculine privilege and (almost) unencumbered speed, celebrating ownership of the snazzy automobile, a home, wife, and masterful fantasies of piloting an airplane. A jazz soundtrack and male voiceover intones, "here in the cockpit, bucket seats." Driving this car is like flying a plane, and "there's no stopping him," according to the narrator, except the cost and possibly his wife. (But perhaps not his girlfriend-to-be. Another commercial for the 1966 Ford Mustang asked, "Should a single girl buy a Mustang, a '66 Mustang?" The secretary character realizes she could win a beauty contest, win an Olympic medal, or win a husband, all thanks to buying a sports car.)

Two years later, in Peter Yates's film *Bullitt* (1968), cinematographer William Fraker graphically and memorably utilized the real streets of San Francisco as a speedway-racing course for exceptionally frenzied, male-action car-chase sequences. Observing the stylistic verve of cinematographer William Fraker's work, David Bordwell reports: "Fraker claims that shooting automobile commercials taught him techniques that he was able to employ in the *Bullitt* chase in order 'to allow the audience to experience the chase like they were in the cars.'"[6] In the twenty-first century, such gendered and reckless imagery is often absent from the automobile commercial narrative; the automobile industry acknowledges that women like to go fast too, but like today's men, all buckle up and drive slowly in the school zone. Some forty-seven years later, the Acura RDX commercial, *Drive Like a Boss* (2015), features an attractive, young woman singing as she drives alone. Late in the commercial, a male voiceover addresses the audience about the car. She experiences her own form of fast, free driving and escape from the men waiting for her at the office, all accompanied by Blondie's familiar song *Rapture* (1980). This soundtrack calculatingly invokes the memory of automobile commercials (and music) past. Images of youthful exuberance advance its consumer messaging to appeal to the purchasing power of twenty-first-century women.

The history of TV commercial cinematography is technological, including the move from shooting with 35mm cameras to 16mm and videotape, and then to digital. But it is also very much an artistic process, being an area in which cinematographers associated with Hollywood have often worked, among them Vilmos Zsigmond, Haskell Wexler, and Jordan Cronenweth. There have also been many important camerapersons who perhaps became best known for their commercials, such as director and cinematographer Henry Sandbank. As Sandbank explained, "You have to create images in your mind. You have to close your eyes in order to see."[7]

The results could be beautiful or horrifying, nostalgic, or even prescient. A 1953 spot for Bromo-Quinine Cold Tablets relied on photographic distortion to depict illness. A 1960 spot for Blue Plate Foods, Inc. intentionally used an antique film camera in order to recreate the "old flicker" of early cinema.[8] Broadcast in 1963, *The Modern Drug for Pain* included an extreme closeup of the human eye; in 1965, a spot for Viz eye drops also featured an extreme closeup of an eye (Fig. 4.2). The television viewer saw both eyes prior to a similar image in Stanley Kubrick's *2001: A Space Odyssey* (1968).

Other commercials could eschew the classical Hollywood style and the composition associated with it. For example, a 1960s spot for Alka-Seltzer showed over thirty characters in composition that cut off their heads, focusing solely on their stomachs. A 1964 commercial for Ozon Fluid Net hairspray showed a beautiful young mother with her child just before leaving the home for a night out. The hands of an unseen husband help her with her coat. In 1986, Stephen Amini directed *Tummy*, a commercial for General Foods Jell-O, in which shots of flat, disembodied stomachs were intercut with the dessert.[9] The following year, a commercial for Guardian Plan, which sold prepaid funerals, showed only the hands of attendees at a burial, as they "twist hankies, pat backs, and balance teacups."[10]

Another example of a TV commercial's compositional strategy is evocative of both silent live action and animated cinema: an iris-out from black reveals a man in a photo booth. He takes numerous photographs of himself.

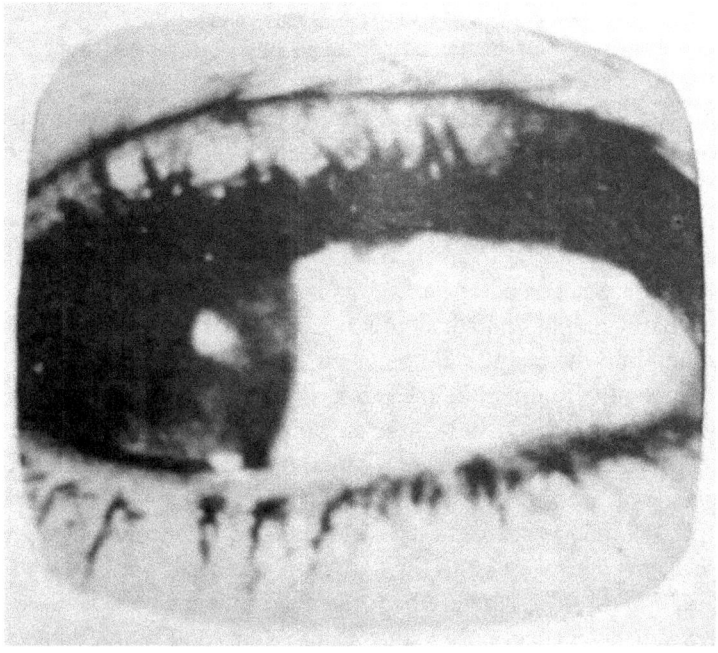

Figure 4.2 Viz Eye Drops (1965)

Then a needle drops on a record player. The man is at home. He cuts the strips of his photos while listening to *Di quella pira* from *Il Trovatore*. Smiling with pure joy, the man then uses his thumb to animate a flipbook of his photos, which has been timed to the music. The moving pictures allow him to "sing" the song. It concludes with an iris-to-black. The sixty-second commercial is *Photobooth* (2001, aka *Photo Booth*), directed by Errol Morris to promote PBS. It interrogates the meaning of cinema while simultaneously offering accessible and memorable imagery.

Film Stock

As of 1958, only one-quarter of American feature productions were filmed in color. By 1967, the percentage had risen to 75%; by 1970, it was 94%.[11] An increasing number of TV commercials were shot in color during the mid- to late 1960s as well.[12] As Richard Misek writes, "When color became cinema's visual default in the mid-1960s, making a black-and-white film became a deliberate choice."[13] The "old" film stock became something of a "new" artistic device, one that could evoke earlier time periods, as in the case of Martin Scorsese's *Raging Bull* (1980) and David Lynch's

The Elephant Man (1980). As Paul Grainge has written, black and white became an "idiom of visual pastness, an aesthetic of memory, and the archive."[14] It is a sign of nostalgia.

But those same two films made much greater use of black and white than merely to picture narratives set in earlier eras, the monochrome helping to convey stark and sometimes bizarre narratives. Other filmmakers embraced black and white to convey wistful and somber themes (Peter Bogdanovich's *The Last Picture Show* in 1971, for example), or the textures of romance (Woody Allen's *Manhattan* in 1979, for example). Here was, as Barry Salt has noted, a "minor trend" that began in the 1970s and continued into the early 1980s.[15]

Since the 1980s, American television commercials have often participated in the trend, one that also became an important component of magazine imagery and print advertisement. Tim Burton famously had difficulty in convincing his studio to let him make *Ed Wood* (1994) in black and white, for example, but monochrome has regularly found acceptance amongst sponsors of television commercials and their audiences. Indeed, from the mid-1980s onward, TV commercials have been the major home for black and white in mainstream cinema, far more so than feature films or TV programs.

One of the earliest television commercials to adopt black and white for artistic reasons was Goodyear's *When There's No Man Around* (circa 1966), which carefully mimics the lighting used in film noir (Fig. 4.3). Its nighttime story begins *in media res*, the first shot being a closeup of a flare that has just been lit. In Shot 2, a woman's hand places the flare beside a flat tire on her car. "This flat tire needs a man," the male voiceover declares. In Shot 3, the lonely and imperiled woman walks away from her car, with the text "When There's No Man Around" appearing on screen. Mysterious and ominous music is heard, along with eerie wind sound effects. Shot 4 depicts her legs walking, in apparent hopes of finding help, while in Shot 5, the woman is in total darkness, save for backlighting that outlines her entire body, vulnerable and in need of assistance. By Shot 7, the woman is at a phone booth. Once she makes the call, the music shifts into an upbeat tune, with narration and onscreen text completing the phrase "When There's No Man Around" by adding "Goodyear Should Be." And the company could be, due to the "new, Double Eagle" tire that "carries its own spare inside," a "tire in a tire" that "keeps on going" after a puncture.

It was not until Richard Avedon's four spots for Calvin Klein's Obsession in 1985 that black and white became a major trend in TV commercial production. They featured black-and-white footage bracketing a narrative otherwise told in color. Academy Award recipient Nestor Almendros,

Figure 4.3 *When There's No Man Around* (circa 1966)

cinematographer of *Days of Heaven* (Terrence Malick, 1978), *Kramer vs. Kramer* (Robert Benton, 1979), and *Sophie's Choice* (Alan J. Pakula, 1982), shot the commercials.[16] The following year, a commercial for the *San Francisco Examiner* depicted William Randolph Hearst III in the "stark black and white style of *Citizen Kane* [Orson Welles, 1941]."[17] By 1987, *Advertising Age* observed the growing number of commercials that were largely or wholly filmed in black and white.[18] Most notable among them was perhaps Nike's *Revolution* (1987), directed by Paula Greif and Peter Kagan. The two used Super 8mm black-and-white reversal stock, a daring move for any mainstream film in an era before Oliver Stone's *JFK* (1991).

In 1988, BBDO relied on the "trendy black-and-white format" for a Dodge automobile commercial in an effort to stand out, to "break through ad clutter."[19] Paul Grainge writes:

> In general, monochrome experienced a resurgence in brand advertising during the 1980s and 1990s by global multinationals such as Nike, Coca-Cola, and Calvin Klein . . . [M]onochrome became a strategic promotional mode, used both for its connotations of time and its association with artistry and style. In the fashion

industry, in particular, black and white was used as a signature of designer legitimacy and high-street chic, advertising anything from the chiaroscuro elegance of Giorgio Armani to the sport/street styles of Adidas.[20]

The use of black and white in commercials became pronounced enough to inspire various parodies of the same, such as *Compulsion by Calvin Kleen* on *Saturday Night Live* in 1987. And its presence has continued in the twenty-first century.

As with their feature-film forebears, these commercials have relied on black and white to create particular moods, which range from nostalgia (as in David Simpson's *Twilight Zone*-style commercial for Arby's in 1989) and humor (as in Pepsi's 1996 commercial *Security Camera*) to romance (as in Lee Jeans' commercial for Riveted Flares in 1997).[21] All of these elements mark Martin Scorsese's Dolce & Gabbana commercial *Street of Dreams* (2013), starring Scarlett Johansson and Matthew McConaughey. And then there is the depiction of sex, which Cross Verve fountain pens used in a 2003 spot featuring "near-naked" talent. *Advertising Age* responded "Hubba hubba!" but told readers, "Don't worry. It's not pornography. It's shot in black-and-white, so obviously its art."[22]

By contrast, other ads have relied on black and white to convey fear or revulsion. In 1988, the GOP ran a spot entitled *I Remember You* that featured "stark" black-and-white images of America during the Carter administration to frighten voters into electing Republicans.[23] And then there is David Lynch's *Rats* (1988), sponsored by the nonprofit organization We Care About New York, Inc. Its narrative preaches against littering by linking the same to the city's rat population. Horrifying closeups of a rat's tail, paws, face, and mouth unfold in slow motion. Conveyed without voiceover narration or character dialogue, the black-and-white commercial's power results from many factors, including its eerie soundtrack. As Colin Odell and Michelle Le Blanc have noted, *Rats* has "all the brooding sinister atmosphere of *Eraserhead* [David Lynch, 1977]."[24] *Advertising Age* reported that *Rats* was filmed in "horror movie style."[25]

Whatever motivates the choice of using black-and-white film stock, a parallel history exists of filmmakers embedding it into otherwise color films. In 1939, Irving Cummings shot *Hollywood Cavalcade* in Technicolor, but used black and white for scenes that recreated footage from old films. Vincente Minnelli's Technicolor film *Meet Me in St. Louis* (1945) used black and white in some scenes to evoke nostalgia. Alain Resnais's documentary *Night and Fog* (1956) framed black-and-white footage of concentration camps with color footage to, as William Johnson has written, "throw the horrors into stark relief."[26] The "amateur" footage screened inside Michael Powell's color film *Peeping Tom* (1960) is in monochrome, which he believed resulted in a "better balance," given that the average person shooting home movies at the time would have still used black and white.[27] And Oliver Stone famously combined color and black-and-white film stocks in such postmodern films as *JFK* (1992), *Nixon* (1995), and *Natural Born Killers* (1996).

Here again, the television commercial has, on many occasions, adopted an effect from feature films, including in the aforementioned ads for Calvin Klein's Obsession. In 1990, Clairol released its *Gray Hair or "Loving Care."* It opens with a black-and-white closeup of a man's face, before cutting to a long shot and then a medium of a woman, both in color. Some of her brown hair is turning gray. The commercial cuts to a black-and-white closeup of the man's lapel, on which is a pin-back button that reads "I'm Gray." Six color shots depict the woman returning to her home, which are followed by two shots of her in black and white; the edit between them is a jump cut. The next image is a color closeup of the product, then two color shots of the woman in public, her hair now dyed. No more gray. Another cut and for the first time we see the man in color, his eyes filling the screen, apparently noticing the change in her. More than just using black and white to depict her graying hair, the commercial also relies on it to express the woman's inner thoughts. "You're planning to wear your gray like a badge," the female voiceover explains when we see the man's pin-back button. Thanks to the narration, it becomes clear that the images of him are externalized projections of how she fears others might see her.

More complicated still is the use of color to tint part of an otherwise black-and-white image, with both thus seen simultaneously. Here is an effect that dates to early cinema, as evidenced by Edwin S. Porter's *The Great Train Robbery* (1903) and many others. Though seldom employed in later decades, the aesthetic was not forgotten. For example, original release prints of King Vidor's *Bird of Paradise* (1932) and Edwin L. Marin's *The Death Kiss* (1932) featured a small number of color tints in otherwise black-and-white shots. However, it would not be until Steven Spielberg's film *Schindler's List* (1993) that the effect returned to Hollywood filmmaking to any major degree.

John Gross in the *New York Review of Books* believed the use of black and white in *Schindler's List* to be "the most important choice Steven Spielberg made."[28] Spielberg himself said, "I have no color reference for that period."[29] Of the film, Harvey Greenberg cited "the crucial use of 40s expressionist/noirish black-and-white," which was "clearly pitched at a more European look, presumably in aid of garnering the cachet of artistic gravitas."[30] And Geoffrey Harman claims that the film's black and white has an "archaizing effect . . . but it seems post-color, so rich a tonality is achieved."[31] But to be "post-color" was not to be without color. For example, a young girl wears a red-tinted coat in scenes that otherwise unfold in monochrome. Killed by the Nazis, her corpse is later recognizable due to that red tinting.

Though with far less thematic import, the effect had been revived in television commercials over five years earlier in *Isn't It Cool in Pink* (which notably did not use a question mark), a series of Leo Burnett-produced ads for Cherry 7Up that launched in 1987 (Figs 4.4 and 4.5). Their approach remained consistent: romantic attractions between young characters unfold in black and white, save for the appearance of cans of Cherry 7Up, as well as the liquid itself, which are tinted pink. A small number of other props would be tinted pink as well, including articles of clothing worn by the two would-be lovers. The pink thus signified the soda and romance, and drew a link between the two.

The most sophisticated of these starred commercials Matt LeBlanc (later famous for the TV sitcom *Friends*) and Terry Farrell (later noted for her role on *Star Trek: Deep Space Nine*). First broadcast in 1988, its narrative is simple: a shy young man purchases a six-pack of Cherry 7Up at a convenient store and quickly shares a mutual attraction with the young lady at the cashier. He gives four of the cans of the soda to his friends and then waits until the store closes. The young lady joins him; the two cans he kept are his and hers. While music and lyrics repeat "Isn't it cool in pink?", nineteen shots have unfolded in thirty seconds. All of them are in black and white, suggestive of budding romance, but all of them feature at least one prop tinted pink. These include cans of the soda seen in seven shots, one closeup of the bubbling pink beverage, and a neon sign hanging on the exterior of the store. It reads "Fast Stop," an indication not only of the store, but also of the speed at which Cherry 7Up can lead to romance. However, more than any other prop, the pink appears on the young man's T-shirt and the scarf in the young lady's hair. This effect appears in fifteen of the nineteen shots.[32]

The use of color tints (or the digital appearance thereof) would continue in television commercials of the 1990s, including a De Beers campaign that began in 1993.[33] In these spots, black and white conveys romance while Karl Jenkins's music *Palladio* is heard. But the appearance of the diamond engagement ring (or other jewelry) was always in color, its sparking gold standing in sharp relief against the otherwise monochromatic figures in the same shots. To be sure, these commercials relied on digital grading to desaturate the image and resaturate other components

Figures 4.4 and 4.5 *Isn't It Cool in Pink* (1988), featuring Matt LeBlanc

of it. And they were well in advance of Gary Ross's *Pleasantville* (1998), which Christopher Lucas cites as exemplifying a "prototype application of digital grading ... to 'de-colorize' and 're-colorize' portions of key shots, which centered on the intrusion of modern life (in color) on the black-and-white world of a 1950s sitcom." For Lucas, *Pleasantville* rightly demonstrated such possibilities in "dramatic fashion."[34] The same had already been true in the De Beers commercials.

The Photofilm

In the 1890s, the Lumière brothers presented an exhibition trick wherein they projected a still image and, by cranking the projector, transformed it into movement, thus astonishing their audiences. The deep relationship between photography and film has spurred an important body of literature, with contributions from such scholars as Roland Barthes, Raymond Bellour, Gilles Deleuze, Christian Metz, and many others. The fact that film as a medium has traditionally resulted from still frames projected to simulate movement makes the kinship to photography stronger, but potentially more difficult to understand.

Bruce Kawin has noted, "the reel of film is a museum full of stills."[35] Tom Gunning refers to the same as "an apparent paradox."[36] And Sean Cubitt writes:

> The moving image moves. But where does that movement come from? For a certain approach in art history, an image is a discrete, whole entity. The move from one image to another is already an immense wrench: even the analysis of a diptych is wildly complex. What then is it to speak of "a" moving image, constructed from thousands of constituent images? In what sense is it *an* image? Cinematic movement is a fundamental challenge to the concept of wholeness and integrity, its becoming a test of the primacy of existence. In particular, it raises the question of temporality: when is the object of cinema? When, indeed, is the moving image?[37]

Nowhere are these issues more pronounced than in the photofilm, or "photo-film," as it is sometimes rendered.

Arnd Schneider has defined the photofilm genre as follows:

> To "animate," that is to bestow life, and to give movement which is already inherent in the sequential nature of photographs, is the underlying principle of photofilm, a minor genre and somewhat arcane visual practice, at the crossroads between film and photography, and which reveals shared principles of, and roots in, animation writ large. The animistic core of photos then is extricated, laid bare, and curiously reanimated through photofilm (defined as the filming in sequence of single still shots, or photographs).[38]

The result exemplifies another apparent paradox, meaning still images that are themselves "moving," if only due to sheer number of film frames on which they appear.

Eivind Røssaak writes, "In a strange way, the history of images between the still and the moving returns to the very origins of cinema; in fact, even earlier."[39] His discussion focuses on precinematic optical toys, and could be augmented by invoking the tradition of illustrated lectures of the nineteenth and early twentieth centuries, as exemplified by such famous speakers as John B. Stoddard and Burton Holmes.[40] Lecturers at such events not only projected lantern slides as a visual aid, but in many cases also verbally interacted with the images, suggesting possible interpretations to the audience in the form of empirical data and humorous anecdotes.

Activating this longstanding tradition was *Weekend Passes* (aka *Willie Horton*), a television commercial first aired on September 7, 1988. Created by Larry McCarthy of McCarthy & Mason and sponsored by supporters of then-Republican presidential candidate George H. W. Bush, the ad attacked his opponent, former Massachusetts governor and Democratic Party nominee Michael Dukakis. It relied on the case of murderer Willie Horton, who in 1987 raped a woman and assaulted a man while on a weekend furlough from prison.

The thirty-second film begins with two still photographs on screen simultaneously, George H. W. Bush and Michael Dukakis, both matted against a gradient blue screen that appears throughout the advertisement. The ad then depicts the same photograph of Bush alone on approximately 20 percent of the screen before dissolving to a different photograph of Dukakis of the same size. The commercial dissolves to what appears to be a mug shot of murderer Willie Horton. That image dissolves to a different photograph of Horton, this time in a medium shot with a policeman. The commercial concludes by dissolving back to the second Dukakis photograph.

When writing about the twenty-five still images that conclude Andrey Zviagintsev's feature film *Vozvrashchenie/The Return* (2003), Philip Cavendish uses the term "photographic slide-show" as a description.[41] The same could be meaningfully applied to *Weekend Passes*, including its accompanying voiceover, which compares the candidates' political positions and describes Horton's crimes, which are further emphasized with onscreen text. Here is an important issue, as the use of narration adds its own form of movement to the photographs, just as it did in illustrated lectures. Liv Hausken has referred to this effect as the "temporality of the narrating voice."[42]

No music is heard in *Weekend Passes*, which serves to make the voiceover potentially starker. The leanness of its audiovisual presentation draws not only on the tradition of the illustrated lecture, but also on its subsequent manifestations, meaning its usage in twentieth-century classrooms (in which slide projections did not normally feature accompanying music), as well as in the home, in which thousands, if not millions, of Americans screened their own slide shows using carousel projectors sold from the mid-1960s and still very much in use in 1988, when *Weekend Passes* was broadcast.

Most scholarship on photofilms has eschewed discussion of slide shows in favor of exploring the usage of still images in avant-garde cinema. Schneider writes:

> Because of their consecutive lining up of still images, photofilms, even when they *narrate* through image order and voice, always question (and push up against) the illusionary time-creating character of mainstream narrative film. In this, they are implicitly close to the preoccupations of experimental filmmakers, interested in making visible and perceptible the conditions of the film-making process itself (for instance, by focusing on the apparatus, i.e., the camera, projector, and film as material).[43]

Examples of experimental photofilms famously include Chris Marker's *La Jetée* (1962), Ernie Gehr's *Serene Velocity* (1970), and Hollis Frampton's *Nostalgia* (1971).

Chronologically parallel to the avant-garde tradition are a small number of notable television commercials that also attempt to draw attention to the medium of cinema, in part by attempting to add motion to still photographs using various techniques, including the aesthetics of the "slide-motion film," which Ira Konigsberg defines as "A film, generally a documentary, that uses a series of still pictures like a filmograph, but in which the camera seems to move among the picture's elements by means of panning or a zoom lens."[44] While Philippe Dubois views the appearance of stilled images in film as something beyond a photograph and a bit less than a film, these commercials suggest that the photofilm might be different than other types of films, but not necessarily *less*.[45] As Kawin has importantly remarked, "There is more movement than fixity in *La Jetée*."[46]

Consider the Chemstrand Corporation's black-and-white commercial for nylon stockings, *A Lady Isn't Dressed Unless Her Legs Are Too*, created by Doyle Dane Bernbach (DDB) in 1958. Here the still image is made temporal not only by voice (in this case a woman singer), but also by music performed by a twenty-piece orchestra.[47] Its narrative is a musical, one in which we learn that a woman in summertime, regardless of how attractive her clothes, shoes, jewelry, hair, physique, and tan might be, is not dressed unless "her legs are too." During the space of sixty seconds, twenty-eight photographs appear on screen, each depicting a woman against a completely white background; on six occasions, a black rectangular box obscures her upper torso in order to emphasize her legs. Eighteen of the images include onscreen text that visually reiterates words and ideas heard in the music, the effect echoing print advertisements that combine still photographs with text.

The commercial notably uses optically printed movements on six of the photographs. Zooms appear in the first, second, tenth, and twenty-seventh images. The seventeenth features a left-to-right pan and the eighteenth features an upward tilt. The result adds a sense not only of visual movement, but also of temporality, given that these effects are orchestrated to the rhythm of the music. However, many more of the photographs try to create a sense of movement that echoes precinematic optical toys and the sequential art of early comics. Thirteen images depict minor changes of the woman's appearance to those that preceded them, whether in her facial expression or the position of her body.

In 1963, Kodak's two-minute color commercial *Turn Around* offered an important variation on Chemstrand's approach (Fig. 4.6). It too is a musical, this time featuring the song *Turn Around* as written by Harry

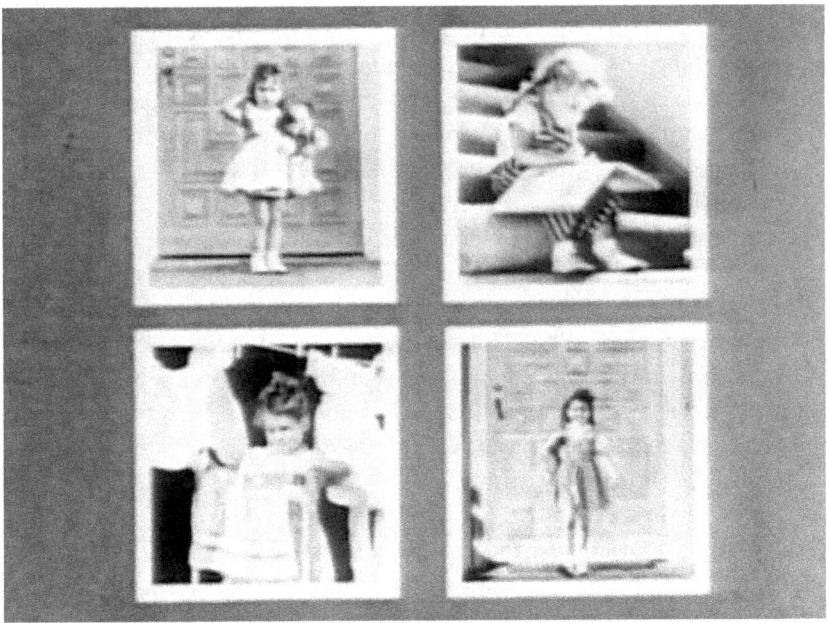

Figure 4.6 Kodak's *Turn Around* (1963)

Belafonte (1959), performed here by another singer. Rather than being upbeat and lighthearted, the tone is wistful, telling as it does the story of Judy, whose life from infancy to becoming mother of her own child is recorded in her father's photo album. The still images anchor these moments in time, but for a variety of reasons the images are not static.

The temporal dimensions of the ad include singing, music, and concluding voiceover, as well as thirteen optically printed moves on the still photographs, specifically nine zooms and two tilts. A unique optically printed move on another causes a vertical photograph to move counter-clockwise horizontally, with its replacement moving in the opposite direction, the result appearing similar to the movement of slides in a carousel projector. Movement also occurs in the opening and closing of the photo album, as well as one page turn in the middle of it, evocative of the Classical Hollywood device of beginning certain feature films, particularly literary adaptations, with a disembodied hand opening the cover of a famous novel.

But *Turn Around* also relies heavily on another device, one that returns to the magic-lantern slide and early cinema: the dissolve, a transition used with projected still images prior to being adopted into the cinema by early filmmakers like Georges Méliès. As Cutting, Brunick, and DeLong remark, "Whereas fades separate scenes, dissolves physically knit them together," sometimes for the purpose of conveying "large-scale temporal sequences": the passage of time.[48] *Turn Around* features seventeen dissolves, four of them used to edit photographs of the same door, presumably that of the family home, in which we see five images of the lead character in the same relative position, but growing older.

Yet another variation of the photofilm appears in *Vietnam*, Richard Nixon's 1968 campaign commercial on the subject of the Vietnam War. The advertisement runs for sixty seconds, fourteen seconds depicting onscreen text, the other forty-six being comprised of still photographs. Temporality is conveyed by voiceover, this time words spoken by Nixon when he accepted the Presidential Nomination at the Republican National Convention on August 8, 1968. The audio track features a repetitive drum beat as well as a far more pronounced use of sound effects than the prior commercials discussed in this section, particularly a thunderous, almost explosive roar created by drums.

Seven of the twenty-five photographs in the commercial feature optically printed movements, the key innovation being that the first image, here a military helicopter, begins with a rapid zoom outward, thus immediately hurling the viewer into a world of action. The commercial also relies on other strategies to imply kinesis as well, including the fact that four of the first ten images are blurred, simultaneously frozen and displaying combat unfolding too fast to be captured in focus. And then there is the sheer rapidity of the photos that appear, which feature an average shot length of 1.84 seconds. As with *Turn Around* and *A Lady Isn't Dressed Unless Her Legs Are Too*, the Nixon photofilm is neither immobile nor cryogenic.

To return to Chris Marker and the avant-garde tradition, the film *La Jetée* richly deserves the level of scholarship it has received. Unfolding as a series of still photographs and edited with straight cuts, fades, and dissolves, its narrative addresses the subject of time travel. It is a film about hybrid temporalities, including in the cinema. But *La Jetée* is not comprised solely of still photographs, as viewers sometimes believe.[49] One shot is an image of a woman in bed, opening her eyes and blinking three times. Moving images are thus juxtaposed with stills, highlighting the respective differences and similarities between the ontologies of each.

In the history of American television commercials, these same questions and concerns perhaps unfold in their most pronounced form in Metropolitan Life's 1974 commercial *Where the Future Is Now*. The ad's title was not announced to viewers, though it suggests its own version of time travel. In the space of thirty seconds, the spot begins with three live-action images of Tommy and Bobby, two children at their lemonade stand. A fourth live-action shot shows two disembodied hands against black screen reaching to shake. Narration explains, "Sometimes your future may be captured in a single moment, in the present," which verbalizes the aesthetic choices the advertisement makes.

The commercial cuts to two still images of Tommy and Bobby's lemonade stand, then cuts to live action of the two hands moving closer to shaking, then to two stills of Tom and Bob (now young adults) at their small vegetable business, then to the two hands finally shaking, then to two still photographs of Tom and Bob even older at their own grocery store (the second showing the store sign being altered to read "Tom & Bob & Sons." A final live-action shot appears, returning Tom and Bob to their youth at the lemonade stand with their mother, the commercial displaying time as both linear and circular, both moving and static. As Kawin has observed, "film arrests," including when it manifests as a photofilm.[50]

The Freeze-frame

Fritz Lang's *Fury* (1936) became the famous director's first American film. It stars Spencer Tracy as an innocent man apparently murdered by a lynch mob comprised of bloodthirsty townspeople. Efforts to pinpoint the guilty parties are undermined by citizens providing fake alibis for one another.

But then the District Attorney (Walter Abel) shows the court newsreel footage of the mayhem. The images are projected but occasionally frozen, paused long enough to draw attention to the clear faces of those involved in the crime. The moving image temporarily ceases to move, transforming in appearance from cinematic footage into still photography. The guilty parties have been captured on screen.

All that said, the use of freeze-frames in *Fury* is situated within larger frames depicting the narrative action, footage that is never frozen. Courtroom time proceeds, even as newsreel time freezes. Moreover, Lang's use of the freeze-frame was hardly the first in film history. James Cruze included one in *Hollywood* (1923). Hitchcock had used the device in *Champagne* (1928), in which dancing characters freeze and then the camera reveals the resultant image to be a framed photograph. And Frank Capra famously used the freeze-frame in *It's a Wonderful Life* (1946) to introduce George Bailey (Jimmy Stewart) as an adult. According to Peter Verstraten, the freeze-frame "literally stops the image and temporarily turns it into a photograph of sorts."[51]

Serge Daney has discussed how television, including commercials, appropriated the freeze-frame from Classical cinema, which has used it somewhat rarely.[52] One of the most important examples is *Daisy Girl* (aka *Daisy*, originally titled *Peace, Little Girl*), created as a campaign commercial for President Lyndon B. Johnson in 1964 (Figs 4.7 and 4.8). Produced by the New York firm DDB, *Daisy Girl* continues to be the best known and most controversial of all American political commercials. Controversy even rages over who developed it creatively. Regardless, *Daisy Girl* has been one of the most analyzed commercials, resulting in—among many other publications—Robert Mann's monograph *Daisy Petals and Mushroom Clouds: LBJ, Barry Goldwater, and the Ad that Changed American Politics* (2011), which remains to date one of the few books devoted to a single American TV commercial. However, consideration of *Daisy Girl* as film art is a topic largely absent in such previous discussions, which have instead concentrated on the commercial's historical context and its role in the 1964 presidential campaign. Equally surprising is that *Daisy Girl* is absent from discussions of Hollywood films of the 1960s that featured atomic and nuclear storylines.[53]

The bulk of the commercial occurs in its first shot, during which the camera gently moves through some weeds towards a little girl standing alone outdoors; the camera gently stops when she is framed in a medium shot. She immediately begins counting the petals that she plucks from a daisy, reaching five and then accidentally saying "seven" before repeating "six" twice and then proceeding to "eight" and "nine." She repeats

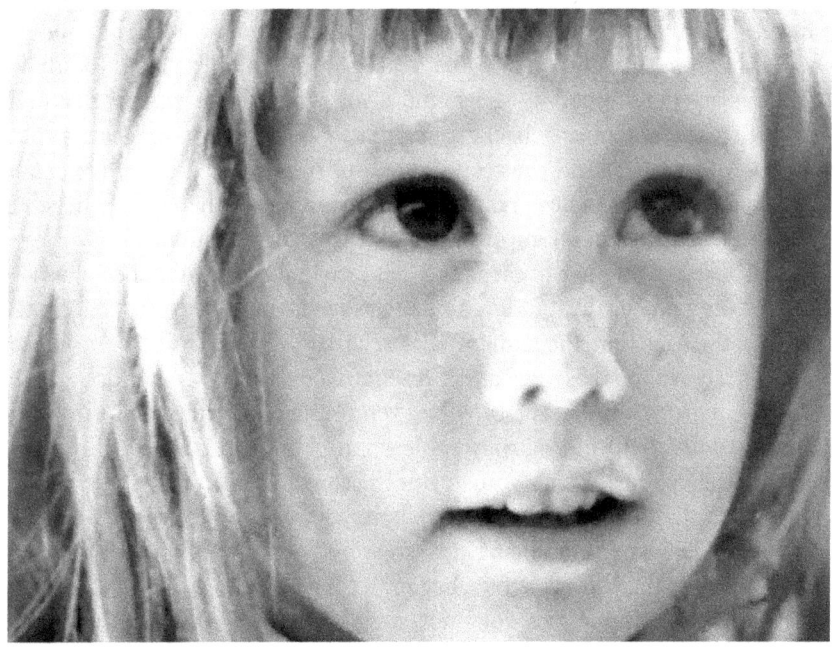

Figures 4.7 and 4.8 *Daisy Girl* (1964)

"nine": at that time, an ominous male voiceover begins his countdown from the number ten to zero. When he reaches "eight," the footage of the little girl is freeze-framed, with optical printing creating a zoom that moves into the darkness of her eye for the rest of the voiceover's countdown. This first shot lasts approximately twenty-nine seconds, roughly half of the sixty-second commercial.

When the voiceover's countdown reaches zero, the commercial features an edit, with the second shot being authentic footage of a nuclear explosion. Another voiceover is heard, this time from a different person, President Johnson, who declares, "These are the stakes." A second cut leads to the image of another atomic blast as Johnson's voice continues: "To make a world in which all of God's children can live." A third cut results in yet another image of a nuclear explosion, with Johnson continuing, "or to go into the dark. We must either love each other, or we must die." The fourth and final cut reveals simple white text against a black background that lobbies, "Vote for President Johnson on November 3." A third male voice immediately begins the closing narration, reading the onscreen text and adding language that is heard but not seen: "The stakes are too high for you to stay home."

The commercial's power results in large measure from its juxtaposition of images, as well as what those particular images suggest. The first shot is set in the countryside, a terrain in which no signs of the modern world are present: no cars, no roads, and no telephone poles. Its idyllic qualities are heightened by the sound of offscreen birds chirping, as well as by the absence of any background music. The result suggests a kind of raw authenticity, and the scene's credibility is assured by two-year-old Monique Corzilius, whose realistic acting is made all the more believable, given her mistakes in attempting to count from one to nine.

The camera moving towards the daisy girl takes the audience closer to her not only physically, but emotionally as well, the latter quality accentuated by the fact that the camera is at relative eye level to her. Audiences might perceive the daisy girl as representative of their own children, or all of the American children of 1964, or even of the children of all future generations who could be—as viewers learn after the cut to the explosion—annihilated in a nuclear holocaust. But the camera movement and eye-level position (in tandem with the setting) invite viewers also to see the daisy girl as a peer, the scene referencing the safety and security of a more innocent age before the nuclear arms race began.

While the commercial does not suggest that a return to that world is possible, it does argue that the security of the daisy-girl scene can be preserved by one of the two outcomes proposed by President Johnson's voiceover: "To make a world in which all of God's children can live, or to go into the dark. We must either love each other, or we must die." The final sentence represents Johnson's appropriation of a line from W. H. Auden's poem *September 1, 1939*, written at the outbreak of World War II; in the context of *Daisy Girl*, it warns of the possible outbreak of World War III. With the eye-level moving camera, the audience is equal to the daisy girl. Together in the commercial, we are "all of God's children." And yet this is potentially terrifying itself, given that the second "move" into the Daisy Girl is the zoom into her frozen eye.

Daisy Girl aired on September 7, 1964, approximately eight months after Stanley Kubrick's *Dr. Strangelove or: How I Learned to Stop Worrying and Love the Bomb* (1964) opened in US theatres, and one month prior to the general release of Sidney Lumet's *Fail-Safe* (1964). The three works represent a triptych of mainstream American cinema of 1964 on the subject of nuclear holocaust, bearing obvious narrative similarities, including the fact that the shadow of World War II looms over the proceedings, whether in the Auden quotation in *Daisy Girl* or in *Dr. Strangelove*'s characters, dialogue, and use of Vera Lynn's 1939 recorded song *We'll Meet Again*. Moreover, the conclusion of both films features nonfiction images of atomic blasts, with both films cutting those particular shots using a faster average shot length than in any their previous scenes. As opposed to *Daisy Girl*'s first shot (twenty-nine seconds), its three images of nuclear detonations unfold in only eighteen seconds. In *Dr. Strangelove*, a film with an overall average shot length of eight seconds, nineteen shots of nuclear detonations unfold in only ninety-seven seconds; the first fourteen of them are edited in the space of only eleven seconds.

While the divergent tones present in the serious *Daisy Girl* and the black comedy *Dr. Strangelove* make comparisons between them somewhat limited, the same is not true of *Daisy Girl* and Lumet's *Fail-Safe*, both of which offer dramatic portrayals of nuclear disasters. Their simultaneous appearance before American audiences also proves fascinating, as they share (in an apparent coincidence) an important aesthetic device. Both films depict the moment of nuclear disaster by freeze-frames of victims that feature inward zooms created by optical printers.

As previously noted, *Daisy Girl*'s first shot ends with this device, the zoom going inside the darkness of Daisy Girl's eye before cutting to the first explosion. Sidney Myers of DDB claimed he thought of this device as a variation on the conclusion of François Truffaut's film *The 400 Blows* (1959), in which the character Antoine Doinel (Jean-Pierre Léaud) runs away and finally reaches waves crashing into a beach.[54] At that point, given that he can run no further, he turns and looks into the camera in a medium shot; the shot becomes a freeze-frame, which quickly becomes a closeup thanks to a zoom created in post-production. Myers was astute in recalling Truffaut's influence, as the effect was at that time rare in Hollywood cinema.

In terms of *Fail-Safe*, every number of a pilot's countdown corresponds to a different shot representing life in New York City, each depicted with its own natural sound. Ten shots unfold in approximately nine seconds (as opposed to *Daisy Girl*'s single character on screen for twenty-three seconds prior to the freeze-frame). Then—after six shots of the aircrew that drops the bomb, one shot of their targeting device, and one aerial shot of New York City—footage from the same ten locations in New York City reappears in the same order that it did during the countdown. The first shot freeze-frames when some birds fly away. The remaining nine either freeze-frame quickly or begin as freeze-frames, but all nine of them feature rapid, optically printed zooms. Together, all ten of these shots unfold in only seven seconds, as opposed to *Daisy Girl*'s eight-second zoom inward.

Whereas Truffaut's usage of the freeze-frame and optically printed zoom (in tandem with Doinel looking into the camera, and the narrative content of the concluding scene) draws attention to an unfinished story that will continue after the film's running time ends, the reverse is true for the same device's appearance in *Daisy Girl* and *Fail-Safe*. Both films use the freeze-frame to draw attention to significant narrative revelations, as would a later film like *Asylum of Satan* (William B. Girdler, 1972), but more specifically to indicate the final, disastrous moment in their characters' lives, an ending, much in the same way that later films like *Butch Cassidy and the Sundance Kid* (George Roy Hill, 1969), *Joe* (John G. Avildsen, 1970), *The Parallax View* (Alan J. Pakula, 1974), and *Race with the Devil* (Jack Starrett, 1975) would do. (A similar, but lighthearted treatment of disasters later appeared in Norelco's 1976 *"Gotcha"* TV commercials, in which the image freeze-frames after a man cuts himself with a competitor's razor.)

In the abstract to her article on freeze-framed violence, Amy Rust speaks about the "conspicuous appearance of freeze frames in commercial cinema of the late 1960s and early 1970s."[55] Inside the article, she rightly suggests that "a number of American films from the late 1960s and early 1970s conspicuously employ freeze-frames in scenes of protracted brutality," proceeding to focus on the documentary *Gimme Shelter* (Maysles Brothers, 1970) and the horror movie *Night of the Living Dead* (George Romero, 1968), though in the case of the latter no moving image freezes;

instead, Romero's film ends with still photographs that operate more akin to a photofilm.[56] Her study claims that films like *La Jetée*, *Blow-Up* (Michelangelo Antonioni, 1966), and *Persona* (Ingmar Bergman, 1966) "influenced their American successors when they couple still images with diegetic incidents of violence."[57]

However, Rust makes no mention of *Daisy Girl* or, for that matter, *Fail-Safe*, both introducing the freeze-frame as a mechanism to convey violence at roughly the same time in 1964. The import of the two in this context should not be underestimated. To be sure, *Daisy Girl* deserves its fame, even if it has been much more often described in conversations about history and politics than film art. It is visually and aurally striking, its impact little diminished over the ensuing decades. Indeed, *Daisy Girl*'s use of the freeze-frame remains potent enough for it to have been mimicked in subsequent political ads.

A 2010 advertisement promoting the New START Treaty recreated the ad and its countdown, including the freeze-frame and zoom into its child actor's eye. When Bill Cooper ran for a US Congressional seat from Michigan in 2011, his campaign updated *Daisy Girl*, the lead character being a girl who counts numbers in the trillions until a freeze-frame zooms into her face. Then, in 2014, Republican Rob Astorino's campaign created a *Daisy Girl*-style attack ad against New York Governor Andrew Cuomo, to the extent of using black and white. None of these three was as effective as the original for many reasons, including their inability to zoom precisely into their characters' eyes. Perhaps that is why, in 2016, Democratic nominee Hillary Clinton released an anti-Donald Trump commercial that used footage from the original *Daisy Girl*, combining it with new narration spoken by Monique Corzilius, by that time Monique Corzilius Luiz.

Certainly, the freeze-frame has had an important life in TV commercials outside of politics, as in the case of an Oxydol commercial of the 1960s, in which a man watching sports spills food and coffee on himself: his freeze-framed image remains visible while an announcer walks on screen to discuss how to remove the resulting stains. Or in *Dodge Rebellion Operation '67*, in which a woman falls off a large windmill, halts in mid-air thanks to a freeze-frame, and then is rescued by a 1967 convertible Dodge Polara. Its voiceover helpfully asks, "How about a lift?" Or in Zenith's 1974 commercial for the Solid State Chromacolor II television, in which an interviewed customer finishes his endorsement but remains on screen in a freeze-frame, with the narrator's spoken words scrolling over his face.[58]

Experimentation with the freeze-frame continued, such that Peter Cooper's 1983 commercial for Advanced Information Systems/American

Bell relied on what *Advertising Age* called "visual legerdemain to create a most unusual commercial." The publication continued, "As the spokesman for American Bell walks through a conference room full of people, the actors freeze, and yet the spokesman continues talking to the audience as he glides through the real-life tableau." Here was an effect far more advanced than that seen in the aforementioned Oxydol commercial. *Advertising Age* asked, "How'd they shoot that?," before proceeding to answer that it was the result of a new technique created by Introvision Systems of Hollywood, one that allowed the filmmaker to project live-action film onto a screen and then "introduce actors inside the projected picture."[59] In short, it was an early and admittedly more rudimentary version of an effect that Dayton Taylor hoped to achieve with his "virtual camera movement" experiments over a decade later.[60]

The continuing use of the freeze-frame led to other innovations as well. In 1996, Associated Advertising used the middle ten seconds of a thirty-second spot to insert 300 different images of Chevrolet cars and trucks. The result was a blistering montage, but that was not the point. Rather, viewers were "asked to record the commercial on videocassette and play it back frame-by-frame for details."[61] As the agency's President said, "It's like delivering a full Chevy catalog over broadcast."[62] The process was called "freeze-frame cataloging."[63]

Moving Camera

Discussing intensified continuity in Hollywood films of the 1990s to the present, David Bordwell writes, "The camera is likely to prowl even if nothing else budges."[64] But of the 1970s and 1980s, he notes, "free-ranging camera movements typically appeared only a few times per film."[65]

A thirty-second Kentucky Fried Chicken commercial from circa 1979 unfolds with the appearance of being a single Steadicam shot. It begins with a character holding a crate of "Grade-A Fresh Chicken" delivered by a truck; he walks into the back of a Kentucky Fried Chicken restaurant, where cooks prepare food. The camera then passes beside a wall into a preparation area, where a worker puts the final piece of chicken into a box and passes it to a cashier. A different cashier then gives the food to a child, who runs to a dining table where Colonel Sanders himself is about to sit down. A single edit is hidden in the commercial: the frame fills with darkness momentarily when it passes beside the aforementioned wall, a trick of the sort Hitchcock employed in *Rope* (1948).

More impressive is another Kentucky Fried Chicken commercial from 1979, in which a young lady arrives at the back of her home

Figure 4.9 Published in *Advertising Age* in March of 1977

with her bicycle (Fig 4.10). She explains to an offscreen narrator that her trio of bags come from "The Colonel's," where she has "gotten dinner." She enters the home, explaining that her parents prefer the original recipe, while her brothers like the extra crispy. The same Steadicam shot lasts twenty seconds, during which time the young lady has entered the family home and stepped into three different rooms. The effect in these two commercials is of an unchained and unedited camera

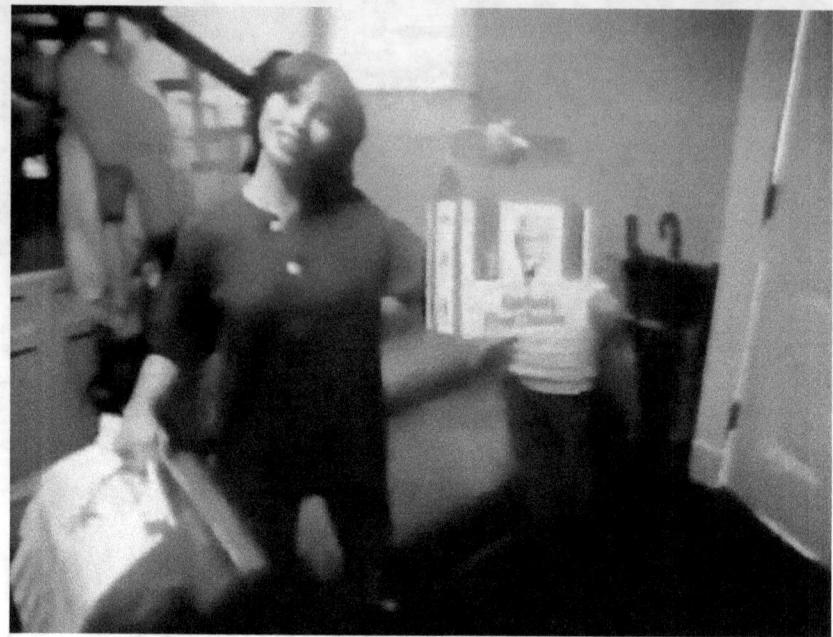

Figure 4.10 Kentucky Fried Chicken and the Steadicam in 1979

move, a kinetic virtuosity; they anticipate the extended Steadicam shots in Stanley Kubrick's *The Shining* (1980) and Martin Scorsese's *Goodfellas* (1990). As Bordwell has written, such shots have become "ubiquitous."[66] But when the KFC commercials first aired, that was not the case. Here is also an indication of the power of high budgets and their impact on cinematic aesthetics. Recalling the making of *The Terminator* (1984), cinematographer Adam Greenberg said that he and director James Cameron had discussed the possible use of Steadicam, but "budgetary constraints precluded that."[67]

Certainly, the greatest innovation in moving camera to emerge in TV commercials is what *Advertising Age* called the "shaky cam," the term here being used to describe a different effect than the "shaky cam" associated with Sam Raimi and his crew for *The Evil Dead* (1981).[68] Leslie Dektor pioneered his own effect a few years later, and unlike Raimi, he placed the camera on a fluid head attached to the solid column on a dolly and then made pans and tilts. The result is marked by sudden, jagged movements to capture an object or person, or even recapture the same if the camera initially passed over them. A creative director who worked with Dektor said the style was one of "searching and probing."[69] "I wanted to get to the moment almost a beat too late," Dektor said of the technique. "I wanted to give an importance to the moment . . . [to] retrieve the moment from its banality."⁷⁰ He added:

> I would let the camera vibrate because I wanted to be prepared to make the next move. It's poised for movement. I wanted [the] frame to be rubbery to prepare myself for the next move. You never wanted it to go rock solid. You wanted to keep the softness, the vibration.⁷¹

Dektor has termed his cinematography "Soviet moves" and "Sovieting," a reference to the crude and "beautiful, but rough-edged" quality he perceived in Soviet photography.⁷² Others have called it "Dektoring."

"Dektoring" famously appeared in his *501 Blues* campaign for Levi Strauss in 1987. *Advertising Age* dubbed it the "Leslie Dektor style," one that quickly became imitated by other filmmakers.⁷³ Dektor relied on the approach in a Maxwell House campaign produced by Ogilvy & Mather in 1987, as well as in numerous other commercials during an illustrious career. *The New Yorker* applauded Dektor for "changing the look of advertising" with his "expressive use of the wobbly camera."⁷⁴

As Grant McCracken has noted, the makers of *NYPD Blue* (1993–2005) consciously adopted Dektor's distinctive "amphetamine photography," as did such television programs as *Battlestar Galactica* (2004–9), and *Friday Night Lights* (2006–11).⁷⁵

Bullet Time

Of all of the aesthetic devices that appeared in fin-de-siècle Hollywood cinema, perhaps none was as visually arresting as what became known as "bullet time." Eivind Røssaak enthuses, "the famous bullet time attraction . . . takes us onto an uncanny ride from an illusion of movement to one of sculptural freeze and back again."⁷⁶ Bob Rehak suggests:

> Graphically, bullet time consists of an extended take during which the camera seems to move in a circle, holding a central actor in focus as action unfolds at different rates and indicating that hero and audience alike are perceiving events at "bullet speed." Ambient noise drops to a lower, sludgy register, only to rev back up to normal as the distortion ends. Often the *mise en scène* contains floating elements—bullets, spent ammunition, water droplets—whose slowed or stilled trajectories enhance the visual uncanniness.⁷⁷

Rehak adds that a scene approximately two minutes into the running time of *The Matrix* (Larry and Andy Wachowski, 1999) "marked the debut of bullet time."⁷⁸

To be sure, *The Matrix* was arguably the first feature film to employ bullet time, thanks to visual-effects supervisor John Gaeta, and it further seems that the Wachowskis created the term "bullet time."[79] However, the effect has much deeper roots in what is more broadly known as "time-slice photography," whether one traces it to Eadweard Muybridge's animal locomotion photographs of the nineteenth century, or to the successful film and video experiments undertaken by Tim Macmillan and Dayton Taylor in the 1980s and 1990s.[80] And with regard to feature films, consider Vincent Gallo's *Buffalo '66* (1998), which predated *The Matrix* by nine months and featured a similar effect. While various technologies were used in pursuit of what became known as bullet time, the effect had very definitely been achieved with success *before* John Gaeta and the Wachowski brothers. It is further important to consider that, even though the term "bullet time" has been applied to all of the effects being discussed herein, there is a necessary distinction to make between time-slice photography, where the actor or object actually freezes in the middle of action, and bullet time, in which extreme slow motion depicts a moving bullet or other object.

The first filmmaker to bring these effects to mainstream audiences was Michel Gondry, first in his 1995 music video for the Rolling Stones' *Like a Rolling Stone*, and then—in a manner closer akin to *The Matrix*, given its use of a projectile prop—a seventy-second television commercial for Smirnoff Vodka entitled *Smarienberg* (1996). The action-packed ad—which includes no dialogue but contains intense music by Dylan Rhymes—features time-slice and bullet time. It begins in a pub with the camera moving towards its lead female actor. In the fifth shot, the male hero yells and jumps, freezing in mid-air while the camera appears to track around him. In the sixth shot, the viewer learns his motivation: the woman has fired a bullet that is heading straight for him. It slowly flies towards a bottle of Smirnoff Vodka, but rather than break, the bottle acts as a visual transition to a new setting.

The commercial's high-adventure narrative then continues into another four settings (a boat, a train, a spaceship attack, and a back alley), each time transitioning when a bottle of vodka becomes the center of the visual spectacle. Breaking into a building, the hero (re-)enters the first location. The hero and his pursuers jump into another freeze, accompanied by a camera move, with the initial bullet now finally shattering the vodka. The bottle then reforms perfectly as the lead male and female characters embrace. The time-bending quality of the visual effect not only plays with the speed of the bullet, but also helps frame and facilitate a short narrative that is not unlike Ambrose Bierce's *An Occurrence at Owl Creek Bridge* (1890) or, given its plunge through alternate worlds, *The Matrix*.

Writing about Gondry in *Shoot* magazine in May 1998, Richard Linnett noted:

> Almost everyone who has ever pondered or practiced the frozen moment cites the Stones video and the 1997 Gold Clio and Cannes Gold Lion-winning Smirnoff spot (via Lowe Howard-Spink, London), in which there appears a famous shot of a bullet frozen in time and space, as the birth of the effect. Although Gondry doesn't claim to have invented the frozen moment, it is fair to say that he pioneered it. His work was the first to bring it to the attention of a wider public and into the world of advertising. As a result of this, and countless other innovations that Gondry has created in a string of incredible music videos and commercials, he has been called a contemporary Georges Méliès, the first special effects filmmaker and illusionist.[81]

Wanda Strauven advances this argument, suggesting that bullet time goes "against" classical narration, not only because it seeks to return to early cinema, but also because it "wants to enunciate itself as non-classical cinema, or even better as non-cinematic cinema."[82]

Gondry used the effect again in *Resignation* (1996), a sixty-second commercial for Polaroid that explores issues of time and memory. In the era before *The Matrix*, bullet time and time-slice correctly became associated with his work, so much so that Linnett called it the "Gondry Effect" because his "use of it has influenced the technique's current popularity."[83] While acknowledging this previous history, Rehak notes:

> [I]t was *The Matrix*'s proprietary packaging of these elements that caught on in the public imaginary. 1999 marked the moment at which bullet time's heretofore itinerant troupe of signifiers stabilized within a particular narrative and stylistic frame, corralling its meanings and kicking off a chain of citation that would end, four years later, in archness and decay.[84]

In *The New York Times*, David Edelstein went so far as to write, "movies as we knew them changed" thanks to *The Matrix*, drawing particular attention to a bullet-time scene. It "cut us loose from the laws of physics in ways that no live-action film had ever done, exploding our ideas of time and space on screen."[85] To be sure, *The Matrix* did popularize the effect for many audiences, and likely inspired subsequent feature films to embrace it, including *Titus* (Julie Taymor, 1999), *Charlie's Angels* (McG, 2000), *Scary Movie* (Keenen Ivory Wayans, 2000), and many others.

It is worth returning to Linnett, though, who wrote in 1998, "According to reliable sources, the software will be used in the upcoming WB feature *Matrix* starring Keanu Reeves. Warner Bros. reportedly has licensed and named the program 'Bullet Time,' after Gondry's frozen bullet gag in the

Smirnoff ad." He then quoted Gondry, who quipped, "Maybe one day I will not be able to use my technique because somebody else has a patent on it."[86]

Indeed, as Eric Huelsman wrote on March 1, 1999, prior to the release of *The Matrix*, "If you are anything like I am about it, watching TV these days is more about checking out the latest commercials and their special effects than the programming itself." He proceeded to discuss the:

> Gap Khakis commercial that people are still talking about. Voted #1 commercial by the *LA Times* & *TV Guide*, *Khakis Swing* . . . is certainly one of the more recognizable recent commercials by virtue of its visual effects . . . One dancer vaults over the head of another, resulting in an impossible freeze frame that appears to allow the camera to arc around these dancers in 3D space.[87]

Directed by Matthew Rolston, *Khakis Swing* (1998) depicted swingers dancing against a solid white background to the music *Jump, Jive An' Wail* (Fig. 4.11). The "impossible freeze frame," as bullet time has also been called, occurs twice during its thirty-second running time. The massively popular commercial was first broadcast during the final episode of *Seinfeld* on May 14, 1998 to an audience of 76 million. In 1998, Linnett

Figure 4.11 Matthew Rolston's *Khakis Swing* (1998)

wrote, the effect "has become a standard gag, repeated in so many different clips and commercials ... that it has created a kind of dizzying overfamiliarity."[88] While his comments proved to become even more true in the years that followed, the pre-*Matrix* advent of what became known as bullet time deserves much consideration.

Here, after all, is a key moment in the dialogue between the TV commercial and the feature film, one that exemplifies the commercial's ability to introduce and adjust mainstream audiences to new aesthetic devices and techniques prior to, parallel with, and even subsequent to their appearance in Hollywood features, an ability that should not be underestimated, given the fragmenting of the modern movie theater audience. Whatever some writers have said of *The Matrix*, in other words, the sheer millions of persons who repeatedly saw commercials using the bullet-time and time-slice effects before its release would be difficult to calculate.

Conclusion

In a 1956 commercial for Piel's beer, the character Bert tells the unseen cinematographer, "Hey, I asked for a better shot of the label on the 12 ounce bottle." The tripod-bound camera then readjusts itself to follow his direction. Bert later tells the cinematographer, "Get a shot of my brother here with this target," the bull's eye of the prop exemplifying the "most dry beer in the supermarket." Once again, the cinematographer follows instructions and roughly reframes his composition. Whether the cinematographer is shooting the feature film or TV commercial narrative, the image is to be measured, framed, and consumed. Nicolas Roeg's initial assertion about the primacy of the cinematographic as the structural, aesthetic, compositional energy creating film art demonstrably extends historically into the commercial advertising short-film narrative. Even Piel's, a locally brewed, uncelebrated beer, a product sold commonly in the nearest grocery, has advertising, artistic potential from a cinematographic perspective, not just studio starlets, Poe's lurid prose, and Corman's colorful set design. Beer cans may be gazed upon, made "interesting" and desired as a commodity. Cinematography is the dynamic means to the realization of the art of the broadcast commercial.

Notes

1. Mário Jorge Torres, "The Phosphorescence of Edgar Allan Poe on Film: Roger Corman's *The Masque of the Red Death*," *The Edgar Allan Poe Review*, vol. 11, no. 1 (Spring 2010), p. 189.

2. Marton's war film is the first adaptation of the eponymous James Jones novel of 1962 and should not be confused with the adaptation directed by Terrence Malick in 1998.
3. Charles Baudelaire, "The Philosophy of Toys," [1853], in *Essays on Dolls*, trans. Paul Keegan (New York: Syrens series, Penguin, 1995), p. x.
4. James E. Cutting, Kaitlin L. Brunick, Jordan E. DeLong, Catalina Iricinschi, and Ayse Candan, "Quicker, Faster, Darker: Changes in Hollywood over 75 Years," *i-Perception*, vol. 2 (2011), p. 574. Available at <http://people.psych.cornell.edu/~jec7/pubs/iperception.pdf> (last accessed November 25, 2018).
5. Jennifer Pendleton, "Hollywood Buys the Concept," *Advertising Age*, November 9, 1988, p. 158.
6. David Bordwell, *The Way Hollywood Tells It* (Berkeley: University of California Press, 2006), p. 158.
7. Hooper White, "Painting with Light," *Advertising Age*, October 20, 1978, p. 50.
8. "Old Flicker Technique Finds New Place in TV," *Sponsor*, October 10, 1960, pp. 39–40.
9. "Jell-O Juggles Light and Varied Forms," *Advertising Age*, July 7, 1986, p. 49.
10. Lenore Skenazy, "Burial Marketer Undertakes TV Spots," *Advertising Age*, November 30, 1987, p. 30.
11. Gorham A. Kindem, "Hollywood's Conversion to Color: The Technological, Economic and Aesthetic Factors," *Journal of the University Film Association*, vol. 31, no. 2 (Spring 1979), p. 35.
12. Arthur Bellaire, "Produce Color Commercials in Four Days with TV Tape," "Here Are Do's and Don'ts for Producing TV Color Commercials," *Advertising Age*, October 29, 1965, p. 122.
13. Richard Misek, *Chromatic Cinema: A History of Screen Color* (Hoboken, NJ: Wiley-Blackwell, 2010), p. 99.
14. Paul Grainge, *Monochrome Memories: Nostalgia and Style in Retro America* (Westport, CT: Praeger, 2002), p. 3.
15. Barry Salt, *Film Style and Technology: History and Analysis*, 3rd edn (London: Starword, 2009), p. 329.
16. Pat Sloan, "Klein's Sultry Avedon Ads for Obsession Hit TV," *Advertising Age*, March 25, 1985, p. 104.
17. "Advertisers Fight Economic Woes," *Advertising Age*, November 3, 1986, p. 9.
18. Sharon Edelson, "Commercials Sing the Blues," *Advertising Age*, January 5, 1987, p. S3.
19. Dee Ann Maki, "Chrysler Set to Soar," *Advertising Age*, February 29, 1988, p. S24.
20. Grainge, p. 102.
21. "Zoned Out," *Advertising Age*, March 6, 1989, p. 4.
22. Bob Garfield, "Sometimes, a Pen's Just a Pen: Forced Sexiness Fells Verve Ads," *Advertising Age*, November 17, 2003, p. 45.

23. Bob Garfield, "GOP Ads May Signal High Noon in America," *Advertising Age*, August 1, 1988, p. 50.
24. Colin Odell and Michelle Le Blanc, *David Lynch* (Harpenden, UK: Kamera Books, 2007), p. 132.
25. "East NewsWatch," *Advertising Age*, December 12, 1988, p. 52E.
26. William Johnson, "Coming to Terms with Color," *Film Quarterly*, vol. 20, no. 1 (Autumn 1966), p. 15.
27. Quoted in *Michael Powell: Interviews*, ed. David Lazar (Jackson: University Press of Mississippi, 2003), p. 27.
28. John Gross, "Hollywood and the Holocaust," *New York Review of Books*, February 3, 1994, p. 14.
29. Yosefa Loshitzky, "Holocaust Others: Spielberg's *Schindler's List* Versus Lanzmann's *Shoah*," in *Spielberg's Holocaust: Critical Perspectives on* Schindler's List, ed. Yosefa Loshitzky (Bloomington: Indiana University Press, 1997), p. 109.
30. Harvey Greenberg, "*Spielberg's Holocaust: Critical Perspectives on* Schindler's List by Yosefa Loshitzky," *Film Quarterly*, vol. 51, no. 4 (Summer 1998), p. 59.
31. Geoffrey Hartman, "The Cinema Animal: On Spielberg's *Schindler's List*," *Salmagundi*, no. 106/7 (Spring–Summer 1995), p. 140.
32. Subsequent directors have used color tints on given props in otherwise black-and-white commercials. A 2005 spot for the Salvation Army featuring Antonio Banderas was black and white, save for the iconic charity kettle, which was red. And *It's Mine*, a 2016 ad for Diet Coke, was in black and white, except for the soft-drink bottle.
33. Another example is *Time Warp* (1991), a Nike commercial featuring Scottie Pippen. Part of the commercial features Pippen playing basketball. The court and other players are in black and white; he remains in color.
34. Christopher Lucas, "The Modern Entertainment Marketplace, 2000–Present," in *Cinematography*, ed. Patrick Keating (London: I. B. Tauris, 2014), p. 134.
35. Bruce Kawin, "Time and Stasis in *La Jetée*," *Film Quarterly*, vol. 36 (1983), p. 18.
36. Tom Gunning, "The Play between Still and Moving Images: Nineteenth-Century 'Philosophical Toys' and Their Discourse," in *Between Stillness and Motion: Film, Photography, Algorithms*, ed. Eivind Røssaak (Amsterdam: Amsterdam University Press, 2011), p. 27.
37. Sean Cubitt, *The Cinema Effect* (Cambridge, MA: MIT Press, 2004), p. 5.
38. Arnd Schneider, "Stills that Move: Photofilm and Anthropology," in *Experimental Film and Anthropology*, ed. Arnd Schneider and Caterina Pasqualino (New York: Bloomsbury Academic, 2014), p. 27.
39. Eivind Røssaak, "The Still/Moving Field: An Introduction," in *Between Stillness and Motion: Film, Photography, Algorithms*, ed. Eivind Røssaak (Amsterdam: Amsterdam University Press, 2011), p. 12.

40. X. Theodore Barber, "The Roots of Travel Cinema: John L. Stoddard, E. Burton Holmes and the Nineteenth-Century Illustrated Travel Lecture," *Film History*, vol. 5, no. 1 (March 1993), pp. 68–84.
41. Philip Cavendish, "The Return of the Photograph: Time, Memory and the Genre of the Photo-Film in Andrei Zviagintsev's *Vozvrashchenie (The Return*, 2003)," *The Slavonic and East European Review*, vol. 91, no. 3 (July 2013), p. 465.
42. Liv Hausken, "The Temporalities of the Narrative Slide Motion Film," in *Between Stillness and Motion: Film, Photography, Algorithms*, ed. Eivind Røssaak, (Amsterdam: Amsterdam University Press, 2011), p. 96.
43. Schneider, p. 29.
44. Ira Konigsberg, *The Complete Film Dictionary*, 2nd edn (London: Bloomsbury, 1997), p. 367.
45. Philippe Dubois, *L'Effet-Film, matières et formes du cinéma en photographie* (Lyon: Galerie Le Réverbère, 1999), pp. 3–4.
46. Kawin, p. 15.
47. Lawrence R. Samuel, *Brought to You By: Postwar Television Advertising and the American Dream* (Austin: University of Texas Press, 2001), p. 110.
48. James E. Cutting, Kaitlin L. Brunick, and Jordan E. DeLong, "The Changing Poetics of the Dissolve in Hollywood Film," *Empirical Studies of the Arts*, vol. 29, no. 2 (2011), pp. 152, 163.
49. Paul Coates addresses this point in "Chris Marker and the Cinema as Time Machine," *Science Fiction Studies*, vol. 14, no. 3 (November 1987), p. 312.
50. Kawin, p. 18.
51. Peter Verstraten, *Film Narratology* (Toronto: University of Toronto Press, 2009), p. 17.
52. Røssaak, "The Still/Moving Field: An Introduction," p. 15.
53. For example, no mention of *Daisy Girl* appears in Joyce A. Evan's *Celluloid Mushroom Clouds: Hollywood and the Atomic Bomb* (Boulder, CO: Westview Press, 1998) or in Jerome Shapiro's *Atomic Bomb Cinema* (New York: Routledge, 2002).
54. Robert Mann, *Daisy Petals and Mushroom Clouds: LBJ, Barry Goldwater, and the Ad that Changed American Politics* (Baton Rouge: University of Louisiana Press, 2011), p. 58.
55. Amy Rust, "Hitting the 'Vérité Jackpot': The Ecstatic Profits of Freeze-Framed Violence," *Cinema Journal*, vol. 50, no. 4 (Summer 2011), p. 48.
56. Rust, p. 49.
57. Rust, p. 51.
58. A similar effect appeared in a 1975 commercial for the White Rock Corporation, in which the model was freeze-framed for the closing voiceover. See Untitled, *Advertising Age*, June 30, 1975, p. 1.
59. Hooper White, "American Bell Freezes Boardroom Action," August 8, 1983, p. 28.

60. Dayton Taylor, "Virtual Camera Movement: The Way of the Future?", *American Cinematographer*, vol. 77, no. 9 (1996), p. 98.
61. Jean Halliday, "Chevy Dealer Spot Freezes Action," *Advertising Age*, July 22, 1996, p. 12C.
62. Quoted in Halliday, p. 12C.
63. Halliday, p. 12C.
64. Bordwell, p. 135.
65. Bordwell, p. 136.
66. Bordwell, p. 135.
67. Quoted in Paul Ramaeker, "The New Hollywood, 1981–1989," in *Cinematography*, ed. Patrick Keating (London: I. B. Tauris, 2014), p. 121.
68. Anthony Vagnoni, "Imagemakers Impart Advertising with Style, Special Effects, and 'Shaky Cam': Lights, Camera, Direction!," *Advertising Age*, March 29, 1999, p. C48.
69. Sharon Edelson, "Soviet Realism in the USA," *Advertising Age*, March 2, 1987, p. 8.
70. Grant McCracken, "Leslie Dektor, Inventing a Camera Inventing a Culture," *CultureBy*, March 6, 2009. Available at <https://cultureby.com/2009/03/leslie-d.html> (last accessed February 20, 2018).
71. McCracken.
72. Edelson, p. 8; Randall Rothenberg, "Rough-Edged Ads Sell 'Reality,'" *New York Times*, July 2, 1988.
73. Bob Garfield, "*Levi's 501 USA* Still Stuck in Leslie Dektor's Blues Funk," *Advertising Age*, July 24, 1989, p. 82.
74. Bernice Kanner, "On Madison Avenue: Soft Focus," *The New Yorker*, May 22, 1989, p. 20.
75. McCracken.
76. Eivind Røssaak, "Figures of Sensation: Between Still and Moving Images," in *The Cinema of Attractions Reloaded*, ed. Wanda Strauven (Amsterdam: Amsterdam University Press, 2006), p. 323.
77. Bob Rehak, "The Migration of Forms: Bullet Time as Microgenre," *Film Criticism*, vol. 32, no. 1 (Fall 2007), p. 27.
78. Rehak, p. 26. Italics in original.
79. Tim Blackmore, "High on Technology; Low on Memory: Cultural Crisis in *Dark City* and *The Matrix*," *Canadian Review of American Studies*, vol. 34, no. 1 (2004), p. 33.
80. Taylor, pp. 93–100.
81. Richard Linnett, "The Gondry Effect," *Shoot*, vol. 39, no. 19 (May 8, 1998), p. 25.
82. Wanda Strauven, "From 'Primitive Cinema' to 'Marvelous,'" in *The Cinema of Attractions Reloaded*, p. 90.
83. Linnett, p. 25.
84. Rehak, p. 38.

85. David Edelstein, "Summer Movies; Bullet Time Again: The Wachowskis Reload," *New York Times*, May 11, 2003.
86. Linnett, p. 25.
87. Eric Huelsman, "Cool Effects That Make for Hot TV," *Animation World*, March 1, 1999. Available at <https://www.awn.com/animationworld/cool-effects-make-hot-tv> (last accessed September 22, 2017).
88. Linnett, p. 25.

CHAPTER 5

Editing

In *The Handbook of TV and Film Technique* (1953), an industrial publication intended for future television commercial productions, Charles W. Curran wrote that commercials

> must be exactly 60 seconds in length, followed by 2 seconds of black. This means on 16mm film, picture portion is 36 feet; 1 foot, 8 frames in black—on 35mm the picture portion is 90 feet; 3 feet is [*sic*] black. All films must be supplied with SMPTE leader at head, the sound track must be 59 seconds in length, and sound track and picture must be physically printed side by side at first frame of the picture.[1]

Curran repeated the same durations and specifications in a revised 1958 manual.[2] By 1968, the thirty-second spot became increasingly common, in part to make television exposure more affordable to sponsors; as of 1972, the half-minute ad had "all but taken over."[3] In the mid-1980s, the fifteen-second commercial was born.[4] In the internet age, commercials are sometimes as short as five or ten seconds.[5] Historically, some commercials span these lengths, meaning variations cut at more than one running time, the shorter version usually broadcast once the longer version becomes well known. This is all in addition to experiments with subliminal cuts in the 1950s and 1960s, as well as time compression editing in the 1970s, the latter being commercials sped up by 20 or 25 percent to squeeze more information into the final running time.[6]

The accelerated continuity and relative velocity of television commercials have resulted in the use of various editing techniques, most borrowed from Classical Hollywood filmmaking. In 1954, *Sponsor* questioned whether optical effects like dissolves and wipes were being overused as transitions in TV spots.[7] In other cases, though, editing techniques in TV commercials have been at the vanguard of the American film industry.

In 1985, a thirty-second commercial promoting Honda Scooters, directed by Steve Horn and edited by Larry Bridges for Wieden+Kennedy, not only relied on swish pans and jump cuts, but innovatively used film leader tape,

Figure 5.1 Steve Horn's 1985 commercial for Honda Scooters

flashes of white screen, and even a frame going overexposed as transitional devices (Fig. 5.1).[8] This commercial possesses an abstract, raw quality, invoking many stylistic practices of postwar American avant-garde film production. The Honda ad was credibly marketed for a younger, 'hip," and mostly urban audience, with its shots of an out-of-focus New York City and its disaffected inhabitants traversing pregentrified lonely streets. There are obvious (now, historical) visual markers such as the Bottom Line nightclub and performer Lou Reed, the man and his posters, narrating in the traditional male, controlling voiceover, with Reed's song, *Walk on the Wild Side*, providing an audio cue facilitating the nostalgia that sells. Martin Scorsese's *Taxi Driver* (1976) stands as the Honda commercial's predecessor: both film and commercial emphasize eccentric perceptions of motion and location. Scorsese's narrator, Travis Bickle, addresses the audience as he expresses his estimation of what he beholds, "the animals come out at night"; in the Honda commercial, Lou Reed offers succor in the form of the motorbike, not a taxi.

As Martin Scorsese told Charlie Rose, when reflecting on the state of filmmaking in the 1960s, "Commercials were affecting—I think, oversimplification, I guess—commercials were affecting cinema editing and logic in a way, continuity at the time."[9] We agree, and would suggest that TV commercials have engaged in an important dialogue with Hollywood editing in terms of average shot lengths (ASLs) and cutting on movement, while diverging from Hollywood in terms of non-Classical editing and even heralding the absence of editing.

Average Shot Lengths

David Bordwell writes, "Rapid editing obliges the viewer to assemble many discrete pieces of information, and it sets a commanding pace: look away, and you might miss a key point."[10] While calculating ASLs for Hollywood feature films of the 1950s, Barry Salt notes that the mean ASL for the period from 1952 to 1957 is 10.13 seconds, whereas the mean ASL for the period 1958 to 1963 is 8.8 seconds, indicating a discernible decrease in the space and time of the short-film narrative's capacity to convince the audience of its consumer-based raison d'être. Salt also notes that:

> During the fifties the modal (most common) value for Average Shot Length remained at close to 9 seconds, where it had stayed for the past 25 years. All of this corresponds to the fact that hardly any new directors were now going in for long-take filming.[11]

Contrary to the then popular European neo-realism filmmaking long-take shot composition, in America, the mean value of ASL for the period 1964 to 1969 fell to 7.1 seconds.[12] Commenting on the increasingly fast-paced edits, Salt writes:

> The cause of this increase in the cutting rate is so far obscure. It seems fairly certain that the trend was not led from methods of scene dissection being used in television production, for a sample of 18 American television programs of all kinds—dramas, Western series, comedy shows—made around 1960 all have ASLs in the range of 7 to 40 seconds, with a mean of 13 seconds. This sample of programmes includes both productions shot on film in the studio, and kinescope recordings of live shows . . . On the other hand, the trend was not led from Europe either, because its beginning at the end of the nineteen-fifties predates the renewed American interest in European film developments.[13]

Salt concludes by noting that some younger European directors of the 1950s and 1960s "used even longer takes than their older predecessors," meaning that they were not the cause of what Salt has called the "Great Speed Up."

In *The Way Hollywood Tells It*, Bordwell also speaks to the changes that Hollywood editing underwent in the 1960s:

> In the mid-1960s, several filmmakers began accelerating their cutting rates. Many A-films of the period contain ASLs of between 6 and 8 seconds, and some have significantly shorter averages. *Goldfinger* [Guy Hamilton, 1964], for example, clocks in at 4.0 seconds, *Mickey One* [Arthur Penn, 1965] at 3.8 seconds, and *Head* [Bob Rafelson, 1968] at a remarkable 2.7 seconds. The pace accelerated in the 1970s.[14]

TV cutting appears to have accelerated over the same years that film cutting did. Before the 1960s, many filmed TV programs had ASLs averaging more than 7.5 seconds. Most programs fall in the 5- to 7-second ASL range, and a few (1960s *Dragnet* episodes, *Moonlighting* during the 1980s) run between 3 and 5 seconds. (Of course, TV commercials tend to be cut even faster. ASLs of 1 to 2 seconds are common for 30-second spots.) Perhaps cutting rates accelerated independently in the two media, or perhaps a feedback loop developed. Rapid editing in influential early-1960s films may have provided a model for television (particularly commercials and shows like *The Monkees* and *Rowan & Martin's Laugh-In*), which in turn encouraged theatrical films to be cut faster.[15]

Given this industrial context, Bordwell's discussion of ASLs of 1–2 seconds (and his mention of 30-second running times) for TV commercials clearly refers to those of a later period than the 1950s and 1960s, though his invocation of them—something that Salt also does in reference to film editing of the 1990s—marks an important, even if brief, indicator of the consideration they deserve.[16]

To address the issues that Salt and Bordwell discuss with specific regard to feature films of the 1960s, we believe that television commercials of the 1950s and early 1960s provide a crucial and hitherto absent piece of the ASL puzzle. Indeed, they offer an answer to Salt's comment that "the cause of this increase in the cutting rate [of Hollywood features in the 1960s] is so far obscure." It is true that, to an extent, Hollywood ASLs had started to decrease from their 1940s high, as Salt notes in the work of Robert Aldrich, Delmer Daves, Byron Haskin, and Robert Parrish.[17] Moreover, Salt has identified a trend of decreasing ASLs in Hollywood features beginning in 1956.[18] He has also identified ASLs of less than five seconds in a small number of Hollywood films made prior to 1956, including animated Disney feature films.[19] All that said, Salt indicates that the mean ASL for the period 1946–51 was 10.47, and that for 1952–7 was 10.13, a minimal decrease, as opposed to the dramatic decrease in the mean for 1958–63, which fell to 8.8 seconds.[20]

As Chapter 1 suggested, television commercials of the 1950s often featured extremely slow ASLs. For example, an analysis of forty commercials produced and broadcast between 1954 and 1958 reveals a collective ASL of 9.1 seconds.[21] Nevertheless, a number of filmed TV commercials of that decade were cut rapidly, as the following examples of ASLs prove:

- 1951: Ford Motor Company (5.7 seconds), Palmolive Soap (5.6 seconds), PET Evaporated Milk (4.6 seconds).
- 1952: B. F. Goodrich (5.8 seconds), Wonder Bread (4.6 seconds), Bab-O (3.5 seconds), Oldsmobile Super 88 (3.8 seconds).

- 1953: Swanson TV dinners (4 seconds), Joy liquid detergent (4 seconds), Campbell's Soup (3.8 seconds), Rice Krispies (3.1 seconds).
- 1954: Kellogg's Sugar Frosted Flakes (4 seconds), Camel Cigarettes (4 seconds), Spin Curlers (3.8 seconds), March of Dimes (3.6 seconds), Orkin termite pest control (3 seconds).
- 1955: Nash automobiles (4 seconds), Ajax the Foaming Cleanser (3.9 seconds), Chevrolet Bel Air (3.6 seconds), Wizard Wick Deodorizer (3.4 seconds).
- 1956: Kodak (4.6 seconds), Chevrolet Trucks (4 seconds), Raid (3.8 seconds), RCA Victor (3.8 seconds), Budweiser (3.3 seconds), Good Luck Margarine (2.9 seconds).
- 1957: Ford (4.8 seconds), Pepsodent (4.3 seconds), Lux Liquid Detergent (4.3 seconds), Greyhound Bus (4.2 seconds).

To that list should be added the following specific examples: Robert C. Mack's 1955 commercial *I Built Me a Dodge*, produced by VanPraag Productions, Inc., featured thirty-seven shots in 120 seconds, resulting in an ASL of 3.2 seconds. In 1956, W. Robert Woodburn's commercial *Alcan Champs* for Chevrolet Trucks featured forty-seven shots in 230 seconds, resulting in an ASL of 4.8 seconds. *Plane in a Fog* (advertising Delco Batteries in 1957) featured fifty-two shots in 187 seconds, with an ASL of 3.5 seconds. *There's Bud* (produced for Anheuser–Busch in 1957) featured nineteen shots in sixty seconds, with an ASL of 3.1 seconds. *Smoking Cowboys* (produced for Liggett & Myers in 1957) featured twenty-one shots in sixty seconds, with an ASL of 2.8 seconds.

And then, in 1958, there is Gerald Schnitzer's *Going to the Dance*. That 120-second commercial unfolds in a series of thirty-four interrelated shots. As a result, it has an ASL of approximately 3.5 seconds. Similarly, Schnitzer's 120-second commercial *Brand New Door* (also for General Motors in 1958) features forty-five shots, with an ASL of approximately 2.6 seconds. As a third example, his *Pour, Pour the Rosé* (for Ernest and Julio Gallo Wines), a sixty-second commercial from 1958 built out of seventeen shots, has an ASL of 3.5 seconds.

However much it predated Schnitzer, rapid cutting became dramatically more common after he began directing television commercials. For example, the Chemstrand Corporation's *A Lady Isn't Dressed Unless Her Legs Are Too*—produced and broadcast in late 1958 after *Going to the Dance* had become well known—featured thirty-one images in sixty seconds, for an ASL of 1.93 seconds (Fig. 5.2). Some individual shots were as brief as half a second, their speed aided by the fact that the shots were still photographs.

Figure 5.2 Chemstrand Corporation's *A Lady Isn't Dressed Unless Her Legs Are Too* (1958)

To be sure, Hollywood feature-film editing was particularly dependent on Schnitzer and those who appropriated his style of "slice-of-life" commercials. Consider, for example, Hollywood films edited after *Going to the Dance* was broadcast, including director Nathan Juran's *The Seventh Voyage of Sinbad*, released in December of 1958, with an ASL of 4.5 seconds, as well as such releases as *Darby O'Gill and the Little People* (Robert Stevenson, 1959), with an ASL of 4.6 seconds, and *The 3 Worlds of Gulliver* (Jack Sher, 1960), with an ASL of 4.1 seconds.[22] Did *Going to the Dance* directly influence those particular fantasy films? That is difficult to say, but not finally the point. More broadly, *Going to the Dance* helped initiate the faster cutting style for TV commercials, and its influence extended, even if in many cases indirectly, to Hollywood features. As Salt has noted after reviewing our data, "just about everybody must have seen those big commercials by Schnitzer from 1958, so it is quite reasonable to suggest that they might well have encouraged the faster cutting trend in the U.S."[23]

As Bordwell suggests, there was a dialogue between television and film in the 1960s with regard to editing, rapid cutting in one media influencing and being influenced by the other, and this also is evidenced in TV commercial editing styles. Indeed, it is important to note that at least a few professionals in the postwar era were simultaneously working on both features and TV commercials. Among them was Otho Lovering, who provides an important case study on the evolution to faster cutting in the post-Classical era. For example, he edited *The Man Who Shot Liberty Valance* (John Ford, 1962) with an ASL of 8.7 seconds, *McLintock!* (Andrew V. McLaglen, 1963) with an ASL of 6.5 seconds, and *Shenandoah* (McLaglen, 1965) with an ASL of 6 seconds; interestingly, Lovering worked on all of these major film productions after he began editing TV commercials for Schnitzer.

While the Schnitzer style of commercials provides an important answer to Salt's query about the faster cutting in Hollywood features of the 1960s, the next logical question would be *why* Schnitzer (and others of the period, many of them influenced by him) edited their television commercials rapidly when no other form of mainstream filmmaking in America was doing the same. In an interview with Gary D. Rhodes, Schnitzer spoke to this issue:

> It was a tendency to advance the action that sped up filmic story telling. The editing merely followed the desired tempo. For example: I recall my first screenplay assignment by my first producer, Burt Kelly, at Columbia, who kept reminding me to "come in high on your following scene."
>
> That meant if two characters agree to meet at a certain street corner, it was not necessary to identify the street corner in the following cut, but to go directly into the action of the next scene, and if the dialogue permits, get into the heat of it. If this approach is followed through the entire film, or commercial, more story information is revealed in less time.
>
> This obviously gave the advertiser more bang for his buck.[24]

Schnitzer's comments reveal the interplay between his early training in feature filmmaking and his later advertising career, as well as the dialogue between TV commercials and feature filmmaking, and, for that matter, the connections between film art and the financial side of the entertainment business. As Bordwell and Thompson have noted, "considerations of money don't necessarily make the artist any less creative."[25] In fact, in the example of Schnitzer, considerations of money made the artist more creative, in this case an artist who rightly viewed himself (by 1970) as an auteur, one who saw editing as a "direct extension of directing."[26]

The dialogue between TV commercials and Hollywood features evolved into a formative trialogue, with television programming—specifically music videos—taking part in the conversation from the 1980s. "There's a definite influence on commercials from music videos," Mary Lambert declared in 1988, having worked as a director on both, as well as of such features as *Siesta* (1987) and *Pet Sematary* (1989).[27]

To explore these issues further, a number of brief case studies—while not representative of commercials as a whole—are worthy of consideration:

- A 1960 campaign commercial for John F. Kennedy features eighty-six shots in sixty seconds, for an ASL of 0.69 seconds. Here the speed is aided by the fact that all of the shots are still images (though three of them have movement added on an animation stand).
- *Bringing People Together*, a 2016 campaign commercial for Bernie Sanders, even more clearly illustrates the potential for speed. It features two live shots of Sanders; twenty still images of text against a white background; twelve still images of the background alone; twenty-six still images of family photographs; thirty-nine still images of individual close-ups; ten live-action images of a hand tearing photographs in half; and 191 images of torn photographs. There is also a closing, expressive montage featuring a large number of still photos on screen at once: it changes sixty-five times. The result means 365 different images in sixty seconds, an ASL of 0.16 seconds.

It must be emphasized that, as with the aforementioned Chemstrand commercial, such rapid editing is aided considerably due to the viewer's perception of narrative consistency depending on shots that are overwhelmingly still images. These two examples should be classified more appropriately as photofilms.

In 2006, David Bordwell wrote that he knew of no feature film "averaging less than 1.5 seconds per shot."[28] In most cases, such shots are narratively comprehensible, though he reports complaints that a fast-cut action sequence in a Michael Bay film, *Armageddon* (1998), was rendered, at least to a degree, illegible.[29] It is thus instructive to consider chronological case studies of live-action commercials that were edited faster than the feature films for which Bordwell calculates ASLs:

- A 1960s commercial for Lucky Draft beer features sixteen shots in twenty seconds, for an ASL of 1.25 seconds.
- Cover Girl's *Clean Make-up* (1969) with Cybill Shepherd features twenty-seven shots in the space of thirty seconds, for an ASL of 1.11 seconds.
- A Bell Telephone commercial from 1977 features sixty-nine shots in the space of seventy-five seconds, for an ASL of 1.08 seconds.
- A Hunt's Tomato Catsup commercial from circa 1966 features sixty-six shots in sixty seconds, for an ASL of 0.9 seconds.

As remarkable as these examples are, it should be added that none of them represents the kind of "slice-of-life" narratives for which Schnitzer became notable. As a result, comparisons of these ads to feature films may well be of limited value, beyond noting the aforementioned trends in TV commercial editing, as presentational commercials likely had far less impact on Hollywood editing than those of the Schnitzer school.

To be sure, there are striking examples of rapidly cut narratives in TV commercials that are akin to scenes and narratives in Hollywood feature films. For example, director Tarsem Singh's *Washroom* (aka *Blind Man*), a 1996 commercial for Levi's, unfolds in fifty-eight shots in the space of sixty seconds, for an astonishing ASL of 1.03 seconds (Fig. 5.3). In a series of atmospherically lit medium and closeup shots, a young lady with sunglasses and blonde hair frantically speeds her car into a gas station parking lot at night, as if lifted from an Edward Hopper landscape of road loneliness, and she enters the men's restroom after finding the women's locked. The electronic jazz soundtrack signals ominous events to come. She sees a young man seated across the room; he wears sunglasses and has a cane, leading her to presume him to be blind. She rapidly removes a wig, revealing her hair to be brunette, and she changes clothes as quickly as

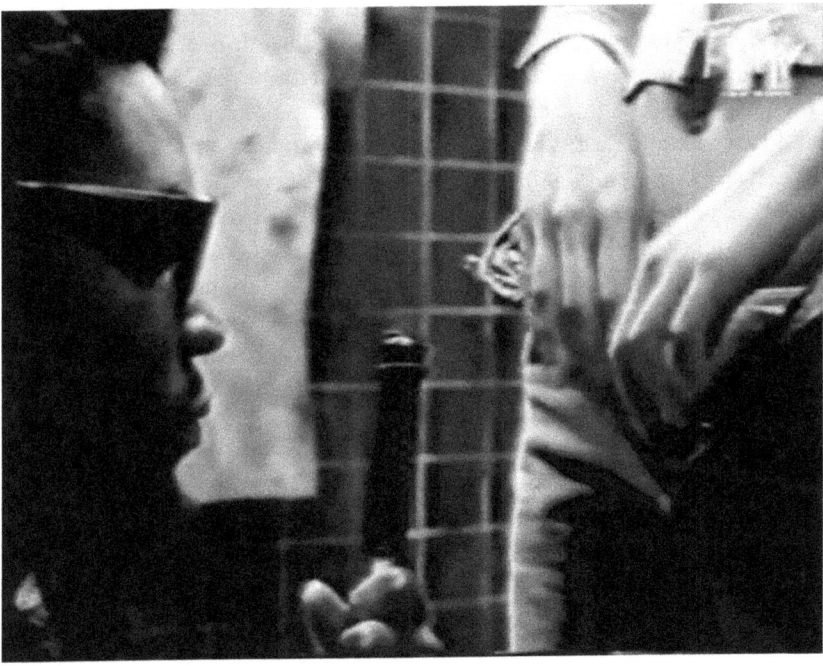

Figure 5.3 Director Tarsem Singh's *Washroom* (1996)

she can. The narrative becomes more clearly evocative of the crime genre due to a closeup of a large amount of cash in her bag, suggesting further considerations for the audience. Despite her rush, she saunters up to the blind man and brazenly buttons her Levi's right in front of his face, thus linking two objects of desire. Then she flees into the night. An older blind man emerges from a stall, with the younger man handing him the cane: he is not blind at all and has in fact seen everything.

Tarsem Singh's *Voodoo* (1996), another commercial for Levi's, is an astonishingly complex short film narrative, featuring 89 shots in ninety seconds for an ASL of 1.01 seconds, and it still amazingly unfolds with varied pacing. The story features seven characters in three distinct locations: an intense romantic encounter between two lovers, a scorned woman visiting a voodoo queen, and three children on the street, one tap-dancing in a manner that recalls—like the entire commercial—Alan Parker's feature film *Angel Heart* (1987). Singh's concluding shots humorously demonstrate the durability and desirability ("an ounce of steel when you need it most") of the button-down brand.

Cut more rapidly than either of those examples is *Shift Sensation* (2003), one of the *Touch* commercials for Nissan Maxima produced by TBWA/Chiat/Day, which features thirty-eight shots in the space of thirty seconds, for an ASL of 0.78 seconds. In it, a man holding an overflowing bag of groceries walks along the street. An orange falls out of it and rolls beside the wheel of the new Maxima. The man picks it up with his right hand and then rests his left on the car. An extreme closeup of his eye indicates that he is thrust into a fantastical vision, one in which the car drives at fast speeds. When he removes his left hand from the car, the fantasy ends. His right hand still holds the orange but he has crushed it due to the intensity of the vision. Closing text explains the fantasy, as well as what a customer could apparently expect: "SHIFT_sensation; SHIFT_expectations; SHIFT_adrenaline; SHIFT_exhilaration; SHIFT_power; SHIFT_excitement."

However, the fastest-cut "slice-of-life" commercial might well be *For People Who Travel* (1971), produced for American Express. Its blistering pace features 136 shots in the space of sixty seconds, for an ASL of 0.44 seconds. Narratively, the speed tries to convey the story of a businessman's kinetic career, travelling internationally from place to place, making business deals and enjoying himself. Its sheer rapidity is aided by the fact that 106 of the shots are still photographs, though thirteen of those do have movement added on an animation stand, and others depict successive motions of the same events, as in eight shots of a belly dancer in different poses, the editing of the same instilling its own sense of movement.[30] By contrast, twenty-nine of the shots are live action, interspersed between the stills, creating a hybrid live action/photofilm. Such commercials exemplify the sheer speeds at which commercials can be cut and remain visually and narratively legible, with their short duration allowing for rapidity that would be difficult to sustain in a feature film.

Despite their speed, it is important to consider that some of these commercials feature sophisticated internal pacing that accelerates or decelerates, rather than unfolding consistently. They feature the changes one might expect in longer-form cinema. For example, the aforementioned JFK campaign commercial features a single shot lasting twelve seconds in the middle of a sixty-second ad comprised of eighty-five other shots. The live-action shots of Bernie Sanders in *Bringing People Together* last six seconds. The four shots that feature the woman buttoning her jeans in front of the title character of *Washroom* unfold in eight seconds, for an ASL of two seconds each, nearly double the norm of the rest of the commercial. *Shift Sensation* creates varied pacing from the early shots of a man who puts his hand on a Nissan (eight shots in approximately eight seconds), to his vision of driving the car (twenty-three shots in approximately eleven seconds), to his return from the fantasy (six shots in approximately eleven seconds).

The overall fact that television commercials have had a major impact on Hollywood feature-film editing since the late 1950s has been acknowledged by filmmakers more often than by scholars. For example, Walter Murch rightly noted:

> as a general trend over the last fifty years, the editing pace of films has been increasing. This is probably due to the influence of television commercials, which have accustomed us to a visual shorthand that was developed to pack more information into expensive time slots and to attract and hold the eye in an environment—the home—where there is much more competition for that attention.[31]

Gerald Schnitzer could hardly have said it better.

Cutting on Motion

It is nighttime in *The Dark Knight Rises* (Christopher Nolan, 2012). Gotham City is in chaos. A heist at the stock exchange spurs the return of the Batman. The police believe they have cornered him down the street where he was last seen on a motorcycle. "Like a rat in a trap, gentlemen," Deputy Police Commissioner Foley (Matthew Modine) announces prematurely. A beaming light shines, and the Batman makes his escape in a new type of aerial conveyance. "You might have the wrong animal, there, sir," one policeman announces just before the Batman flies overhead. The wind from the superhero's escape sweeps across the dumbfounded authorities. It blows the cap off of a mustachioed cop, who watches the skies intently even as his colleagues keep their heads down. The camera moves towards him. At least some viewers will anticipate the teleology of the shot: the cop in question will appear in a closeup, or at least medium shot, once the camera halts. But that outcome does not occur. It is subverted when the film cuts while the camera is still moving.

Bordwell writes, "The quickening of editing has affected other techniques. While studio directors avoided cutting in the middle of a camera movement, today's filmmakers feel no hesitation."[32] To be sure, there was one notable exception in the Classical Hollywood era. Aerial shots featured moving camera, with editors usually left to cut on movement simply because the plane or helicopter was not itself able to stop mid-air. But the point remains the same. Cutting on camera movement before the camera reaches an expected static endpoint was, in fact, little seen in Hollywood features before the 1990s.

By contrast, the "quickening of editing" in TV commercials at times caused their editors to implement the effect at least as early as the 1960s. For example, a 1960s commercial for Hamm beer cuts in the middle of a camera movement on an actor standing on a small stage. And while a 1976 commercial for Exxon self-service gas stations does not cut during a moving camera shot, it strikingly cuts during four zooms and two pans. The reason? Presumably to incorporate a then current aesthetic device, the zoom, while also giving, to quote Schnitzer, the commercial's client "more bang for his buck."

Consider also the aforementioned 1977 commercial for Bell Telephone, in which we learn:

> Technology has given America the best phone system in the world. Behind that technology are people. Bell people. Using technology to solve all kinds of communications problems and provide a wide range of new services. New technologies, such as light wave communications, micro-circuitry, teleconferencing, electronic switching systems, computerized speech, microwave communications, and improving existing technologies to serve you in new and less costly ways. Making your life easier and less complicated. Bringing people closer together.

The fast-paced commercial cuts on camera movement *eight* times. It also cuts *during* two pans, two tilts, and eight zooms.

Also important in this lineage is Joe Pytka's *Two Kids* (Fig. 5.4), a 1991 Pepsi commercial produced by BBDO and starring Cindy Crawford. The song *Just One Look* by Doris Troy plays in the background while the commercial shows two young boys apparently ogling the supermodel, who has driven up to a rural gas station in a Lamborghini. The comedic twist is that they are, in fact, enraptured by the new look of the Pepsi can. The

Figure 5.4 Joe Pytka's *Two Kids* (1991)

commercial unfolds in twenty shots in sixty seconds, for an ASL of 3 seconds. The first example of cutting on motion occurs on the second edit and is quite minimal. The next occurs as Crawford walks from her car to the Pepsi machine; it is much more noticeable but tempered by a dissolve transition. The third, however, is a straight cut on her movements towards the Pepsi machine, the most visible in the commercial. The fourth and final occasion is more minimal, the camera moving down Crawford's body to show her torso and hand holding the Pepsi can.

To be sure, such cuts would have been acceptable in a post-Classical Hollywood film prior to the Pepsi commercial, and they do not represent teleological disruptions of the type seen in *The Dark Knight Rises*. However, the visibility and popularity of *Two Kids* and the sheer number of these cuts in such a short film may have influenced others. In 1995, actor Ray Walston appeared in a commercial for AT&T. Reviving his character Uncle Martin O'Hare from the CBS TV program *My Favorite Martian* (1963–6), he makes sure that the company's new pricing applies to calls made to everyone in America, including Martians. It features eighteen shots in thirty seconds, for an ASL of 1.66 seconds. And it cuts on movement five times.

The cut on camera movement became so common during and after the 1990s as to provoke little reaction, either in Hollywood films or in TV commercials. But a final example is salient, suggestive of the convergence of both styles. In 2009, Michael Bay directed the first of what became his four commercials for Victoria's Secret. It features eighty-one shots in ninety seconds, for an ASL of 1.11 seconds. And it cuts on movement thirty-four times.

Non-classical Editing

Bordwell observed that, "as faster cutting became salient . . . so did tighter framing."[33] He has likewise noted, "Tighter framings permit faster cutting."[34] This relationship occurred in American television commercials prior to the same in Hollywood feature films. For example, *Going to the Dance* features seventeen closeups (three being extreme closeups), eight medium shots, and eight long shots; the commercial also features one moving camera shot that begins on a closeup and dollies backwards to a long shot. *Brand New Door* opens with a moving camera shot that begins on a closeup and dollies back to a long shot; the remaining forty-four shots in the commercial include thirty-two closeups, but only nine medium shots and only three long shots. In other words, the ASLs of TV commercials not only influenced the "rapid cutting" that Bordwell sees as intrinsic to "intensified continuity" in the post-Classical Hollywood era, but also encouraged the "reliance on close shots" in the same.[35]

The larger question, though, is whether considerations beyond ASLs led to the increased use of focalizing closeups, specifically the fact that most commercials advertise retail products. Most products are relatively small in physical size and thus lend themselves to closeups, particularly given the need for potential customers to see them clearly on the television screen. Consider *The Modern Drug for Pain*, a sixty-second commercial for Bufferin broadcast in 1963. It is comprised solely of closeups and extreme closeups, not merely of the pills and the bottle that contains them, but also of a human hand (holding the medicine) and a pocket watch (its second hand illustrating how quickly the medicine works).

The exclusive use of closeups to construct a film is decidedly non-Classical in its approach. Slavko Vorkapich once noted that the closeup "appears somehow dissociated from its context," and was "thus more or less liberated."[36] With regard to editing the same with other types of shots, he added:

> We react bodily, kinesthetically, to any visual change. As a rule the bigger the change the stronger the reaction. For example, in a sudden cut from a long view of an object to a very close view of it there is always an inevitable optical and kinesthetic impact, an explosive magnification, a sudden leap forward.[37]

EDITING 143

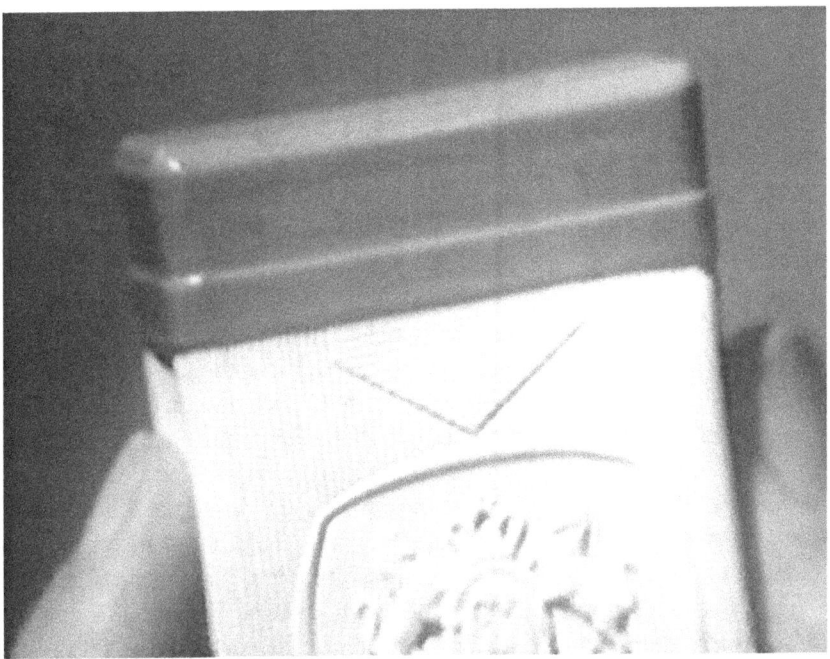

Figure 5.5 Paxton cigarette commercial from 1963

But what of cinema that consciously avoids what Vorkapich called a "visual dynamic language," and instead edits together only closeups?

Consider a 1963 commercial for Paxton cigarettes that unfolds as a series of nineteen closeups and extreme closeups for the duration of sixty seconds, with an ASL of 3.1 seconds (Fig. 5.5). Shot 1 begins with a closeup of a human hand. A package of Paxton's magically floats into it, angled directly towards to the camera to be viewed clearly. Shot 2 is an extreme closeup of the top of the cigarette package being opened by a thumb and index finger; the package is positioned at a forty-five-degree angle to the camera. Shot 3 is a match-on-action edit to closeup of a hand holding the package, angled directly to the camera so as to show the front of it clearly. Another hand removes the cellophane. Shot 4 is a jump cut to a closeup of a hand holding the top of a package, and then pushing the same downward.

Shot 5 is a closeup of fingers dunking the package into water (to illustrate that it is made of "moisture-proof plastic") and then lifting it back upwards. Shot 6 is a closeup of fingers pulling up the package and shaking water droplets off of it. Shot 7 is a closeup of a hand moving into an empty frame and squeezing the package. Shot 8 is an extreme closeup of two fingers squeezing the package. Shot 9 is a closeup of fingers lifting the top off of the package "with ease." Shot 10 is a closeup of the top of the package at a forty-five-degree angle, with fingers tearing into its foil seal. After a dissolve, Shot 11 is a closeup of fingers knocking the package, which is displayed horizontally; the action causes two cigarettes to emerge. Another dissolve reveals Shot 12, a closeup of a cigarette held by fingertips. Shot 12 is a closeup of a finger and thumb displaying the bottom of the cigarette, angled slightly so as to show its "menthol blend" tobacco. After a dissolve, Shot 13 shows a closeup of one hand holding the package while another fits the original plastic top onto the bottom of the same, in order to keep it "in reserve."

After another dissolve, Shot 14 is a closeup of the plastic top flying out of a hand (to "throw it away") before flying back into the same. The camera then tilts downward away from the hand. Shot 15 is a closeup of a hand holding the plastic top, and Shot 16 is a closeup of a hand putting the top back on top of the package, thus illustrating the third option of what the buyer can do with it. The commercial dissolves to Shot 17, a closeup of a hand snapping its fingers. Thanks to a special effect, a lit cigarette magically appears in between its thumb and index finger, resulting in a "new world of flavor." Shot 18 is a closeup of another hand, with a package flying into its grip. The camera zooms inward to show the label. The commercial dissolves to Shot 19, an extreme closeup of the brand name on the label.

To be sure, the commercial relies on various devices to instill variance to given shots and edits of the same: shot scale (three extreme closeups versus sixteen closeups), blocking (hand movements), cinematography (a camera tilt and a zoom), and editing transitions (six dissolves), for example. It also features music and two narrators, one male and one female. Nevertheless, the lack of medium and long shots is noticeable and a clear departure from the Classical Hollywood Style. By contrast, the commercial for Paxton cigarettes is more akin to, say, Carl Dreyer's affect shots in *La Passion de Jeanne D'Arc/The Passion of Joan of Arc* (1928), but even here, the eye and hand—traditional synecdochic images—are not affiliated with an onscreen face. In his landmark essay on the closeup, Béla Balász writes, "We have said that the isolated hand would lose its meaning, its expression, if we did not know and imagine its connection with some human being."[38] But that is not the result of this commercial, save for the implication that the disembodied hand belongs to the viewer, the (potential) customer.

Many TV commercials have been edited solely out of closeups, particularly presentational commercials, marking the most notable and repetitive usage of the same in mainstream American filmmaking. Consider a 1970 commercial for the product "Chills & Thrills" that features twenty-five shots in sixty seconds, for an ASL of 2.4 seconds (Fig. 5.6). The product was a frozen concentrate in a can that, once combined with

Figure 5.6 Chills & Thrills commercial from 1970

water, transformed into a thick "soft drink" that had to be eaten with a spoon: "cold and cherry and very magical . . . like nothing the world has ever known before." Its reliance on closeups and extreme closeups of the product is at times mediated by dissolves, which soften the effect of a closeup to another closeup. In other cases, though, straight cuts and even jump cuts draw further attention to the lack of medium and long shots.

Not all commercials that make exclusive use of closeups are necessarily cut quickly. Consider *Get a Little Closer* (1986), a Ted Bates Advertising commercial for Arrid Extra Dry deodorant spray starring Brooke Shields. Shot 1 depicts a closeup of Shields's head; she speaks to the viewer in direct address. The camera slowly tracks inward. The commercial dissolves to Shot 2, a bigger closeup of Shields's face. Shot 3 is a closeup of a can of Arrid Extra Dry spray deodorant, held by a woman's hand. It is a photograph, with downward movement added, presumably on an animation stand. Shot 4 is a closeup of Shields. The commercial rapidly dissolves to Shot 5, another closeup of Shields. The commercial dissolves to Shot 6, another closeup of Shields. The commercial then dissolves to Shot 7, yet another closeup of Shields. A can of the deodorant spray appears as well. The presentational commercial features an ASL of 4.28 seconds. The result eschews traditional Hollywood editing in favor of a non-Classical approach, exhibiting the same to mainstream audiences.

The Absence of the Edit

Walter Murch rated "emotion" as the number one reason that constitutes the "ideal cut."[39] But what of those occasions when emotion suggests *not* cutting? Lee Smith, editor of *Master and Commander: The Far Side of the World* (Peter Weir, 2003), *The Dark Knight* (Christopher Nolan, 2008), *Inception* (Nolan, 2010), *The Dark Knight Rises* (Nolan 2012), *Interstellar* (Nolan, 2014), and *Dunkirk* (Nolan, 2017), remarked in an interview:

> I always say to the guys I work with, "You've got to have a reason to cut. Don't just cut." Anyone can do that. You sit there and you're bored, so you cut. You're bored, so you cut. It's terrible. It's not a good reason. You cut for dramatic reasons. You cut to shift emphasis. You cut for a reaction that's stronger than a line. That's how you cut in my opinion.[40]

Jake Roberts, who has edited such films as *Hell or High Water* (David Mackenzie, 2016), adds, "I think there's something more authentic in a moment if there *isn't* a cut, then you know that that moment hasn't been contrived by the editor. It feels more real."[41]

Since the 1950s, the narratives of many television commercials have unfolded as a single unbroken shot, sometimes juxtaposed with one or more other shots of the product and/or sponsor name, which operate akin to film credits rather than as part of the narrative proper. In the story, there are no temporal leaps. The space is completely determined. The result invokes nineteenth-century cinema with its proscenium-style viewing perspective, as well as individual scenes in Classical Hollywood that unfold as a single master shot. While Valerie Orpen observes, "editing exists only *in relation to*, as a *counterpart* to, the shot," it is worth considering another point of view, one in which the absence of the edit is itself a type of editing, a conscious choice, with one or more factors leading to a decision quite opposed to, say, the type that Schnitzer would have made.[42]

A 1953 commercial for the Remington 60 Deluxe electric shaver featured three shots, the first being approximately five seconds of large onscreen text that instructs the viewer to "Forget Everything You Ever Heard," with voiceover speaking those words and the rest of the sentence, "about electric shavers." For ten seconds, Shot 2 displays the Remington 60 Deluxe in its case; after four seconds, text reading "Remington 60 Deluxe" appears on screen over the image. Then, Shot 3, which initiates the narrative, lasts sixty seconds. It is a closeup of a man removing his beard with the new product, as well as a superimposed clock. The clock's second hand and the absence of edits both illustrate a "demonstration no other shaving instrument has ever dared attempt."

Here the lack of editing is akin to the onscreen treatment of Fred Astaire dancing in some of his feature films, or of Harpo and Chico Marx playing their instruments, the unbroken shot underscoring that they could and did perform the same in a single take, rather than piecemeal. Here is real time, more "real," arguably, than that which a film like Fred Zinnemann's *High Noon* (1952) created, even with its emphasis on unfolding in something akin to real time.

As a followup to *Daisy Girl*, Lyndon B. Johnson's presidential campaign broadcast *Girl with Ice Cream Cone* (aka *Ice Cream Girl* and *Ice Cream Cone*) on September 14, 1964, one week after its predecessor aired. Also produced by DDB, the sixty-second commercial features a single closeup of a young girl lasting for fifty-three seconds. There are no edits. The camera does not move. Aside from eating her ice cream cone, the seated four-year-old actress does not move. Shot 2, which lasts for seven seconds, is white text on a black background that reads "Vote for President Johnson on November 3." The uninterrupted image of the young girl unfolds while a woman narrator explains that children need vitamin A and calcium, but they do not need radioactive poison. The voiceover proceeds to herald the nuclear test ban treaty and decries Senator Barry Goldwater for voting against it. Shot 1 ends with a freeze-frame of the young, innocently attractive actress, who peers beyond the frame and, arguably, the audience into an uncertain future, and this shot lasts for less than one second.

Apple's advertisement *Hal* (1999) heralded the company's computers for being immune to the threat of the Y2K bug. Created by Ken Segall for TBWA/Chiat/Day, *Hal* debuted online, receiving much attention before being broadcast during Super Bowl XXXIII. Shot 1 lasts fifty-six seconds. It is a parody of the HAL-9000 computer in Kubrick's *2001: A Space Odyssey* (1968). Actor Tom Kane imitates Douglas Rain, who provided HAL's voice in the feature film and who refused to participate in the commercial.[43] HAL concludes by saying, "You like your Macintosh better than me, don't you, Dave? Dave? Can you hear me Dave?" Shot 2 lasts four seconds, being the Apple logo against a black screen; white text underneath reads, "Think different." *Hal*'s narrative thus lasts fifty-six seconds, marked by a slow track into the computer's infamous red eye. Its reliance on camera movement arguably mitigates the sheer length of its single shot.

By contrast, eTrade's 2008 commercial *E Trade Baby*, created by Tor Myhren at Grey New York, featured an infant "speaking" to the camera. Like *Hal*, *E Trade Baby* also made its on-air debut during a Super Bowl. In webcam style, the infant sits at a computer inside his bedroom; in the background, a turning carousel hangs above his crib. The purpose was to illustrate how easy it was to invest with the online company. "If I can do it, you can do it," the infant explains. Shot 1 lasts twenty-four seconds, the baby looking directly at us and talking, thanks to CGI manipulation and voiceover from comedian Pete Holmes. The shot ends with the infant vomiting. Shot 2 lasts six seconds and features the company's animated name, logo, and slogan against white screen, the image once again akin to onscreen film credits.

But perhaps the most remarkable example is a sixty-second commercial for California-produced prune juice featuring Olan Soule, broadcast in the late 1960s or early 1970s (Fig. 5.7). A character actor from radio, film, and television, Soule had roles on such popular programs as *The Donald O'Connor Show*, *Dragnet*, and *Perry Mason*. One of his most memorable recurrent characters was as the choir director on *The Andy Griffith Show* (1960–8). Here was a trustworthy and wholesome face and voice,

Figure 5.7 Olan Soule promotes prune juice in the late 1960s/early 1970s

but not that of a star: immediately recognizable and yet simultaneously little known.

Shot in one unedited closeup against a white background, the commercial is completely unadorned, featuring no onscreen graphics or text. Except for occasional, admiring glances at the glass of prune juice that he holds next to his face, Soule looks directly at the viewer through his eyeglasses, an unthreatening and unassuming presence who seems to know what he is talking about, but who actually enjoys it as well. When the commercial begins, he is drinking prune juice. He soon happily finishes the glass and pours another, which he drinks as the commercial fades to black.

Soule's friendly gaze and dialogue spoken directly to the camera overtly attempt to convince the viewer that prune juice not only provides energy, but also is a delicious beverage, anticipating and attempting to overcome the unspoken argument that prunes might not taste good. His breaking of the fourth wall—in tandem with the closeup—also avoids explicit discussion of the digestive benefits of the drink, which is hinted at only in his closing dialogue: "To your health," a double meaning, as it also acts as a toast, given that he proceeds to drink the beverage again.

By looking at the viewer, and the viewer not being able to look at the rest of Soule's body, the issue of prunes aiding defecation is simultaneously present and absent. And the commercial is truly a single-shot commercial to the extent that no other image appears, not even white text on a black background. This cleverly recalls the strategy of the authoritative, realistic male voice from earlier broadcast commercials; this time, the audience reassuringly sees a material presence.

Conclusion

Francis Ford Coppola succinctly concluded: "The essence of cinema is editing. It's the combination of what can be extraordinary images of people during emotional moments, or images in a general sense, put together in a kind of alchemy."[44] Editing is the informing, creative work of making film a more coherent expression of magic, for any classification of film; the processed narrative illuminates meanings, whether in a closeup, medium, or long shot, or another compositional strategy.

In 1986, the Bloom Agency of Dallas created a thirty-second commercial for Maybelline's Shine Free Mascara, one marked by a bright, colorful mise-en-scène and then contemporary pop music (Fig. 5.8). It features sixty-one shots, an assemblage of images of the product juxtaposed with different women happily applying the makeup and ecstatically enjoying its effects.

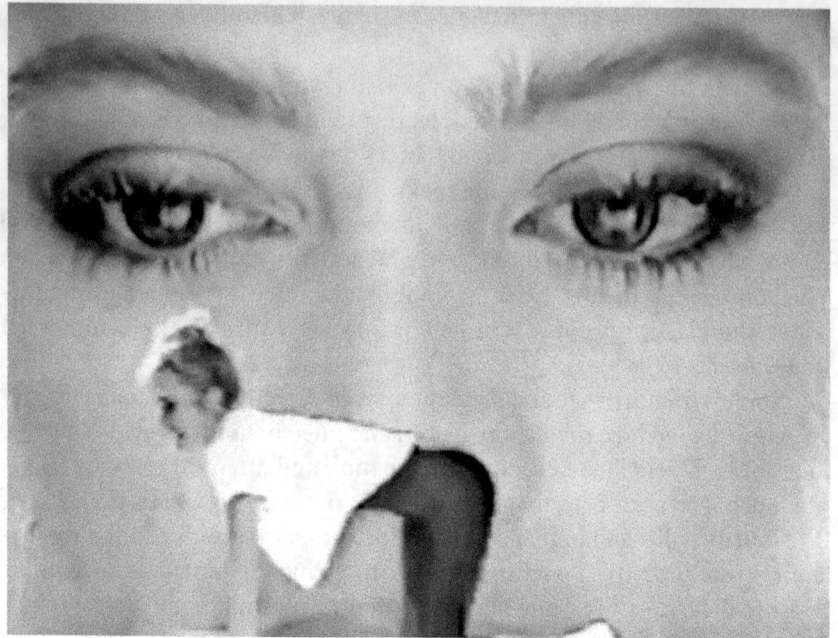

Figure 5.8 Maybelline's *Shine Free Mascara* (1986)

This engaging and abbreviated visual fantasy, composed like a music video, is a variation on the theme of idyllic bourgeois living in the mid-1980s. Maybelline's *Shine Free Mascara* ASL is a staggering 0.49 seconds, with some of the cuts so fast as to cause a strobe or "flicker effect." NBC and ABC agreed to broadcast the commercial. The Standards and Practices Department at CBS refused, fearing that its rapid editing could cause seizures in some epileptics.[45]

Director Howard Deutch's *Pretty in Pink* was released in 1986, the same year that the aforementioned Maybelline's *Shine Free Mascara* commercial was initially televised. Deutch's film was another effort at attracting the purchasing power of the youth market. In both the long and the short films, the rock music soundtracks successfully demonstrate the influence of the MTV phenomenon and demonstrably produce a dynamic "after-life" beyond their respective broadcast parameters: the audience wanted "more." These two films market images geared toward gendered identification via the artfully edited to create desire that sells its product, whether tickets to reveal fables of alienated youth in medium closeup, as viewed on the big screen, or to "wildly" apply eye makeup, as viewed on the small screen. Editing makes meaning.

Notes

1. Charles W. Curran, *The Handbook of TV and Film Technique* (New York: Pellegrini & Cudahy, 1953), p. 67.
2. Charles W. Curran, *Screen Writing and Production Techniques: The Non-Technical Handbook for TV, Film and Tape* (New York: Hastings House, 1958), p. 93.
3. "30 Second TV Ads Dominate, Records Show," *Advertising Age*, March 26, 1973, p. 104; Arthur Bellaire, "Shrink the 30-Second Spot? No! Here Are Better Ways to Get Your Money's Worth," *Advertising Age*, February 10, 1975, p. 40.
4. Timothy D. Taylor, *The Sounds of Capitalism: Advertising, Music, and the Contest of Culture* (Chicago: University of Chicago Press, 2012), p. 119.
5. Ten-second commercials date to at least the 1970s. See "Advertisers Put Over Big Ideas in 10-Second Spot Commercials," *Advertising Age*, July 21, 1975, p. 32; "Wave of TV Ad Future the 10-Second Spot?", *Advertising Age*, March 6, 1978, p. 74.
6. "James Vicary: Subliminal Svengali?", *Sponsor*, November 30, 1957, pp. 42–3, 70; "Subliminal Cuts Show 'Hot Car' in New Toyota Push," *Advertising Age*, September 19, 1966, p. 3; Hooper White, "Do Commercials Run Faster?", *Advertising Age*, February 18, 1980, p. 50.
7. "Is the Use of 'Opticals' a Problem in Today's Film Commercials?", *Sponsor*, October 1954, p. 60.
8. Hooper White, "Honda Commercial Walks on the Wild Side," *Advertising Age*, June 20, 1985, p. 38.
9. *Charlie Rose*, with guests Martin Scorsese, Jan Harlan, and Christiane Kubrick, 2001. Available at: <https://www.youtube.com/watch?v=VrtJXH2hRGI> (last accessed May 30, 2019).
10. David Bordwell, *The Way Hollywood Tells It* (Berkeley: University of California Press, 2006), p. 180.
11. Barry Salt, *Film Style and Technology: History and Analysis*, 3rd edn (London: Starword Press, 2009), p. 277.
12. Salt, p. 302.
13. Salt, p. 302.
14. Bordwell, p. 121.
15. Bordwell, p. 150.
16. Salt, p. 358.
17. Salt, p. 277.
18. Barry Salt, "The Shape of 1959," *New Review of Film and Television Studies*, vol. 7, no. 4 (December 2009), p. 403.
19. Examples include: *Target Earth* (Sherman A. Rose, 1954, with an ASL of 4.00 seconds), *The Story of Robin Hood and His Merrie Men* (Ken Annakin, 1952, 4.70 seconds), *Flying Leathernecks* (Nicholas Ray, 1951, 4.74 seconds), and *The Master of Ballantrae* (William Keighley, 1953, 4.84 seconds). As for Disney films, Salt has noted *Alice in Wonderland* (Clyde Geronimi,

Wilfred Jackson, and Hamilton Luske, 1951, 3.7 seconds) and *Peter Pan* (Clyde Geronimi, Wilfred Jackson, and Hamilton Luske, 1953, 3.4 seconds).
20. Salt, *Film Style and Technology: History and Analysis*, p. 358.
21. The commercials used to compile this data are as follows (with year of broadcast and ASL indicated in parenthesis): *Ale Puppet* (1957, 4.6 seconds), *Battlin' Danny* (1956, 6.6 seconds), *Beer Parade* (1957, 5 seconds), *Bert & Harry* (1955, 20 seconds), *Bop Corn* (1955, 7.5 seconds), *Busy Day* (1955, 8.5 seconds), *Cacklin' Fresh* (1955, 8.5 seconds), *Chicken Zoop* (1954, 22.5 seconds), *Chalk Talk* (1955, 12 seconds), *Chinese Baby* (1957, 12 seconds), *Cleanest Clean* (1958, 6.6 seconds), *Does She or Doesn't She?* (1957, 6.6 seconds), *Dot's Peanut Butter* (1954, 12.8 seconds), *Dry Bones* (1954, 12 seconds), *Flavor Buds* (1956, 17.4 seconds), *Funny Bandages* (1957, 6 seconds), *Good Manners* (1957, 4.6 seconds), *The Great A&B Race* (1952, 5.4 seconds), *Here's a Band* (1956, 7.5 seconds), *Hey, Mabel!* (1954, 4.2 seconds), *Hey, Hey, Hey* (1954, 6.6 seconds), *I Want My Maypo* (1956, 7.5 seconds), *Instant Money* (1955, 10 seconds), *John & Marsha* (1956, 8.5 seconds), *Ladder Drop* (1954, 7.5 seconds), *Life of a Baby* (1955, 12 seconds), *Look, Ma!* (1958, 6 seconds), *Meet Mr. Clean* (1958, 4.2 seconds), *Mum's the Word* (1955, 5 seconds), *Over the Falls* (1955, 4.4 seconds), *Peach of a Shave* (1954, 7.5 seconds), *Pee Wee Reese* (1955, 6 seconds), *Pepsodent* (1956, 5 seconds), *Smoker* (1955, 6.6 seconds), *Smoking Penguin* (1954, 8.5 seconds), *Soup Twins* (1957, 15 seconds), *Stalled Auto* (1957, 12 seconds), *Take Tea* (1956, 15 seconds), *Was It Paris?* (1955, 7.5 seconds), and *Watch the Birdies* (1954, 20 seconds).
22. Barry Salt, email to Gary D. Rhodes, July 19, 2014.
23. Barry Salt, email to Gary D. Rhodes, January 18, 2019.
24. Gerald Schnitzer, email to Gary D. Rhodes, May 3, 2013.
25. David Bordwell and Kristin Thompson, *Film Art: An Introduction*, 9th edn (New York: McGraw-Hill, 2010), p. 3.
26. "Selling the Soft-Sell: Gerald Schnitzer Carries the Auteur Viewpoint into Television Commercials," *Entertainment World*, January 30, 1970, p. 15.
27. "Loosening Up with Lambert," *Advertising Age*, April 4, 1988, p. 8.
28. Bordwell, *The Way Hollywood Tells It*, p. 123.
29. Bordwell, *The Way Hollywood Tells It*, p. 123.
30. Along with ninety-three still images and thirteen still images featuring movement, there is also a single image of the text logo, with movement added, that ends the commercial. Our overall calculation of 136 shots includes that single image in the total.
31. Walter Murch, *In the Blink of an Eye: A Perspective on Film Editing*, 2nd edn (Los Angeles: Silman–James Press, 2001), p. 119.
32. Bordwell, *The Way Hollywood Tells It*, p. 123.
33. Bordwell, *The Way Hollywood Tells It*, p. 142.
34. Bordwell, *The Way Hollywood Tells It*, p. 137.
35. Bordwell, *The Way Hollywood Tells It*, p. 121.
36. Slavko Vorkapich, "Creative Use of the Motion Picture," *Educational Theatre Journal*, vol. 2, no. 2 (May 1950), p. 144.

37. Vorkapich, p. 144.
38. Béla Balász, "The Close-Up," in *Film Theory and Criticism*, 6th edn, ed. Leo Braudy and Marshall Cohen (New York: Oxford University Press, 2004), p. 316.
39. Murch, p. 18.
40. Quoted in Steve Hullfish, *Art of the Cut: Conversations with Film and TV Editors* (New York: Routledge, 2017), p. 75.
41. Quoted in Hullfish, p. 72. Italics ours.
42. Valerie Orpen, *Film Editing: The Art of the Expressive* (London: Wallflower Press, 2003), p. 3. Italics in original.
43. "The Making of Apple's HAL," Ken Segall's Observatory: A Watchful Eye on Technology & Marketing, February 17, 2003. Available at <http://kensegall.com/2017/02/the-making-of-apples-hal/> (last accessed on November 17, 2017).
44. See <http://www.theyshootpictures.com/coppolafrancis.htm> (last accessed April 25, 2018).
45. Pat Sloan, "CBS Nixes Maybelline's SFX," *Advertising Age*, October 27, 1986, p. 41.

CHAPTER 6

Sound

America believes in Coke. In 1979, Martin Esslin noted the dynamic function of music in the television commercial as he focused on one spectacular, effervescent example:

> It is significant [in some cases] that the more abstract the imagery of the TV commercial becomes the more extensively it relies on music: around the giant soft drink bottle revolves a chorus of dancing singers; the mountain range of a trademark is surrounded by a choir of devoted singing worshippers. The higher the degree of abstraction and pure symbolism, the nearer the spectacle approaches ritual forms. This intriguing observation and description refers to an especially significant short film narrative.[1]

In 1971, a new Coca-Cola commercial begins to air on the networks: a young lady starts singing a cappella, "I'd like to buy the world a home, and furnish it with love," as the camera encircles her in closeup. The camera pulls back to reveal another young lady and a young man, who join the first in song (Fig. 6.1). The young man holds an open bottle of Coca-Cola. Dissolves lead to Shots 2 and 3, the camera moving from screen right to left across a line of many young adults from around the world. All sing, and many enthusiastically hold opened Coke bottles. A dissolve to Shot 4 reveals that there is a second and third line of singers behind the first. In Shot 6, we see the first camera move from right to left, which concentrates on hands and the bottles they hold; in Shot 7, a caroling face is seen in closeup. It is then superimposed over an aerial shot of the engaged, singing crowd. The face disappears, but the aerial image remains. Scrolling text explains, "On a hilltop in Italy/We assembled young people/From all over the world.../To bring you this message/From Coca-Cola Bottlers/All over the world." There is an engaging, nearly communal (religious?), and mysteriously vital experience watching and, especially, listening to this song of buoyant youth. Coke is celebrated in a song of utopian terms in this incredible, visionary landscape that usually exists only as an escape plan for the decommissioned audience.

Figure 6.1 Roberto Malenotti's *Hilltop* (1971)

Thus, director Roberto Malenotti's sixty-second musical *Hilltop* (1971, aka *I'd Like to Teach the World to Sing*) concludes, produced by McCann–Erickson for Coca-Cola, and using a melody written by Cook and Greenaway. At a budget of $250,000, it became for its time the most expensive commercial ever made.[2] More intriguing than its immediate economic impact on the advertising and beverage industry, *Hilltop* led to followup commercials, and the song itself, *sans* mention of Coke, was released as a single from the Hillside Singers in 1972.

Coke marketed the fantasy of a worldwide youth culture that could exist only in a politically air-brushed commercial. The success of the Coke commercial not only is marked by statistics and hypertextual references, but, most effectively, is measured even now by the audience's recollection of the song and the faces of people who really did not exist, except for these staged-innocent moments. The people and faces in the Coke commercial became "the real thing," to be perpetually consumed, in a life beyond the margins of the image and sound of the time of its initial broadcast. We still know the words to the song. We still remember the commercial.

Hilltop proved to be a genuine cultural and media phenomenon, and it provided the culminating moment in the final episode of the AMC television program *Mad Men* in 2017, as the contemplative adman Don

Draper envisions this sixty-second creation as his own. The audience can nearly feel and hear his thoughts, as they recall their own memory and impressions, and the program segues into the broadcast commercial. The conceptual Coke commercial of Draper's fictional imagination is the future—his and our future—and it remains, in reality, one of the most famous and beloved of all TV commercials. Film narrative revises and reimagines both collective and personal history, yet another hypertextual citation; Draper is not real, but Coke is best served chilled.

As Hilary Lapedis has written, "music may claim a place for itself as a primary conveyor of emotion and affective experience in the cinema."[3] The same has been true of TV commercials, which have relied on a varied and, at times, sophisticated usage of film sound. During a September 1950 broadcast of the CBS program *Studio One* (1948–58), famed TV commercial spokesperson Betty Furness spoke on camera about the advantages of the new Westinghouse television set. Its single dial was so simple, she said, that it could be tuned with "one hand behind my back." In a rather remarkable live simulation of the problems plaguing other, lesser TVs, Furness asked the home viewer: "In the set you are watching now, does the channel ever come in like this and give you only sound?" When she says "this," her own broadcast image rapidly blinks to black screen on three occasions, the commercial intentionally mimicking picture troubles known to many audiences.

Furness then asks, "Or, when the picture comes in clear like this, is the sound ever so hard to get that all you hear is this?" For the next four seconds, her direct address to the camera continues. Furness's lips move, but no audio is heard whatsoever. There is an intentional "loss of intelligibility," to quote Michel Chion.[4] The early TV commercial manipulated sound to an extent that there was a loss of sound. The possibilities of the sonic landscape were already being explored and would continue to be in the years that followed. *Ike . . . Bob*, one of Adlai Stevenson's political ads against Dwight D. Eisenhower in 1952, featured an image of two hearts pierced by a single arrow, with a narrative that attempted to suggest the renewed and perhaps suspect coalition of Eisenhower and Robert A. Taft. While Mel Blanc provides voiceover imitations of both men, sentimental background music of a type associated with soap operas plays at erratic speeds, slowing down at times to underscore the troubled relationship.

The use of offscreen sound effects in which the source of the audio is not revealed also became a component in the TV commercial. One of Hubert Humphrey's ads for the 1968 presidential election decried Richard Nixon's selection of Spiro T. Agnew as a running mate. The entire soundtrack is one unseen man laughing hysterically. The camera slowly zooms outward to reveal a prop television with onscreen text that asks, "Agnew for Vice-President?" The cause of the laughter is made clear, though its source is not: the laughter continues when the commercial cuts to black screen with text that advises, "This would be funny if it weren't so serious . . ." As the commercial ends, the laughter changes to a brief cough, as if the unseen character is choked up by the impact of the final text.

More commonly, and much to the chagrin of many viewers, TV commercials have explored dynamic range, usually in the effort to have their volume louder than the program they sponsor in order to attract greater attention.[5] But dynamic range can have other impacts as well. "Listen to the sounds of freshness," a 1960s advertisement for Baggies Plastic Bags instructs, aurally emphasizing the sounds of foods stored in the plastic bags and of teeth biting the same, all crunchy because the food has remained fresh. It over-signals the functional. A commercial produced in the same era for County Fair Rolls emphasized the sounds of various food being barbecued over an open grill, the sizzle being dramatically louder than offscreen conversations taking place at an unseen backyard party.

Despite the limitations of television speakers during the bulk of the twentieth century, commercials were, at times, at the vanguard of new technologies to maximize clarity and what *Advertising Age* once called "aural gloss."[6] By 1981, for example, the publication heralded the use of digital sound in commercials, even though at the time only a dozen or so sound studios around the world even had the necessary equipment. Such recordings allowed directors to avoid transferring their soundtracks to film prints and the possible quality loss that could result.[7]

However, the most pronounced usage of sound in TV commercials from the 1950s to the present day has been, as *Hilltop* suggests, music. As Timothy D. Taylor notes, "Music has power. Musicians know it, listeners know it. And so do advertisers."[8] From jazz singers like Frank Sinatra and pop giants like Michael Jackson to unknown studio musicians, some of the most important talents of the twentieth and twenty-first centuries have taken part.[9] In 1981, executive Joe Kilgore suggested,

> Only the most amateurish use of music will normally hurt a spot. Used well, it can make your words and pictures come to life as nothing else can. So when you're creating the spot at your typewriter, think about music.[10]

The emphasis on music evolved from it merely consisting of jingles to the use of pre-existing popular songs. In 1985, *Advertising Age* wrote:

> The hot and hip look of music videos is quickly invading TV advertising. Commercials for products ranging from jeans to junk food are trading in hard-product sells for foggy imagery, fantasy sequences and pulsating rock music . . . The result is a whole new advertising genre—the 'product video.'[11]

But the "product video" actually had deep roots, dating to Schnitzer's *Going to the Dance* in 1958, if not earlier. Schnitzer very definitely believed in the integration of sound and cinematography.

The Silent Movie

Richard Abel and Rick Altman have made clear how "ubiquitous" the "presence of sound" was "in the so-called silent cinema."[12] James Lastra writes, "That the silent cinema was never silent has become one of the great revisionist clichés of film studies."[13] To be sure, there were exceptions, but in general, musical accompaniment was the norm. There was sound, but the audiovisual experience was different than what "sound cinema" became as a result of the "talkies."

For various aesthetic and thematic reasons, a number of commercials have adopted silent film aesthetics, presenting them to mainstream audiences who otherwise have little exposure to pre-talkies. A series of American commercials for Molson beer in 1981 incorporated clips from "vintage silent movies," for example.[14] That same year, Suzanne Somers starred in a spot for Ace Hardware that featured a "silent movie format," in which she rescued a "struggling cowboy with the aid of her helpful hardware man, who provides the material for the quick construction of a ladder." No dialogue was heard during the narrative, but the commercial featured an intertitle that declared, "Gasp!"[15]

One commercial from circa 1965–6 parodied silent film serials by depicting a dark-costumed villain. He has placed a victim on railroad tracks; a train rapidly approaches. A nearby cowboy, dressed in white and on horseback, surveys the pending murder. Melodramatic piano music plays while the villain's and victim's lips move, the latter clearly pleading for her life, even though no dialogue is heard. The hero's approach frightens the villain, who announces to the camera—thanks to an intertitle—"Curses—Foiled Again!" The hero rescues the victim and speaks unheard words to the camera. An intertitle translates, "Us Tareyton Smokers would rather fight than switch!," a slogan created by James Jordan of BBDO and used by the company during the 1960s and 1970s.

While the Tareyton commercial relied on music, it did not use sound effects, which had, at times, been part of silent film exhibition practices. Touting the possibilities, René Clair wrote in 1929:

> The talking film is not everything. There is also the sound film—on which the last hopes of the advocates of the silent film are pinned. They count on the sound film to ward off the danger represented by the advent of talkies, in an effort to

convince themselves that the sounds and noises accompanying the moving picture may prove sufficiently entertaining for the audience to prevent it from demanding dialogue, and may create an illusion of 'reality' less harmful for the art than the talking film.[16]

Clair's particularized use of the term "sound film" and its sonic landscape did not gain currency, but some television commercials have adopted the technique he described, including spots that Martin Scorsese and David Lynch directed for Giorgio Armani in 1986 and 1992, respectively.

In the 1960s, the American Cancer Society sponsored a commercial featuring a man on a train platform. He starts to read a newspaper before noticing a poster that asks, "Do you know the seven warning signs of cancer?" Below the question a large photographic hand obscures the text of the signs. The man carefully examines the poster, returns to his newspaper, and then, with a worried expression, looks at the poster again. When he gets on his train and the door closes behind him, he stares at the poster through the window. The reflection of a man dressed in black, a subtle visual reference to the Grim Reaper, partially obscures the man's face. Once the train begins moving, it becomes even more difficult for the poster to be read.

As the man's train rides away, scrolling onscreen text announces each of the seven signs, allowing the viewer to learn information that was previously withheld. The commercial utilizes no voiceover, no dialogue, and no music. The only sounds heard are the wind, the man's feet as he walks, an offscreen child, a conductor, a whistler, and the sound of the trains.

In 2012, Hans Knaapen directed *Thief*, a sixty-second commercial for LG televisions that relied on just a single sound effect (Fig. 6.2). Its story appears to unfold in four shots, for an ASL of fifteen seconds. Each shot mimics the point of view of a security camera, heightened by the fact they appear as high-contrast black and white. Each of the four "shots" is actually comprised of numerous edits that give the appearance of the type of drop-frame recording associated with security cameras.

The first shot depicts the interior of an electronics store that has over twenty-five LG flat-screen televisions for sale. A young male character enters the frame and walks towards and finally under the security camera, looking directly into it as he does so. In Shot 2, the character enters another section of the store, walking backwards as his eyes remain fixed on a different security camera. In the high-angle, medium Shot 3, he appears in yet another section of the store, again walking backwards and staring into yet another security camera, his blocking making him ever the more suspicious. As he makes his way to the exit, he turns and looks at a clerk.

Figure 6.2 Hans Knaapen's *Thief* (2012)

Shot 4 depicts the store exterior, with a prominent window sign promoting LG as "The World's Slimmest Television." The character walks backwards out of the store and onto the sidewalk.

For the first time, it is apparent that he is holding one of those slim TVs. The thief runs away, with a store clerk chasing after him. Somebody was watching as we were listening. There is no music and no dialogue. The only sound is a consistent room tone, an aural suggestion that the film results from security camera footage, even though most security cameras do not record audio. Here is not only the kind of "sound cinema" that Clair imagined, but one with a sonic landscape that opts for the opposite dynamic range used by most commercials, meaning loud volumes to capture viewer attention.

Neill Blomkamp's *Evolution* (2004), a thirty-second commercial for Nike Huarache 2K4, appears to unfold as a single, unedited thirty-second shot of a tennis shoe. Scratches, light leaks, and even the superimposition of leader tape visually imply time-lapse film photography, as does the changing background sky. The shoe visually undergoes eight transformations until becoming the Huarache. Here is the evolution of a product, witnessed in the form of science-fiction, the permutations each occurring on their own, unguided by any helping hand or visible force. The only sounds heard during the first twenty-four seconds of the ad are effects that are synchronized to the evolution of the shoe, adding to the sense of transformation. During the final six seconds of the commercial, the sounds of an offscreen basketball game are heard, but the individual voices are not intelligible. The fact that the sound effects unfold consistently, as if unedited (even though they are), reinforces the commercial's visual desire to be understood as a single, unbroken shot. But here is a clear example of what Stanley Kubrick meant when he discussed how sound can "bend" time: the image is allegedly time-lapsed over years, but the effects do not at all sound as if they have been recorded over a lengthy period of time. Sound and image are simultaneously integrated and asynchronic.

Other commercials feature more complicated interplay between silence and sound. In the 1960s, actor Jack Gilford starred in commercials for Cracker Jack that featured no character dialogue or music. One of them, broadcast in 1965, features a young boy sitting next to Gilford on a train. Having been to the circus (as is apparent by a circus flag in his hand), the boy is tired and quickly shuts his eyes. Gilford spies the box of Cracker Jack in the boy's pocket, looks into the camera, peeks around the railroad car, and then sneaks a bite of Cracker Jack. Not content, he takes the box from the sleeping boy and eats even more. After he replaces the box, the boy wakes up and confronts him nonverbally.

At the end of the sixty-second spot, the narration explains, "When it comes to Cracker Jack, some kids never grow up." Until that time, the only sound heard is the train rolling down the tracks, Gilford's newspaper making a noise, and Gilford's teeth crunching the snack. Here is Clair's "sound film," with an ending that invokes the tradition of lecturers who at times spoke during screenings in the early cinema period.[17] Much the same was true of *Gum Goes to Work*, a commercial introducing Leaf's Xylifresh Gum in 1990, in which onscreen talent chewed gum "to the sounds of jackhammers and drills while construction signs pound home the plaque-righting message." A voiceover warned viewers, "Don't expect to find Xylifresh loafing in the candy aisle."[18]

The combined approach of music and sound effects is particularly apparent in Android's nondialogue commercial *Rock, Paper, Scissors* (2016, aka *Be Together, Not the Same*). Produced by Droga5, it features John Parr's 1985 song *St. Elmo's Fire (Man in Motion)* as background music in an animated story about a personified sheet of paper in a school hallway. He fearfully walks past a group of personified scissors, only to be bullied by other sheets of paper. A pair of scissors helps him; the two walk home together, only to see two personified rocks bullying a third, smaller rock. With newfound courage, the paper frightens the two larger rocks. He and the smaller rock join the scissors as onscreen text informs us, "Be together. Not the same." Sound effects, though less prominent than the music, are heard throughout.

The Musical

Advertising jingles date to the late nineteenth century and became an important feature on the radio in the 1930s and 1940s.[19] "The sound of jingles changed little with the advent of television," Timothy D. Taylor writes, "probably because advertising agencies' lack of understanding of television in its early years meant that radio practices continued."[20] He adds that, for their first few decades, "jingles tended to track trends in popular music—with some lag time—though they were almost always unremittingly cheerful and upbeat, using happy tunes to sweeten the frequently bland information contained in the lyrics."[21] Though early TV commercial jingles featured simple accompaniment, by 1960, the use of "modern" musical styles and orchestras of thirty-five pieces became increasingly common.[22] Composer Raymond Scott even created an electronic machine for his radio/TV commercial firm, the Jingle Workshop, which made news in 1960 for its ability to select, modify, and combine sounds produced by musical instruments.[23]

And yet, the popularity of the jingle waned significantly, certainly by the 1980s and 1990s. Replacing jingles were pre-existing pop songs, which sometimes featured variations, including lyrics rewritten to promote given products.[24] Taylor observes the "decrease—to negligibility—of the difference between 'advertising music' and 'music.'"[25]

For several years, rumor had it that Bill Gates and Microsoft paid the Rolling Stones between $8 and $13 million for the use of the band's 1981 song *Start Me Up* to help launch Windows 95, notably in a sixty-second commercial produced by Wieden+Kennedy in 1995. According to Microsoft's then Chief Operating Officer Bob Herbold, the actual amount was closer to $3 million.[26] Nevertheless, even that amount underscores how important particular music has been to given advertising campaigns.

Consider a 1967 commercial for Noxzema's shaving cream (Fig. 6.3). Produced in extreme to traditional closeup shots, it depicts a blonde female seductively caressing a can of shaving cream next to her face while directly addressing the viewer, in a controlling female voice, with a vaguely "European"-sounding accent (this was Swedish model, Gunilla Knutsson): "Men, nothing takes it off like Noxzema Medicated Shave." The commercial cuts to four closeups of a man shaving, as well as one shot of him rinsing his razor. David Rose's burlesque instrumental *The Stripper* is heard in the background. Some of the man's hand movements are intentionally timed to the music. As the music continues, a closeup of the blonde encourages the viewer, "Take it off. Take it all off." After another closeup of the man shaving in time to the music, the blonde reappears, explaining

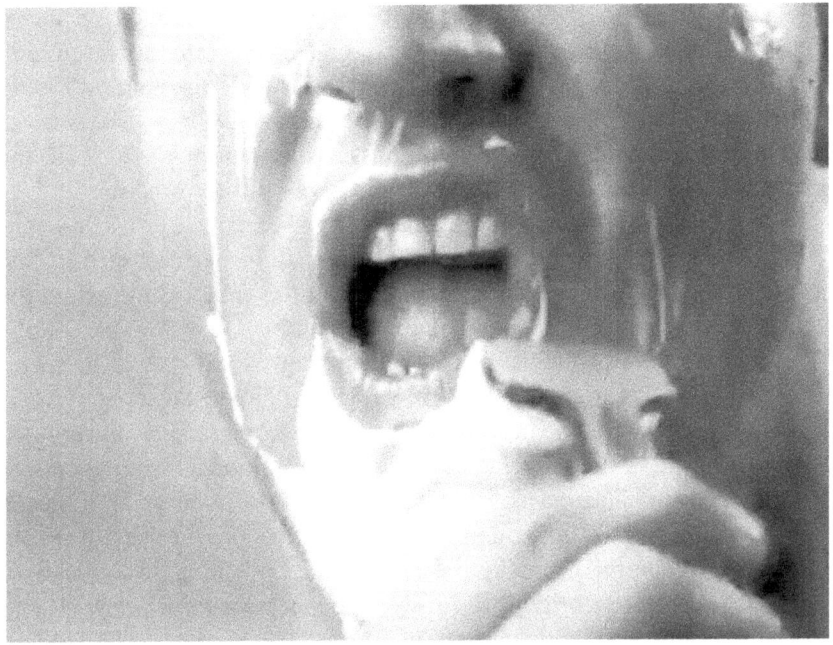

Figure 6.3 Noxzema shaving cream commercial (1967)

"Nothing takes it off like . . ." She pauses during five quick shots of the man washing his freshly shaved face with water; her sentence concludes with "Noxzema Medicated Shave" over the commercial's final shot, an image of the product's label. The commercial humorously depicts the actors as sexual, but inverts traditional gender roles by making the man "strip."

Given their emphasis—at times, audio focalization—on music, it is not surprising that TV commercials would adopt and adapt the musical genre, invoking a tradition for mainstream audiences during eras after its popularity had waned in Hollywood. In 1976, for example, Kenyon & Eckhardt went so far as to hire Tony Award-winning librettist and Broadway director Burt Shevelove, known for *A Funny Thing Happened on the Way to the Forum* (1962) and the revision of *No, No, Nanette* (1971), to direct a musical commercial for the Savings Bank Association of New York State. He insisted that the video and audio be shot live, rather than dubbing the sound in post-production. "You're competing with the programs," he said, justifying the added cost, "so you have to make something that makes them watch."[27]

Singer Julie London appeared in Marlboro commercials in the early 1960s. All were intended to be romantic, even seductive, featuring her in elegant attire. In one of the series, broadcast in 1963, voiceover introduces "Julie London sings the Marlboro song" as the camera—beginning in long shot and showing a pianist—moves through a restaurant dining room. The lights are low and all tables are empty, save hers. She sings to her dinner companion, the lyrics addressing him and, by extension, the audience: "Why don't you settle back, and have a full-flavored smoke?" As she continues the song, she flicks ashes from her cigarette into an ashtray, intentionally and provocatively touching the tip of her cigarette against the tip of his. In this case, the commercial features source music, from the visible pianist and from an unseen orchestra.

In the late 1960s, Thomas Scott Cadden, known for his work on Procter & Gamble's Mr. Clean commercials, wrote and directed a series of spots for Bold laundry detergent known collectively as *The Bold Sound*. Each unfolded more in the tradition of opera than traditional film musicals, at least in so far as all of the dialogue in them was sung to music. There is no "myth of spontaneity," no nonmusical sequence to provide a comparison. Two of these commercials featured a housewife explaining to her neighbor how Bold achieved "bright" results. Another featured a window cleaner advising a housewife of the same.

The most elaborate of the series featured a young lady on trial. A singing judge charges her with "improper laundry." The jury harmonizes that she did not "wash with Bold." She pleads that she had "never been told." Two witnesses swear that other detergents "can't hold a light to new Bold bright!" Exhibit A is the detergent poured into a clear cup. The jury and witnesses continue to sing the virtues of Bold, leading the defendant to see the "error of her ways," and thus bringing a happy ending to the proceedings. The judge hammers his gavel and sings for his next case.

In some cases, musical commercials have been self-reflexive, integrating the audience into the story through song. In a 1973 advertisement entitled *The Little Fisherman*, a young boy (Andrew "Andy" Lambros) fishes on a pier while singing a song about Oscar Mayer bologna:

> My bologna has a first name, it's O-S-C-A-R.
> My bologna has a second name, it's M-A-Y-E-R.
> Oh, I love to eat it every day,
> And if you ask me why I'll say,
> Cause Oscar-Mayer has a way
> With B-O-L-O-G-N-A.

The boy sings directly into the camera, in a manner akin to Warner Bros. Vitaphone shorts of the late 1920s. Then, at the end of the commercial, he asks "How's that?" while still peering into the camera, as if seeking approval as an actor not only from the company who hired him, but, more importantly, from the viewing audience at home.

Other commercials have appropriated a narrative approach associated with some music videos, meaning visual narratives set to music, but without featuring images of their singers or band members in performance. For example, when writing the song for what became Chevrolet's campaign *Heartbeat of America* in the late 1980s, Robin Batteau tried to convey a three-act narrative through music that associated Chevy with rock music. Bill Ludwig of Campbell-Ewald enthused that it was an "anti-jingle."[28]

Against heartbeat sound effects, the music begins with a folk sound, "travels" to Motown, and reaches a rock destination.[29] In a sixty-second spot broadcast in 1987, the music is visualized with an automobile journey through geography relevant to the music. Director Peter Dowd shot in thirty locations, including San Francisco, Los Angeles, Las Vegas, and New York. The commercial featured a total of fifty-one shots, for an ASL of 1.17 seconds.[30] "Kudos are coming from all directions," *Advertising Age* observed of the song's popularity, to the extent that releasing the song as a record became a viable possibility.[31] General Motors relied on *Heartbeat of America* for a series of commercials until 1991, recording the theme in different styles and genres.[32]

Intertextuality

Though premiered in 1829, Rossini's *William Tell Overture* became most famous in America during the 1930s and 1940s as the theme music to *The Lone Ranger* on radio, an association that intensified when the program moved to television from 1949 to 1957.[33] Thanks to syndication, as well as subsequent incarnations of the character, the overture has retained its cultural identification. Even Gore Verbinski's *The Lone Ranger* (2013) relied on it.

Aware of this history, commercials for Lark cigarettes in the 1960s featured actors holding signs asking others on city streets to "Show us your Lark pack," a phrase that became so famous as to inspire a George Carlin joke on his 1972 album *FM & AM*. Music in these commercials featured the *William Tell Overture*, performed with new lyrics:

> Have a lark, have a lark, have a lark today!
> Have a lark, have a lark, have a lark today!
> Have a lark today!
> There's nothing, nothing, nothing like a lark!
> There's nothing, nothing, nothing like a lark!

Here was musical palimpsest, with the Lone Ranger remaining a vivid association even as a new one became etched into American culture of the 1960s. As Andy Birtwistle observes, "The issue ... is not that one type of relationship determines audiovisuality, but rather that film and video are host to multiple, shifting sound–image relations."[34] Lark, the Lone Ranger, and the *William Tell Overture* converged in a series of shot sequences.

In 1968, Stan Freberg drew upon these multiple sound–image relationships to create an intertextual and interaural sixty-second commercial for Jeno's Pizza Rolls, one that was simultaneously simplistic and complex, and ultimately humorously brilliant (Fig. 6.4). In this case, new lyrics to the *William Tell Overture* dramatically request that the viewer "Have a pizza, pizza, pizza roll!" Various attendants at an upper-class party reveal boxes of Jeno's in a manner that visually echoed smokers showing their Lark packs, a sign of earlier audiovisual practice. Fourteen seconds into the commercial, a waiter pushes a cart from screen right to left with a sign that reads, "Show us your pizza roll pack!", the general image and specific usage of the word "pack" intentionally and overtly echoing Lark's commercials.

Figure 6.4 Stan Freberg's 1968 commercial for Jeno's Pizza Rolls

Various party attendants enjoy the pizza rolls, and the waiter pushes his cart again, this time from screen left to right. Then, after nearly thirty seconds, an on-camera character speaks for the first time. "I'd like to talk to you about that music you're using," he says while putting a cigarette into his mouth, the prop clarifying that he is from Lark Cigarettes, and potentially unhappy about the repurposing of the *William Tell Overture*. But a hand immediately appears on the speaker's shoulder. His face and body are not seen until the next shot, when it is revealed that he is the Lone Ranger. "That's funny," he tells the emissary from Lark, "I've been meaning to speak to you people about the same thing." As he sternly folds his arms, his companion Tonto asks him, "Have a pizza roll, *Kemo sabe*?" The Lone Ranger declines but Tonto partakes. While their costumes alone indicate who they are, the actors' recognizable voices underscore this fact: Clayton Moore and Jay Silverheels, who portrayed the characters on television, reprise their roles for Jeno's.

For the commercial's conclusion, an on-camera spokesman explains how easy and quick the pizza rolls are to prepare, followed by a woman asking a variation on the question so often heard on *The Lone Ranger* program: "Who was that masked man, anyhow?" It then ends with another variation on the program's dialogue, with Clayton Moore's offscreen voice shouting, "Hi-ho, pizza roll, away!" Reaction to the commercial was positive, so much so that Johnny Carson recalled an audience applauding it when it was first shown on *The Tonight Show*, the only time he ever saw such a reaction to an advertisement. Sound made this Jeno's commercial especially memorable, along with its flow of supporting humorous images.

Audiovisual Dissonance

Whether drugs are strictly medicinal or cosmetic in their application, the legal drug narrative reveals contradictory reactions and impulses, and dissonant spaces, especially in the broadcast commercial produced for the marketing of these products. For the television audience in 1958, perhaps immersed in the early phase of a Schnitzerian golden age of broadcast commercials produced as short-film narratives, a child-like, animated spokes-character, "Speedy," and a familiar (albeit, older) emblematic presence from American film culture, Buster Keaton, demonstrate the wonders of the over-the-counter drug, Alka-Seltzer. In medium and close-up shots, Keaton expresses stomach trouble and incipient relief via his comedic performance. Few actors could internalize suffering more comically than Keaton's affective and recognizable face.

In this sixty-second spot, Keaton, Speedy, and a male voiceover work in concert to facilitate the consumer messaging via dialogue and jingle singing to chronicle and resolve Keaton's perturbance.[35] Keaton plays a suburban, tired mailman, and, as the camera pans and follows his daily work ritual, there is a revealing trick shot recalling the shock transitions and editing in Keaton's earlier film career. As one house slowly moves away from him as he attempts to make a delivery, its swift departure reveals it to be a mobile home, thus signaling Keaton's closeup expressions of verbal and visual perplexity. Speedy, the cheerful animated trademark figure signifying the product, pops out of a mailbox to offer succor. A magical, illustrative cartoon demonstrates the mock-biological process of relief, as the cartoon figure transitions into the formerly beleaguered mailman on a motorbike catching up a trailer to deliver mail: the product "delivers." Complementing the narrative is the clever, well-known product's theme song, whose lyrics capture the experience of the drug's promise of relief. A child-like voice intones, "relief is just a swallow away," and the crisis is resolved. The postwar fascination with the marketing and distribution of new and/or improved pharmaceuticals continues to the present era and frequently saturates the medium's commercial programming. Yet not all drugs, whether sold to consumers over the counter or professionally prescribed, are as safe as Speedy might indicate, or even necessary for the survival of the individual.

What is especially compelling for the contemporary audience is the corrosive subtext involving side effects, rendered alongside the imagery and sounds of media-inspired life and success, in drug commercials. Many legal drug commercials, marketing products for medical or cosmetic purposes, are inferentially absurd, occasionally horrifying, contradictory narratives, full of ironic sound and fury, signifying serious, often lethal, complications. Would the reader take pills or injections if it leads to puffier cheeks and lips, but also to death?

Forget Speedy and his encouraging smile: what are the sounds and images of a postmodern drug commercial, especially as the product subversively underplays the deleterious effects of its usage? Since 1999, the Food and Drug Administration (FDA) has required American television commercials to disclose potential side effects of the medicines in a manner akin to declarations of their potential benefits. But narrators reading lists of side effects are sufficient: accompanying images do not have to picture them, and so they do not. Images continue the aura of the beneficial, while audio tells a very different story. The frequent result is what Chion has called "audiovisual dissonance," when the "image goes its own way and the commentary goes another." They "follow two different tracks," he writes.[36]

SOUND   169

In a sixty-second commercial broadcast in 2018 for Enbrel, a drug marketed to combat arthritic pain and inflammation, medium two shots and a closeup of hands playing the piano (*ergo*, not in pain) shows a mother-patient and daughter harmoniously playing the instrument as a female voiceover informs the audience about the drug's potential side effects: "infection, tuberculosis, lymphoma, other cancers . . ." A cute dog completes the commercial experience and this family's renewal; the drug worked, despite the side effects, apparently. And the sixty-second Humira commercial *Not Always Where I Needed to Be* (2018) features a hip, young, attractive group of musicians in a rock band that might miss the performance schedule if the lead singer cannot gain control over her Crohn's disease and the inflammation that prevents her from rocking out live (Fig. 6.5). She will perform; the drug works, but voiceover messaging warns the potential consumer about adverse side effects that similarly invoke the ironic counterpoint previously referenced.

Produced in a frenzied, cinematic, refreshingly experimental collage style, the ad directly invites the audience to witness several unidentifiable fetish objects—attractive young women—as they reform into new, better selfhoods as facilitated by legal drugs. Produced in 2018, the Juvederm *Work It* advertisement for "dermal filler"—cosmetic injections—directly appeals to a mostly female audience via messaging different in tone and style from Speedy's general marketing strategies. The Juvederm commercial is less sexual in its visual appeal and marketing than it is a stylish tour-de-force of female-in-control attitude in medium and closeup shots,

Figure 6.5 Humira's *Not Always Where I Needed to Be* (2018)

coupled with a dynamic contemporary soundtrack, both of which are ironically juxtaposed with what is heard about deadly side effects in the voiceover. The Juvederm narrative is a sensational example of the short-film commercial narrative. Images of young women appear rapidly as the viewer hears a nearly incomprehensible but fetching "bounce" dance-music soundtrack entitled *Karaoke*, performed by Big Freedia. This sixty-second commercial features an accelerated, music-video editing style, and a female voiceover providing details and descriptions.

The Juvederm product basically creates inflated body parts like lips and cheeks for fashionable purposes; these are cosmetic applications. Juvederm's abstracted, attractive women signify parts of a whole image; they are contemporary, voguish props with big lips and cheeks inviting a response as they peer directly into the camera in a self-reflexive pose of heightened awareness of their attractiveness.

This commercial is artfully manipulative in its disharmonious aural descriptions and comments: rapidly edited, boldly colorful images of fabricated "hip" settings and exotic women, an informative, female voiceover that offers industrial messaging, and a dance-hall soundtrack that would appeal to a younger audience suggest its classification as a contemporary short-film narrative. As the voiceover in the commercial refers to "common side effects include . . . swelling, pain . . . lumps, bumps, bruising . . . vision abnormalities, blindness, strokes . . . scarring," there is the concurrent appearance on screen of bright, large, color graphic print urging the consumer to PLUMP IT—COMMAND IT—BOSS IT, over the dance music. Earlier in the commercial, in small text printed toward the bottom of the screen, there is a message—"[Juvederm] may increase risk of infection, bleeding, or bruising at the application site" —but the later, larger-print message at the end of the commercial informs the viewer that a website will help to locate a participating "Juvederm doctor" if assistance is needed by the consumer; it did not include the sound of a speeding ambulance. Nevertheless, unlike the approach of so many Hollywood films, the audio goes one way starkly, while the images go beautifully in another direction.

Disrupted Teleology

A 1960s commercial for the Zenith color television with Space Command remote control featured a voiceover that asked viewers, "Wish you could stay right where you're sitting now and turn to the next channel to see what's on? Or the next? And the next?" At the beginning of the question, a loud racecar roars down the road, interrupted abruptly by a channel change to a couple walking on a peaceful beach, which changes to a gun-firing cavalry, which changes to a jazz combo.

Even without owning a remote control, viewers were familiar with such abrupt transitions. Changing channels could cause what was not possible at a movie theater. The key difference was that, even while cutting on sound effects like the fast-moving automobile, the editing of Zenith's commercial softened the effect to an extent by choice of footage. For example, no channel change occurs in the middle of a word of character dialogue, thus cutting it noticeably short, a pronounced effect that viewers would have often encountered during their own channel selections.

Efforts to incorporate abrupt changes to soundscapes are also noticeable in a 1960s Coca-Cola commercial that features a single shot of a sweating Coke bottle. Various sound effects are heard, many related to the beverage only metaphorically. For example, offscreen effects convey birds chirping in the morning, the words of a weather report about hot temperatures, glass bottles clanking, a tennis ball being hit, Coke being poured, a vocalist singing "Life is much more fun when you're refreshed," kids playing, a child complaining "I'm so hot, I'd like to take my skin off," ice dropping into a glass, a vocalist singing "It has the taste you never get tired of," Coke being poured again, a different vocalist singing "Things go better with—," a bottle being opened, a woman laughing, and Coke being poured for a third time.

The result is a key example of the ability of given sound effects to create narrative legibility, as well as—due to the single image on screen—a unique audiovisual event. More specifically, the commercial creates greater aural disruptions than the Zenith ad, with the sound of playing children beginning so close to the final articulation of the word "refreshed" as to be pronounced; the same occurs with the words "tired of" to the sound of the beverage being poured. Here the absence of a pause and/or sound bridge is striking, but not nearly so much as the lyric "Things go better with—," which ends so abruptly as the delete the expected word "Coke," as would have been heard in earlier commercials using the same jingle. In some respects, the brand name here is emphasized due its aural absence.

Of course, it is true that some films cut to music already in progress. Biancorosso writes at length on the straight cut to a concert *in media res* in Woody Allen's *Manhattan* (1979).[37] And Kevin Donnelly observes:

> Sound bridges are the points where the joins are problematized but also dramatized. They manifest a form of montage and fashion a momentary asynchrony quickly resolved by the payoff of returning to synchrony. Sound bridges are one of the best illustrations of the principles of montage, where different ideas of spaces can be joined through a transition that is more than simply functional.[38]

But the Coca-Cola commercial represents a different form of asynchronic sound, and one that exceeds the channel changing in the Zenith ad.

In some cases, this is the denial of what Chion calls "temporal vectorization," where the listener can accurately "anticipate the moment of coming to a cadence" or the "last word" of a sentence.[39] Commercials of this type disrupt aural teleology in a manner akin to Jean-Luc Godard's use of music in such films *A Woman Is a Woman* (1961), in which vocal music stops mid-word and mid-note, and sounds effects like crowd "walla" abruptly disappear. Experiments of this type have also occurred in television commercials, including edits made *during* the middle of a character's dialogue, cutting away from it and disallowing its completion.

Consider Charles Stone III's extremely popular sixty-second commercial *Whassup?* (aka *Wazzup?* and *Wassup?*), which Anheuser–Busch first broadcast in December 1999. It was based on Stone's short film *True* and produced by DDB Worldwide Chicago. During the ad, a group of middle-class friends, some watching "the game" and having a "Bud," ask each other "Wassup?," a slang corruption of "What's Up?" The question is clearly articulated twice, and then slips into a slurred version of the same on two occasions. At that point, three characters ask the question once each, the image cutting while the phrase continues to be heard in the form of a sound bridge.

The commercial continues with the characters repeating the question, but the editing style changes. On eleven occasions, the film cuts *during* the question, not allowing for its completion. With no pause whatsoever, another person's version of the question replaces it. This is an evolution of the kind of clipped audio heard in the aforementioned Zenith commercial, but without the narrative device of channel changing to explain it. Instead, this is a repeated and much-intensified version of the "Things go better with—" edit in the Coca-Cola ad.

Here is a unique cinematic rupture, an aggressive form of what Donnelly has called "punctuation," meaning the "sonic emphases on an element such as a cut . . . [that] tends to 'underline' narrative activity."[40] The disrupted teleology of "Wassup?" draws attention to the entire word, even as part of it is not heard. As a result, it is an instance where a filmmaker is able, in the words of Jay Beck, to "utilize the film sound track as an effective medium for expanding the dimensions of the narrative."[41]

In addition to winning the Grand Clio and Cannes Grand Prix awards, *Whassup?* was inducted into the Clio Hall of Fame in 2006. The commercial spawned seven subsequent Budweiser commercials and was parodied in Keenen Ivory Wayans's *Scary Movie* (2000). Stone later directed *Wassup 2008*, a two-minute short that resituated the characters as suffering from various effects of President George W. Bush's two terms in office.

With regard to the larger issue of disrupted aural teleologies, examples have since occurred in such feature films as Jonathan Glazer's *Under the Skin* (2013) and Dan Trachtenberg's *10 Cloverfield Lane* (2016), as well as in such television programs as *Family Guy* (1999–2003, 2005 to present) and *American Dad* (2005 to present). The effect occurs at the end of the opening credits of *Better Call Saul* (2015 to present), and has been adopted by various internet programs, such as the film reviews of "Mr. Plinkett" for Red Letter Media.

Conclusion

Beginning in 1950, Old Gold cigarette commercials featured a woman tap-dancing in white boots to various familiar songs while male voiceover extolled the virtues of the product. According to *Sponsor* magazine, the woman's legs were "eye-arresting."[42] The rest of her body was not seen, as the actress ("Miss X") wore a costume made to look like a huge package of Old Gold cigarettes. Next to her danced a box of matches or, in other cases, a pack of "King-Sized Old Gold." Disembodied legs enticed the viewers to smoke tobacco without saying a word.

Over six decades later, in *By the Pool*, a 2015 commercial for Schick Hydro Silk Trim Style, three bikini-clad women, conceived as Barbie doll fantasies—eroticized, imaginary, and voiceless—pose in front of a shimmering pool of calming water: sprites engaged in acts of voluptuous, ironic, and masterful strokes (Fig. 6.6). The audience, like invisible voyeurs, witnesses the marketing of wet dreams.

Figure 6.6 *By the Pool* (2015)

A spirited rock soundtrack, featuring child-like singing of nonsensical phrases, completes the viewing experience, while a female, controlling voice informs the audience about the wondrous product. Each young woman trims the metaphorical bushy plant poised in front of her genitalia, as the camera tracks from screen left to right, stopping on the last successfully trimmed, heart-shaped, verdant shrubbery. This transformation has been possible only thanks the new shaver. As the female voiceover confidently intones how this product is "the tool you've been waiting for," the happy, shaved woman will jump into the pool. Not one of the three models in the shaving commercial says a word, but sounds, soundtrack, and image in this commercial arguably form a successful and coherent narrative, however ludicrous this *Dada Meets Freud* fantasy may be read.

Sound production in commercials reached a sustained level of artistic achievement, whether involving modes of narration, source and underscore music, dialogue, and special effects, for sound is directly or inferentially linked to the visual images it complements. As Noël Burch writes, "The *necessary* interrelationship of sound and image today appears to be a definitely established fact, as even the most doubting critic must concede once he has examined the history of film."[43] Or, as Hooper White claimed in *Advertising Age* in 1978, "Whether you start first with the words, the music, the pictures—or attempt to start with all three, the composition of your sound track should fit hand-in-glove with your visual to make an entire video experience."[44] Perhaps Michel Chion states it best: "There is no soundtrack," he proclaims, meaning that (A) the sounds do not form a coherent entity without the image, and (B) the audio is in a simultaneous, vertical relationship with the image.[45] The commercial is a prime field of narrative discourse in which to perceive this verticality. According to Lastra, "Sound space, no longer theoretically defined by the passive perceptions of a securely located (and physically real) observer, is now shot through with the hierarchies of 'dramatic' relationships."[46] As it is with the case of film and television productions, sound is a vital, instrumental element of broadcast commercial production.

What one *hears* during the broadcast of any commercial, including calculated screen-time silence, is a signifying link to the visual schema, another narrative strand, engaging acoustic experiences ranging from sublime orchestrations, controlling voiceovers, strange and memorable effects, and other auditory considerations. Both pleasing and gauche sounds of all kinds complement the space and time of the commercial narrative. In particular, the structural composition of the commercial's sound(track), involving modes of narration, underscore and source music, dialogue and special effects, are directly or inferentially linked to the visual images.

Sound in commercials, either real or imagined, loud or silent, sells the product. That's "whassup."

Notes

1. Martin Esslin, "Aristotle and the Advertisers: The Television Commercial Considered as a Form of Drama," *The Kenyon Review*, vol. 1, no. 4 (Autumn 1979), p. 103.
2. Ted Ryan, "The Making of *I'd Like to Buy the World a Coke*," *Coca-Cola Journey*, January 1, 2012. Available at <http://www.coca-colacompany.com/stories/coke-lore-hilltop-story#TCCC> (last accessed February 15, 2018).
3. Hilary Lapedis, "Popping the Question: The Function and Effect of Popular Music in Cinema," *Popular Music*, vol. 18, no. 3 (October 1999), p. 370.
4. Michel Chion, "Wasted Words," in *Sound Theory/Sound Practice*, ed. Rick Altman (New York: Routledge, 1992), p. 109.
5. For an early example of viewer discontent about the dynamic range of commercials in comparison to the programs they sponsored, see: "What Viewers Dislike in Commercials," *Sponsor*, July 26, 1958, p. 34.
6. Hooper White, "Sights, Sounds of '80s," *Advertising Age*, August 25, 1981, p. 52.
7. White, p. 52.
8. Timothy D. Taylor, *The Sounds of Capitalism: Advertising, Music, and the Contest of Culture* (Chicago: University of Chicago Press, 2012), p. 1.
9. "Jazz Set Tunes Tourism Spot's Tone," *Advertising Age*, June 30, 1986, p. 42.
10. Joe Kilgore, "TV's Creative Boundaries," *Advertising Age*, May 4, 1981, p. 64.
11. Susan Spillman, "Commercials Dance to Video Beat," *Advertising Age*, January 10, 1985, p. 48.
12. Richard Abel and Rick Altman, "Introduction," in *The Sounds of Early Cinema*, ed. Richard Abel and Rick Altman (Bloomington: Indiana University Press, 2001), p. xii.
13. James Lastra, *Sound Technology and the American Cinema: Perception, Representation, Modernity* (New York: Columbia University Press, 2000), p. 98.
14. "Martlett Importing Co.," *Advertising Age*, September 7, 1981, p. 71.
15. "Ace Adopts Silent Movie Format for Suzanne Somers," *Advertising Age*, May 4, 1981, p. 2.
16. René Clair, "The Art of Sound," in *Film Sound: Theory and Practice*, ed. Elizabeth Weis and John Belton (New York: Columbia University Press, 1985), p. 92.
17. Rick Altman, "The Living Nickelodeon," in *The Sounds of Early Cinema*, p. 232.

18. Julie Liesse, "Leaf Unwraps Gum with Xylitol," *Advertising Age*, October 8, 1990, p. 34.
19. See: Taylor, pp. 69–95.
20. Taylor, p. 97.
21. Taylor, p. 98.
22. "What's New in the Use of TV Commercial Music and Jingles," *Sponsor*, January 2, 1961, pp. 46–7.
23. "Commercials Go Off the Beaten Sound Track," *Sponsor*, November 28, 1960, pp. 38–9.
24. Taylor, pp. 108–9.
25. Taylor, p. 1.
26. Paul McNamara, "What Microsoft Paid The Stones to Help Launch Windows 95," *Network World*, June 29, 2011. Available at <https://www.networkworld.com/article/2220097/data-center/what-microsoft-paid-the-stones-to-help-launch-windows-95.html> (last accessed November 4, 2017).
27. Bob Donath, "N.Y. Savings Banks Gets Broadway Director for Its Musical TV Spots," *Advertising Age*, December 1, 1976, p. 50.
28. Julie Halpert, "Chevy's Most Enduring Advertising Campaigns," *Advertising Age*, October 31, 2011, p. 82.
29. Taylor, p. 117.
30. Hooper White, "Pulse Is Strong in Chevy Ads," *Advertising Age*, November 17, 1986, p. 56.
31. Raymond Serafin, "*Heartbeat*: New Ads Pump Life into Chevy's 'American' Image," *Advertising Age*, January 12, 1987, p. 3.
32. Raymond Serafin, "Chevy Ads Pull Plug on *Heartbeat* Music," *Advertising Age*, September 28, 1992, p. 45.
33. For more information, see Ed Andreychuk, *The Lone Ranger on Radio, Film and Television* (Jefferson, NC: McFarland, 2018).
34. Andy Birtwistle, *Cinesonia: Sound Film and Video* (Manchester: Manchester University Press, 2010), p. 19.
35. In this popular series of commercial spots produced for Alka-Seltzer, Keaton plays a ship captain, a Canadian Mountie, a zoo worker, a compulsive overeater, and a window washer.
36. Michel Chion, *Audio-Vision: Sound on Screen*, ed. and trans. Claudia Gorbman (New York: Columbia University Press, 1994), p. 37.
37. Giorgio Biancorosso, *Situated Listening: The Sound of Absorption in Classical Cinema* (Oxford: Oxford University Press, 2016), pp. 29–34.
38. K. J. Donnelly, *Occult Aestheticism: Synchronization in Sound Film* (Oxford: Oxford University Press, 2014), p. 89.
39. Michel Chion, *Film, A Sound Art*, trans. Claudia Gorbman (New York: Columbia University Press, 2009), pp. 266–7.
40. Donnelly, p. 32.
41. Jay Beck, *Designing Sound: Audiovisual Aesthetics in 1970s American Cinema* (New Brunswick, NJ: Rutgers University Press, 2016), p. 5.

42. "Legs and the Girl," *Sponsor*, February 12, 1951, p. 28.
43. Noël Burch, "On the Structural Use of Sound," in *Film Sound: Theory and Practice*, ed. Elizabeth Weis and John Belton (New York: Columbia University Press, 1985), p. 200.
44. Hooper White, "What Comes First When You Write that TV Commercial—The Words, Music or Pictures?," *Advertising Age*, May 8, 1978, p. 46.
45. Chion, *Film, A Sound Art*, p. xi.
46. Lastra, p. 207.

Conclusion

In this book, we have sought to reimagine the historical and aesthetic parameters of the television commercial, to be placed now within the broader context of Film Studies. The intertextual framework we suggest indicates an ongoing, dynamic interrelationship among narrative media, and whether thirty or sixty seconds in length, multiple examples of the historical and contemporary advertising commercial demonstrate that each is, in fact, a short-film narrative, informed by ideologies and technologies of the past and present cultural time. In *TV By Design* (2008), media critic Lynn Spigel cites *Art Direction* columnist Ralph Porter's comments made in 1962 concerning standard and experimental cinematic praxis, as evident in commercial productions made for television. Interestingly, Porter focuses on one example to illustrate his point that is especially germane to this study: "Jerry Schnitzer's TV commercial for Clairol Hair Color was a contemporary version of Eisenstein's techniques . . . essentially an analytical study of a woman's hairdo rendered with a montage-type photographic layout of a female head."[1] In this advertisement, entitled *Silk & Silver*, a controlling, male voiceover excitedly describes this transformative hair-dye product in glowing terms: "hairdressers love the magic of it . . . your family will love it." Schnitzer's stylized black-and-white commercial targets a maturing female audience. The product transforms their hair from "mousy gray" into a "silky, gleaming, glimmering" silver. Cinematography focuses on heads and hair, with the commercial likening the same to bright, blinking lights.

A year earlier, Schnitzer directed an episode of the popular television show, *Lassie*, entitled *Lassie and the Greyhound*, which featured a family, a farm, a dog, and a guaranteed resolution for every heart-warming event, however dangerous or absurd. In this case, a dog "desires" a bejeweled collar owned by Lassie, and a poor bet is made that results in its loss: another tenuous postwar fantasy narrative for unencumbered consumption. While not stylistically identifiable as a Schnitzer film, this *Lassie* episode suggests that the relationship between network productions and television commercials merits critical analyses and additional research. The impact of TV commercials on the medium of television is another area of untilled promise. Even when considering production restraints and network demands imposed upon the *Lassie* show, Schnitzer's *Silk & Silver* was arguably a more complex, engaging, and creative narrative, however abbreviated in space and time. Porter astutely interprets this quality of Schnitzer's hair commercial; the narrative promiscuously engages "high" art in closeup, synecdochic head shots, and especially via its playful, visual messaging, creating a need/desire to consume.

Future studies should explore the dialogue between television commercial and television programming, just as others should advance the discussions herein regarding the TV commercial and the feature film. For example, the subject of the television commercial and the avant-garde awaits inquiry, as does the history of popular music underscores in the television commercial. Likewise, historical studies of the jump cut could be meaningfully augmented to include those present in TV commercials of the 1950s. And to be sure, our present work is an invitation to a conversation that needs to continue.

Like theatrically released feature films, or those films produced today for various media platforms, television commercials are informed by historical and/or contemporary ideological, frequently external sources, which exhibit discernible cinematic movements, genre, compositional strategies, auteurism, and other creative and production factors. The TV commercial is a significant part of the retrieved historical and artistic composite of the twentieth and twenty-first centuries. Whether intertextualities are encoded or evident, cinematic or emanating from a variety of narrative sources, the TV commercial is a dynamic film praxis, no less aesthetically complex or significant than generically interrelated, industrial releases produced for the big screen. It is a viable and indeed crucial component of the history of national and international cinemas.

The television commercial impacts both the individual and the collective conscience of the viewing audience. Even in the space and time of thirty, sixty, or even 120 seconds, technique and artistry may be exhibited while selling cold cream, fake college degrees, or used cars. These short films function like a glimpse into the socio-political order of the postwar self and home, and beyond, into today's technology-addled, media-saturated consumer. In his article, "On Advertising's Relation to Moving Pictures," Patrick Vonderau provides a succinct, working definition of advertising directly applicable to this study of the cinematic television commercial:

> Advertising, understood as an institutionalized process associated with a set of codified practices and a host of content types or cultural forms designed for promoting consumption, evidently emerged through an intimate relationship with communication technologies that included moving pictures.[2]

180 CONSUMING IMAGES

Figures C.1 and C.2 The culmination of Ridley Scott's *1984* (1984)

CONCLUSION

We believe that Vonderau's aptly phrased "intimate" relationship between communication media—film and the television commercial—has flourished. Television commercials, when understood as short films, signify an interpretive and historical range of images that lead to active audience acts of consumption. The TV commercial initiates personal and social acts of desire; they make the audience *want* something. We see and we desire. The film, either produced in long, feature form or in short form lasting mere seconds, becomes a part of the whole media experience informing modern and contemporary narrative, whether during the evening's programming, relocated on the internet, or in the collective or individual memory of the viewer.

In the 2015 feature film *Steve Jobs*, the title character, played by Michael Fassbender, discusses Apple's famous TV commercial *1984*. He declares, "Two days ago we ran a Super Bowl ad that could have won the Oscar for Best Short Film."

We couldn't agree more. In contemporary media culture, aesthetic and industrial practices involving commercial production are far more complex than William Heise's *Admiral Cigarette* party could have imagined in 1897. In a decidedly postmodern gesture to the real/imaginary past, while filming a television commercial produced in the late 1960s for a cigarette brand, Rick Dalton (Leonardo DiCaprio), a fictional American film and television star, adopts a familiar, folksy gaze of confident masculinity. Dalton directly addresses the audience—real film attendees and imaginary television viewers—in Quentin Tarantino's homage to a bygone social era, *Once Upon a Time in Hollywood* (2019). As Dalton moves within the frame, he smokes a Red Apple cigarette. The fake tobacco brand dates to 1862. Characters in various time periods and countries smoke it in other Tarantino films, a group even more diverse than Heise assembled.

Dalton oozes salesmanship and sincerity. As the credits of *Once Upon a Time in Hollywood* roll, this fake commercial is wholly realistic and historically contextualized. Famous actors such as Lee Marvin and John Wayne appeared in similar character-driven marketing campaigns for cigarette companies, yet Tarantino's audience also witnesses an unrehearsed moment after the commercial stops filming. Dalton reveals to the crew (and audience) that he hates the brand. But the staged commercial must go on, very likely, even in reruns.

Here is the convergence of film art and the American television commercial.

Notes

1. Lynn Spigel, *TV By Design: Modern Art and the Rise of Network Television* (Chicago: University of Chicago Press, 2008), p. 209.
2. Patrick Vonderau, "Introduction: On Advertising's Relation to Moving Pictures," in *Films That Sell: Moving Pictures and Advertising*, ed. Bo Florin, Nico de Klerk, and Patrick Vonderau (London: British Film Institute, 2016), p. 6.

Index

Note: *italic* page numbers refer to illustrations

Abel, Robert, ii, 82, 83, 158
Abel, Walter, 110
Acker, Kathy, 37
Acord, Lance, 48, 49, 55
Acura, 96
Adidas, 100
Admiral Cigarette (1897), 1, *2*, 6, 181
Adventures of Ozzie and Harriet, The (1952–66), 18
Advertisements for Myself (1959), 32
Advertising Now (2008), 14
Agnew, Spiro T., 156
Ajax, 78, 133
Alcan Champs (1956), 133
Alcoa, 23
Aldrich, Robert, 92, 132
Alien (1979), 65
Alka-Seltzer, 69, 78, 167
Allen, Woody, 2, 98, 171
Almeida, Laurindo, 29
Aloma of the South Seas (1941), 27
Altman, Rick, 43, 53, 158
Almendros, Nestor, 98
American Cancer Society, 159
American Dad (2005–present), 173
American Express, 138
American Gothic (1930), 69
American Tobacco Company, The, 23
Amini, Stephen, 96
Ampex Digital Optics, 82
Anacin, 80
Anchors Aweigh (1945), 80
Andy Griffith Show, The (1960–8), 148

Anheuser-Busch, 133, 172
Antonioni, Michelangelo, 115
Apple Macintosh, 2, 63, 64, 65, 147, 181
Arby's, 100
Armageddon (1998), 136
Aronofsky, Darren, 2
Associated Advertising, 116
Astaire, Ava, 85
Astaire, Fred, 84, 85, 147
Astaire, Robyn, 85
Astorino, Rob, 115
Asylum of Satan (1972), 114
Atomic Films, 85
Auden, W. H., 112
Avedon, Richard, 98
Avildsen, John G., 114
Avrett, Free & Ginsberg, 80

Bab-O, 132
Back Door to Hell (1964), 92
Badham, John, 2
Baggies Plastic Bags, 157
Baker, William F., 16
Bald, Ken, 45
Ball, Lucille, 14
Ballard, Carroll, 2
Bark Side, The see *Dog Strikes Back, The*
Barthes, Roland, 36, 104
Batteau, Robin, 165
Batten, Barton, Durstine & Osborn (BBDO), 52, 75, 99, 140, 158
Battlestar Galactica (2004–9), 119

Baudelaire, Charles, 94
Bay, Michael, 2, 136, 142
Be Together, Not the Same see *Rock, Paper, Scissors*
Beck, Jay, 172
Belafonte, Harry, 107–8
Bell Telephone, 23, 136, 140
Bellaire, Arthur, 52
Bellour, Raymond, 104
Ben-Hur (1925), 27
Benton, Robert, 99
Berenguer, Manuel, 92
Berger, Arthur, 3
Bergman, Ingmar, 2, 115
Berlin, Irving, 79
Better Call Saul (2015–present), 173
B. F. Goodrich, 132
Biancorosso, Giorgio, 171
Bierce, Ambrose, 120
Bikel, Theodore, 19
Bird of Paradise (1932), 101
Biroc, Joseph F., 92
Birtwistle, Andy, 166
Black Maria, The, 69
Blackton, J. Stuart, 82
Blade Runner (1982), 65
Blanc, Mel, 156
Blind Man see *Washroom*
Blomkamp, Neill, *160*
Bloom Agency, The, 149
Blow-Up (1966), 115
Blue Angel, The (1930), 49
Blunt, Roy, 73
Boddy, William, 13
Bogdanovich, Peter, 98
Bold laundry detergent, 164
Boone, Richard, 19
Bordwell, David, 5, 44, 95, 116, 118, 131, 132, 134, 135, 136, 140, 142
Bowery at Midnight (1942), 22
Boy Meets Impala see *Going to the Dance*
Boyle, Laura Flynn, 39
Brand Name (1977), 82, *83*

Brand New Door (1958), 133, 142
Brecht, Bertolt, 69
Bresson, Robert, 92
Breton, André, 9
Brian's Song (1971), 45
Bridges, Larry, 129
Brilliance (1985), 83, *84*
Bringing People Together (2016), 136, 139
Brock, Jerry, 29
Bromo-Quinine, 96
Browne, Nick, 72
Bubbles (1974), *ii*, 82
Budweiser, 73, 133, 172
Buffalo '66 (1998), 120
Bullitt (1968), 95
Bunny, Bugs, 80
Buñuel, Luis, 37
Burch, Noël, 174
Burk, Robert, 92
Burns, Ken, 52
Burton, Tim, 98
Bush, George Herbert Walker, 105
Bush, George W., 172
Butch Cassidy and the Sundance Kid (1969), 114
By the Pool (2015), *173*, 174

Cadden, Thomas Scott, 164
California Oil, 23
Calvin Klein, 37, 40, 98, 99, 101
Cambell-Ewald, 18, 22, 23, 24, 165
Campbell's Soup, 133
Camel cigarettes, 133
Cameron, James, 118
Campari, 5
Canada Dry, 54
Canned Food Information Council, 83
Capra, Frank, 110
Captain Crunch, 80
Carlin, George, 165
Carr, Ed, 68
Carson, Johnny, 50, 167

Carter, Benny, 29
Casablanca (1942), 80
Castle, Nick, 83
Cavendish, Philip, 105
Chabrol, Claude, 39
Champagne (1928), 110
Chanel No. 5, 44
Chaplin, Charlie, 27, 87
Charlie Rose (1991–2017), 69
Charlie's Angels (2000), 121
Charmin, 50, 55
Chase, Carlton, 3
Chase and Sanborn, 72
Chemstrand Corporation, 106, 107, 133, 134, 136
Cherry 7Up, 102
Chesterfield cigarettes, 72
Chevrolet, 19, 25, 68, 70, 72, 75, 116, 133, 165
Chex cereal, 80
Chiat/Day, 65, 138, 147
"Chills & Thrills," 144, *145*
Chion, Michel, 156, 168, 172, 174
Christine, Virginia, 54
Cimino, Michael, 2
Citizen Kane (1941), 99
Civil War, The (1990), 52
Clair, René, 158–9, 160, 161
Clairol, 23, 25, 101, 178
Clairol Story about the Adams Family, The see *Do Blondes Really Have More Fun?*
Clean Make-up (1969), 136
Cline, David & Mann, 74
Clinton, Bill, 51
Clinton, Hillary, 115
Coca, Imogene, 26
Coca-Cola, 44, 99, 154, 155, 156, 171, 172
Cody, Iron Eyes, 44
Coke Zero, 49
Cole Swimwear, 68
Colgate-Palmolive, 26
Columbia bicycles, 6

Compulsion by Calvin Kleen (1987), 100
Cooper, Bill, 115
Cooper, Merian C., 49, 82
Cooper, Peter, 115
Copperfield, David, 81
Coppola, Francis Ford, 45, 149
Coppola, Sofia, 2
Corman, Roger, 92, 123
Corra, Henry, 43
Cortez, Stanley, 28
Corzilius, Monique, 112, 115
Count Chocula, 80
Country Fair Rolls, 157
Cover Girl, 136
Cracker Jack, 161
Cramer-Krasselt, 52
Crawford, Broderick, 55, *56*
Crawford, Cindy, 140, *141*
Crews, Terry, 55
Crispin Porter Bogusky, 49
Cronenweth, Jordan, 96
Crowther, Bosley, 31
Cruze, James, 110
Cubitt, Sean, 104
Culhane, Shamus, 78
Cummins, Walter, 5
Cuomo, Andrew, 115
Curran, Charles W., 129
Curtiz, Michael, 27. 80

Dahlquist, Mike, 86, 87
Daisy Girl (1964), 110, *111*, 112, 113, 114, 115, 147
Dali, Salvador, 37
Daney, Serge, 110
Darby O'Gill and the Little People (1959), 134
Dark Knight, The (2008), 146
Dark Knight Rises, The (2012), 139, 141
Daves, Delmer, 132
Davis, Fred, 70
Days of Heaven (1978), 99

De Beers, 102
Death Kiss, The (1932), 101
DeGeneres, Ellen, 47
Dektor, Leslie, 3, 118–19
"Dektoring," 118–19
Del Monte, 53
Delco batteries, 133
Deleuze, Giles, 104
DeMille, Cecil B., 17, 27
Deneuve, Catherine, 44
DeRosa, Vincent, 29
Dessart, George, 16
Deutch, Howard, 150
Deutsch, Donnie, 48
Devil Doll (1964), 92, 94
Dewar's Scotch, 6
Diamant, Lincoln, 17
DiCaprio, Leonardo, 181
Dickens, Charles, 37
Dickson, W. K. L., 69
Dietrich, Marlene, 49
Dirt Devil, 84, 85
Disney, Roy, 79
Disney, Walt, 29, 80
Disneyland, 27
Dixon, Wheeler Winston, 71
Do Blondes Really Have More Fun? (1962), 25, 27
Dog Strikes Back, The (2012), 48
Dole, Bob, 74, 75
Donner, Richard, 85
Dr. Jekyll and Mr. Hyde (1932), 27
Dr. Pepper, 85
Dr. Strangelove or: How I Learned to Stop Worrying and Love the Bomb (1964), 113
Dodge Rebellion Operation '67 (1967), 115
Dolce & Gabbana, 100
Donahue, Peter, 3
Donen, Stanley 84
Donnelly, Kevin, 171, 172
Doritos, 53
Douglas, Donna, 26

Dowd, Peter
Doyle Dane Bernbach (DDB), 106, 110, 113, 147, 172
Dragnet (1951–9), 18, 49, 148
Dragoti, Stan, 2
Drake, Philip, 66
Dream of a Rarebit Fiend (1906), 79
Dreyer, Carl, 66, 144
Drive Like a Boss (2015), 96
Droga5, 161
Drugstore (1994), 41, *42*
Dubois, Philippe, 106
Dukakis, Michael, 105
Dunkirk (2017), 146
Dusenberry, Ruriani, & Kornhauser, 49
Dwan, Allan, 27

E Trade Baby (2008), 148
Easter Parade (1948), 84
Ebert, Roger, 3
Ed Wood (1994) 98
Edelstein, David, 121
Edison Manufacturing Company, 69, 70
Edison, Thomas, 45
Eisenhower, Dwight D., 51, 79, 80, 156
Elephant Man, The (1980), 98
Elliott, Bob, 76
Enbrel, 169
Ephraim, Lin, 29
Eraserhead (1977), 100
Esslin, Martin, 7, 8, 44, 52, 154
Esurance, 62
E. T. The Extra-Terrestrial (1982), 7
eTrade, 148
Evans, Linda, 26
Evil Dead, The (1981), 118
Evolution (2004), 160–1
Exorcist, The (1974), 49
Exxon, 140
E-Z Pop popcorn, 76

Fail-Safe (1964), 113, 114, 115
Fallon McElligott, 85
Family Guy (1999–2003, 2005–present), 173
Farrell, Terry, 102
Fassbender, Michael, 181
Feldon, Barbara, 26
Fellini, Federico, 5
Fiddler on the Roof (1964), 29
Filmack, 16
Fincher, David, 2, 45
Flaubert, Gustave, 37, 39, 40, 41
Florida Citrus Commission, 23
Food and Drug Administration (FDA), 168
Footloose (1984), 28
For People Who Travel (1971), 138–9
Force, The (2011), 48, *49*
Ford, John, 28, 135
Ford Motor Company, 76, 95, 132, 133
Fort Apache (1948), 37
48 Hrs. (1982), 28
400 Blows, The (1959), 113
Foucault, Michel, 40
Fowles, Jib, 43
Fox Photo, 80
Fox, Wallace, 22
Fraker, William, 95
Frampton, Hollis, 106
Frankenheimer, John, 10, 95
Franklin, Deborah, 50
Freberg, Stan, 166
Frees, Paul, 78
Freund, Gary, 29
Friday Night Lights (2006–11), 119
Friedkin, William, 49
Frito-Lay, 49
Froemke, Susan, 43
Fruit of the Loom, 49
Full Metal Jacket (1987), 36, 57–8
Funny Thing Happened on the Way to the Forum, A (1962), 163

Furness, Betty, 16, 72, 156
Fury (1936), 109

Gaeta, John, 120
Gallo, Vincent, 120
Gallo Wine, 23, 27, 28, 133
Gandolfini, James, 86
Gap, 12, 122
Garfield, Bob, 40
Gately, Fred, 18
Gates, Bill, 71, 162
Gaudreault, André, 45
Gehr, Ernie, 106
General Foods, 96
Get a Little Closer (1986), 145
Get a Mac (2006–9), 71
G. I. Bill, The (1987), *58*, 59
Gibb, Gerald, 92
Gilford, Jack, 161
Gilliam, Terry, 2
Gimme Shelter (1970), 114
Giorgio Armani, 100, 159
Girdler, William B., 114
Girl with Ice Cream Cone (1964), 147
Glazer, Jonathan, 173
Gleghorn, Arthur, 29
Godard, Jean-Luc, 2, 5
Godfrey, Arthur, 72
Godfrey, Peter, 27
Godzilla, 53
Going to the Dance (1958), *19, 20, 21,* 22–3, 24, 26, 133, 134, 158
Goldfinger (1964), 131
Goldwater, Barry, 147
Gondry, Michel, 2, 11, 41, 120, 121, 122
Good Luck Margarine, 133
Goodfellas (1990), 118
Goodyear, 98
Gordon, George, 4
Goulding, Ray, 76
Grainge, Paul, 98, 99
Grand Prix (1966), 95

Gray Hair or "Loving Care" (1990), 101
Great Caruso, The (1951), 27
Great Dictator, The (1940), 27
Great Train Robbery, The (1903), 101
Greif, Paula, 99
Green Berets, The (1968), 54
Greenberg, Adam, 118
Greenberg, Harvey Roy, 48, 101
Greene, Lorne, 26
Greene, Mean Joe, 44, 49, 52
Grey New York, 148
Greyhound Bus, 133
Grierson, John, 22
Gross, John, 101
Guardian Plan, 96
Guitar and the Eye, The, 22
Gum Goes to Work (1990), 161
Gun Crazy (1950), 47
Gunn, Donald, 8
Gunning, Tom, 45, 81, 104

Hal (1999), 147, 148
Halas, John, 75, 80
Halberstam, David, 22
Halo shampoo, 26
Halo Top ice-cream, 86, *87*
Hamilton, Guy, 131
Hamm beer 140
Hammond Organs, 49
Handbook of TV and Film Technique, The (1953), 129
Hardy, Oliver, 71
Harman, Geoffrey, 102
Harnick, Sheldon, 29
Harris, Matthew, 3
Haskin, Byron, 132
Haunted Hotel, The (1907), 82
Hausken, Liv, 105
Hawkey, Penny, 45
Head (1968), 131
Hearst III, William Randolph, 99
Heartbeat of America (1987), 165
Heck on Wheels see *Longest Chase, The*

Heinze, Rüdiger, 49
Heise, William, 1, 6, 181
Helena Rubinstein, Inc., 68
Hell or High Water (2016), 146
Hellman, Monte, 92
Henke, Mel, 29
Herbold, Bob, 162
Hey Kid, Catch! (1979), 44, 45, 49
H. G. Willis & Associates, 49
Hi, Heidi (1964), 93–4
Hidden Persuaders, The (1957), 8–9
Hidden Valley Ranch, 73
High Noon (1952), 147
Highway Patrol (1955–9), 55
Hill, Walter, 28
Hillside Singers, 155
Hilltop (1971), 154, *155*, 156, 157
Hitchcock, Alfred, 92, 116
Hodgman, John, 71
Hollywood (1923), 110
Hollywood Cavalcade (1939), 100
Holmes, Burton, 105
Holmes, Pete, 148
Honda Scooters, 129, *130*
Hope (1992), 51
Hopper, Edward, 137
Horn, Steve, 129
Horton, Willie, 105
Hotpoint appliances, 78
House of Wax (1953), 27
How a Bottle of Cocktails Was Smuggled into Camp (1898), 53
How Bridget Served the Salad Undressed (1898), 53
How the Dressmaker Got Even with a Dead Beat (1898), 53
How Farmer Jones Made a Hit at Pleasure Bay (1898), 53
How a Rat Interrupted Afternoon Tea (1897), 53
Hoyt, Harry O., 82
Hubley, John, 76
Hudson, Hugh, 2

Huelsman, Eric, 122
Humira, 169
Humphrey, Hubert, 156
Hunt's Tomato Catsup, 136
Hush . . . Hush, Sweet Charlotte (1964), 92

I Am Not a Witch see *I'm You*
I Built Me a Dodge (1955), 133
I Love Lucy (1951–7) 16
I Remember You (1988), 100
Ice Cream Cone see *Girl with Ice Cream Cone*
Ice Cream Girl see *Girl with Ice Cream Cone*
I'd Like to Teach the World to Sing see *Hilltop*
Ike . . . Bob (1952), 156
Ike for President (1952), 79
I'm You (2010), *70*
Impromptu Interview, Dennis O'Keefe, 51
Inception (2010), 146
Interstellar (2014), 146
Introvision Systems of Hollywood, 116
Irwin, May, 45
Isn't It Cool in Pink (1987), 102, *103*
Isuzu Motors, Ltd., 72
It's a Wonderful Life (1946), 110

Jackson, Michael, 157
Jell-O, 96
Jenkins, Karl, 102
Jeno's Pizza Rolls, 54, *166*
Jetée, La (1962), 106, 115
JFK (1992), 99, 101
Joe (1970), 114
Joe, the Educated Ourangoutang (1898)
Johansson, Scarlet, 100
Johnson & Johnson, 76
Johnson, Lyndon B., 110, 112, 147
Johnson, William, 100
Jones, Kensigner, 22, 23

Jonze, Spike, 2
Jordan, James, 158
Jordan, Michael, 80
Journey (1992) see *Hope*
Joy liquid detergent, 133
Julian, Rupert, 49
Juvederm, 169, 170

Kagan, Peter, 99
Kander, Jason, 73, 74
Kane, Tom, 147
Kawin, Bruce, 104, 106
Keaton, Buster, 26, 167, 168
Keel, Howard, 29, 31
Keep America Beautiful (1971), 44
Kellogg, Ray, 55
Kellogg's Sugar Frosted Flakes, 133
Kelly, Burt, 135
Kelly, Gene, 80
Kennedy, John F., 136, 139
Kentucky Fried Chicken, 45, 116–18
Kenyon & Eckhardt, 163
Khaki's Swing (1998), 12, *122*
Kilgore, Joe, 157
King Kong (1933), 49
Kiss, The (1896), 1, 45
Kleenex, 81
Klose, O. W., 23
Knaapen, Hans, 159, 160
Knight, Shirley, 26
Knutsson, Gunilla, 162
Kodak, 23, 29, 31, 107, 133
Konigsberg, Ira, 106
Korine, Harmony, 2
Krämer, Lucia, 49
Kramer vs. Kramer (1979), 99
Kubrick, Stanley, 1, 36, 41, 57, 58, 59, 86, 96, 113, 118, 147, 161
Kulik, Buzz, 45

Lacy, N. Lee, 45
Lady in the Lake (1947), 73

Lady Isn't Dressed Unless Her Legs Are Too, A (1958), 106–7, 109, 133, *134*
Lambert, Mary, 135
Lambros, Andrew "Andy," 1644
Lang, Fritz, 64, 109, 110
Lapedis, Hilary, 156
Lark cigarettes, 165, 166, 167
Lassie (1954–73), 178, 179
Lassie and the Greyhound (1961), 178
Last Picture Show, The (1971), 98
Last Starfighter, The (1984), 83
Lastra, James, 174
Laughton, Charles, 28
Le Blanc, Michelle, 100
Leaf Xylifresh Gum, 161
Léaud, Jean-Pierre, 113
Leave It to Beaver (1957–63), 50
LeBlanc, Matt, 102, *103*
Lee Jeans, 100
Leech, Ian, 82
Leisure, David, 72
Lennen & Mitchell 78
Leo Burnett agency, 8, 102
Levenson & Levenson, 80
Levi Strauss, 41, 82, 119, 137
Levinson, Peter J., 85
Lewis, Joseph H., 47
LG televisions, 159–60
Life with Father (1947), 27
Liggett & Myers, 133
Lincoln MKC, 46
Lindon, Lionel, 95
Linnett, Richard, 121, 122
Lipton tea 72
Little Fisherman, The (1973), 164
Living Doll (1964), 93
Loebel, Herb, 82
London, Julie, 163–4
Lone Ranger, The (1949–57), 165
Lone Ranger, The (2013), 165
Long, Justin, 71
Longest Chase, The (2016), 55
Lost World, The (1925), 82

Love Happy (1949), 27
Lovering, Otho, 28–9, 135
Lucas, Christopher, 104
Lucas, George, 45, 71
Lucky Draft beer, 136
Lucky Strike cigarettes, 80
Luhrmann, Baz, 2
Lumet, Sidney, 113
Lunch (2017), 43
Lux Liquid Detergent, 133
Lynch, David, 1–2, 5, 13, 37, 39, 40, 41, 97, 100, 159
Lyne, Adrian, 2
Lynn, Vera, 113

M&M's, 52
Mac Tonight (1987), 69
McCann Erickson, 45, 82, 155
McCarthy, Larry, 105
McCarthy & Mason, 105
McConaughey, Matthew, *46*, 47, 100
McDonald's, 7, 69
McG, 121
McGuire, Pat, 68
Mack, Robert C., 133
Mackenzie, David, 146
McKinley Taking the Oath (1897), 1
McLaglen, Andrew V., 135
McLintock! (1963), 135
McLuhan, Marshall, 32
Macmillan, Tim, 120
McNally, John J., 46
McRuer, Robert, 86
Mad Men (2007–15), 155–6
Madame Bovary (1856), 37, 39, 40
Magnificent Ambersons, The (1942), 28
Maher, Bill, 69
Mailer, Norman, 32
Maillard's chocolates, 6
Make Room for Daddy (1953–65), 29
Malenotti, Roberto, 155
Mamoulian, Rouben, 27
Man Who Shot Liberty Valance, The (1962), 135

Manchurian Candidate, The (1962), 10, 95
Manhattan (1979), 98, 171
Mann, Richard, 110
Manvell, Roger, 75, 80
March of Dimes, 133
Marchand, Nancy, 86
Marin, Edwin L., 101
Marker, Chris, 106
Marlboro cigarettes 163–5
Marley, J. Peverell, 27, 28
Marnie (1964), 92
Marquette, Jacques, 92
Marshall, Penny, 2
Marton, Andrew, 92
Marvin, Lee, 181
Marx Brothers, The, 71
Marx, Chico, 147
Marx, Harpo, 147
Masque of the Red Death, The (1842), 92
Masque of the Red Death, The (1964), 92
Master and Commander: The Far Side of the World (2003), 146
Matrix, The (1999), 119–20, 121, 123
Max Factor, 27
Maxwell House, 119
Maya Memsaah (1993), 39
Maybelline Shine Free Mascara, 149, 150
Maypo Oat Cereal, 76
Maysles, Albert, 2, 43, 68
Maytag, 72
Medicare, 74
Meet Me in St. Louis (1945), 100
Mehta, Ketan, 39
Méliès, Georges, 81, 108, 121
Metropolis (1927), 64
Metropolitan Life, 109
Metz, Christian, 104
Meyer, Nicholas, 83
MGM, 26
Michelob, 36

Mickey One (1965), 131
Micrin Oral Antiseptic, 76, *77*, 78
Microsoft, 162
Mike Wallace Interview, The (1958–9), 69
Milius, John, 28
Miller, David, 27
Mini Darth Vader see *Force, The*
Minnelli, Vincente, 27, 100
Misek, Richard, 97
Mr. Clean, 164
Mr. Death (1999), 3
"Mr. Plinkett," 173
Mr. Whipple, 50
Modern Drug for Pain, The (1963), 96, 142
Modern Times (1936), 87
Modine, Matthew, 139
Molson beer, 158
Mondale, Walter, 50
Mongols, The (1961), 55
Monkey Business (2005), 52
Monogram Pictures, 22
Montand, Yves, 5
Montgomery, Robert, 73
Moore, Clayton, *166*, 167
Morris, Errol, 3, 13
Murch, Walter, 139, 146
Muriel cigars, 78, *79*
Murnau, F. W., 27
Murrow, Edward R., 51
Musser, Charles, 69
Muybridge, Eadweard, 120
My Favorite Martian (1963–6), 141
Myers, Sidney, 113
Myhren, Tor, 148

Naked and the Dead, The (1958), 54
Natural Born Killers (1996), 101
Nestlé, 68
Night and Fog (1956), 100
Night of the Hunter, The (1955)
Night of the Living Dead (1968), 114
Nike, 80, 99, 160

1984 (1984), 2, 52, 63, *64*, 65, 86, *180*, 181
Nissan, 138
Nixon (1995), 101
Nixon, Richard, 108, 109, 156
No, No Nanette (1971), 163
Nolan, Christopher, 139, 146
Norelco, 114
Nostalgia (1971), 106
Not Always Where I Needed to Be (2018), *169*
Noxzema, 162, *163*
Nuveen Investment Corporation, 85
NYPD Blue (1993–2005), 119

O'Brien, Conan, 47–8
O'Brien, Willis 82
Obsession for Men (1990), 1, 37, *38*, 39–40, 101
Occurrence at Owl Creek Bridge, An (1860), 120
Odell, Colin, 100
O'Donnell, Christine, 69–70, 71
Ogilvy & Mather, 119
Okun, Tommy, 44
Old Gold cigarettes, 173
Old Spice, 55
Oldsmobile, 132
Once Upon a Time in Hollywood (2019), 181
1-USA '57 Chevrolet (1957), 72–3
Only God Forgives (2013), 48
Orkin termite pest control, 133
Oscar Mayer, 164
Our Town (1938), 25
Ovation Marketing, 68
Oxydol, 115, 116
Ozon Fluid Net Hairspray, *66*, 96

Pabst Blue Ribbon, 78
Packard, Vance, 8–9
Pakula, Alan J., 99, 114
Palance, Jack, 55, *57*
Palmolive Soap, 132

Pan Productions, 80
Parallax View, The (1974), 114
Paramount Pictures, 26
Parker, Alan, 2
Parr, John, 161
Parrish, Robert, 132
Passion de Jeanne d'Arc, La (1928), 66, 144
Passion of Joan of Arc, The (1928) see *Passion de Jeanne d'Arc, La*
Paul Masson, 68
Paxton cigarettes, *143*, 144
Peace, Little Girl see *Daisy Girl*
Peeping Tom (1960), 101
Peller, Clara, 50
Penn, Arthur, 131
Pepsi Cola, 75, 100, 140
Pepsodent, 133
Person to Person (1953–61), 51
Pet Milk Company, 82, 132
Pet Sematary (1989), 135
Pfizer, 74
Phantom of the Opera, The (1925), 49
Photobooth (2001), *4*, 96–7
Piel's beer, 6, 76, 123
Pillsbury Doughboy, 82
Plane in a Fog (1957), 133
Pleasantville (1998), 104
Poe, Edgar Allan, 92, 123
Polamalu, Troy, 49, 50
Polaroid, 121
Politically Incorrect (1993–2002), 69
Porter, Edwin S., 79, 101
Porter, Ralph, 178, 179
Post Cereal, *18*
Pour, Pour the Rosé (1958), 133
Powell, Michael, 101
Prestone, *67*
Pretty in Pink (1986), 150
Previn, André, 29
Price, Vincent, 92
Private Lives of J. Edgar Hoover, The (1977), 55

Procter & Gamble, 55, 164
Progressive Insurance, 43
Proyas, Alex, 2
Purina Dog Chow, 25
Pytka, Joe, 3, 43, 80, 140, 141

Quaid, Dennis, 62, *63*

Race with the Devil (1975), 114
Rafelson, Bob, 131
Raging Bull (1980), 97
Raid House & Garden Bug Killer, 78, 133
Raimi, Sam, 118
Rain, Douglas, 147
Raleigh cigarettes, 81
Rapture (1980), 96
Rasca, Nonong, 92
Rats (1988), 100
Ray, Aldo, 54, *56*
RCA Victor, 133
Red Apple cigarettes, 181
Red Dawn (1984), 28
Red Letter Media, 173
Reed, Lou, 67, 130
Reese's Pieces, 7
Reeve, Christopher, 85, 86
Reeves, Keanu, 121
Reeves, Rosser, 79
Refn, Nicolas Winding, 46, 47
Rehak, Bob, 120, 121
Reiner, Carl, 31
Reinhardt, Gottfried, 27
Remco toy company, 93
Remington shavers, 146–7
Renoir, Jean, 26
Resignation (1996), 121
Resnais, Alain, 100
Return, The see *Vozvrashchenie*
Revolution (1987), 99
Rhymes, Dylan, 120
Rice, John, 46
Rice Crispies, 133
Robert Lawrence Productions, 18, 24

Roberts, Jake, 146
Robin, Larry, 44
Robt. Burns cigars, 73, 74
Rock, Chris, 51
Rock, Paper, Scissors (2016), 161
Rockwell, Norman, 81
Roderick-Jones, Alan, 69
Roeg, Nicolas, 92, 123
Rolling Stones, 120, 162
Rolston, Matthew, 122
Romero, George, 114
Rope (1948), 116
Rose, Charlie, 130
Rose, David, 162
Ross, Gary, 104
Ross, Herbert, 28
Ross, Katherine, 68
Røssaak, Eivind, 105, 119
Royal Appliance Manufacturing Company, 85
Royal Wedding (1951), 84–5
Russell, David O., 76
Rust, Amy, 114, 115

Salt, Barry, iv, ix, 98, 131, 132, 135
Sandbank, Henry, 96
Sanders, Bernie, 136, 139
Sanders, Colonel, 45, 116, 117
Santell, Albert, 27
Saturday Night Live, 100
Savings Bank Association of New York State, 163
Saxon, David, 28
Scary Movie (2000), 121, 172
Schick Hydro Silk Trim Style, 173
Schindler's List (1993), 101–2
Schneider, Arnd, 105
Schnitzer, Gerald "Jerry," iv, ix, 10, 18–32, 43, 50, 53, 68, 133, 134, 135, 139, 140, 158, 178, 179, 167
Schoedsack, Ernest B., 49, 82
Scognamillo, Gabriel, 26
Scorsese, Martin, 2, 97, 100, 118, 130, 159

Scott, Raymond, 162
Scott, Ridley, 2, 44, 52, 63, 65, 86, 180
Scott, Tony, 2
Scotties Tissues, 76, *77*
Screen Test (1966), 67
Season Sardines, viii
Security Camera (1996), 100
Security First National Bank & Trust Company, 23
Sedelmaier, Joe, 3, 50, 51
See It Now (1951–8), 51
Segrave, Kerry, 7
Seinfeld (1989–98), 122
Serene Velocity (1970), 106
Serpentine Dance, Annabelle (1897), 1
Seven Days in May (1964), 10, 95
7-Up, 82
Shane, David, 62
Shenandoah (1965), 135
Shepherd, Cybill, 136
Sher, Jack, 134
Shevelove, Burt, 163
Shields, Brooke, 145
Shift Sensation (2003), 138, 139
Shine Free Mascara, *150*
Shining, The (1980), 118
Sholem, Lee, 27
Shontoff, Lindsay, 92, 94
Siesta (1987), 135
Sign of the Cross, The (1934), 27
Sign of the Pagan (1964), 55
Silk & Silver (1962), 178, 179
Silverheels, Jay, *166*, 167
Simpson, David, 100
Sinatra, Frank, 157
Singh, Tarsem, 137, 138
Sirk, Douglas, 55
Siskel, Gene, 3
Sloan, Pat, 39
Smarienberg (1996), 11, *12*, 120, 121, 122
Smell is Power (2012), 55
Smirnoff, 11, 120, 121, 122

Smith, Lee, 146
Smoking Cowboys (1957), 133
Sokolsky, Mel, 85
Somers, Suzanne, 158
Sophie's Choice (1982), 99
Soule, Olan, *148*, 149
Spencer, Dorothy, 29
Spigel, Lynn, 8, 178
Spielberg, Steven, 7, 45, 101
Spin Curlers, 133
Stagecoach (1939), 28
Staiger, Janet, 44
Stairs (2014), 45
Star Trek II: The Wrath of Khan (1982), 84
Starrett, Jack, 114
Start Me Up (1981), 162
Stevenson, Robert, 134
Stewart, James, 110
Story of Three Loves, The (1953), 27
Strangler, The (1964), 92
Strauven, Wanda, 45, 82, 121
Steve Jobs (2015), 181
Stevenson, Adlai, 80, 156
Stoddard, John B., 105
Stone III, Charles, 172
Stone, Oliver, 99, 101
Street of Dreams (2013), 100
Stuart, Mel, 28
Struss, Karl, 27
Studio One (1948–58), 156
Suez (1938), 27
Sunrise: A Song of Two Humans (1927), 27
Sunrise, Sunset (1966), 29, *30*, 31
Superman (1978), 85
Surfin' Bird (1963), 58
Swanberg, Joe, 5
Swanson TV dinners, 133

Taft, Robert A., 156
Take Stock in America (1977), 78
Tarantino, Quentin, 181
Tareyton cigarettes, 158

Tate, Sharon, 26
Taxi Driver (1976), 130
Taxi Driver and Dog (1956), 51
Taylor, Dayton, 120
Taylor, Timothy D., 157, 162
Taymor, Julie, 121
Ted Bates Agency, 79, 145
10 Cloverfield Lane (2016), 173
Terminator, The (1984), 118
Thanks, Easter Bunny (1984), 52–3
There's Bud (1957), 133
Thief (2012), 159, *160*
Thin Red Line, The (1964), 92
This Is Your Brain on Drugs (1987), 51
Thompson, Kristin, 5, 44, 135
Thorpe, Richard, 27
Three Kings (1999), 76
3 Worlds of Gulliver, The (1960), 134
THX 1138 (1971), 71
Titus (1999), 121
Tobor the Great (1954), 27
Tony the Tiger, 80
Topper, Burt, 92
Torres, Mário Jorge, 92
Tout va bien (1972), 5
Trachtenberg, Dan, 173
Tracy, Spencer, 110
Trashmen, The, 58
Trip to the Moon, A see *Voyage dans la Lune, A*
Troy, Doris, 140
Truffaut, François, 113, 114
Trump, Donald, 115
Tummy (1986), 96
Turn Around (1963), 107–8, *109*
20th Century Fox, 69
Twilight Zone, The, (1950–64), 93, 100
Two Kids (1991), 140, *141*
Two Mrs. Carrolls, The (1947), 27
2001: A Space Odyssey (1968), 87, 96, 147

Un Chien Andalou (1929), 37
Under the Skin (2013), 173

United Productions of America, 76
Universal Pictures, 26

VanPraag Productions, Inc., 133
Verbinski, Gore, 3, 165
Vernet, Marc, 71
Verstraten, Peter, 54, 110
Viagra, 74, 75
Victoria's Secret, 142
Visa, 74
Viz eye drops, 96, *97*
Volkswagen, 48
Vondereau, Patrick, 179, 181
Voodoo (1996), 137
Vorkapich, Slavko, 142
Voyage dans la Lune, A (1902), 81
Vozvrashchenie (2003), 105

Wachowski Brothers, 119
Waite, Ric, 28
Walsh, Raoul, 54
Walston, Ray, 141
Walters, Charles, 84
Wareheim, Eric, 55
Warhol, Andy, 67
Warner Bros., 26, 121, 164
Warwick, Welsh & Miller, 49
Washroom (1996), *137*, 138, 139
Wassup? see *Whassup?*
Wassup 2008 (2008), 172
Way You Look Tonight, The, 29
Wayans, Keenen Ivory, 121, 172
Wayne, John, 55, 181
Wazzup? see *Whassup?*
Weekend Passes (1998), 105–6
Weinstein Associates, 49
Weir, Peter, 146
Welles, Orson, 28, 68, 99
Wenders, Wim, 3
West, Adam, 26
West, Mae, 78
Western Airlines, 76
Westinghouse, 156
Wexler, Haskell, 96

Whassup? (1999), 172
When the Future Is Now (1974), 109
When There's No Man Around
 (ca. 1966), 98, *99*
Where's the Beef (1984), 50
White, Hayden, 13
White, Hooper, 76, 174
White, Jesse, 72
Widow Jones, The (1895), 46
Wieden+Kennedy, 45, 55, 129, 162
Wilder, Thornton, 25
William Tell Overture, 165, 166
Willie Horton see *Weekend Passes*
Willy Wonka & The Chocolate Factory
 (1971), 28
Wilson, Dick, 50
Windows 95, 162
Wingard, Adam, 5
Winston cigarettes, 78
Wire, The (2002–8), 55

Wizard Wick Air Deodorizer, 133
Woman Is a Woman, A (1961), 172
Wonder Bread, 132
Wood, Grant, 69
Woodburn, W. Robert, 133
Woolite, 54
Work It (2018), 169–70
Wylde Films, 69

Yates, Peter, 95
Young and Rubicam, 76, 82
You're Next (2015), 5

Zanger, Anat, 48
Zenith televisions, 115, 170–1
Zeplin Productions, 82
Zieff, Howard, 13, 14
Zinnemann, Fred, 147
Zsigmond, Vilmos, 96
Zviagintsev, Andrey, 105

EU representative:
Easy Access System Europe
Mustamäe tee 50, 10621 Tallinn, Estonia
Gpsr.requests@easproject.com

www.ingramcontent.com/pod-product-compliance
Lightning Source LLC
Chambersburg PA
CBHW070356240426
43671CB00013BA/2528